THE
SPIDER

By

JOHN CROMPTON

Nick Lyons Books

Printed in the United States of America

10 9 8 7 6 5 4 3 2 1

Published by arrangement with William Collins Sons & Co. Ltd.

Library of Congress Cataloging-in-Publication Data

Crompton, John, 1893–
    The spider.

    Reprint. Originally published: London : Collins,
1950.
    Includes index.
    1. Spiders.   I. Title.
QL458.4.C76   1987   595.4'4   87-5634
ISBN 0–941130–29–0

CONTENTS

THE VOICE OF JOHN CROMPTON

Let's begin with a pair of small but pertinent mysteries. Who was John Crompton? And why should any sensible person (by which I presume to mean you and I) read a decades-old, stubbornly unscientific book on the subject of spiders?

First, the riddle of Crompton. Available facts are meager. We know he was an Englishman who wrote, lovingly and idiosyncratically, about the natural world. We know that he favored especially certain groups of animals that are commonly thought of as vermin. Spiders, wasps, ants, snakes. To each of those he devoted a whole book. He also wrote two other volumes, one about bees (toward which the conventional attitude is favorable, and which were therefore initially suspect to Crompton), and one about the sea. These books were published in England (several also in America) between the end of World War II and the early 1960s, but there is some confusing uncertainty about the original dates and the original titles. There is also a nimbus of confusion about the author's identity. Was his name really "John Crompton"—or was it "J. B. C. Lamburn," as the copyright information on a few of the old editions seems to suggest? Why should a chronicler of spiders have two names? We know from dustjacket copy that, in addition to the nature books, he wrote several novels, but we don't know whether those novels

3

were ever published. If so, did they appear under the authorship of "Crompton" or of "Lamburn"? Were they good novels or lousy ones? Was a serious novelist named "Lamburn" perhaps shamefaced about his work as a light-hearted nature-writer named "Crompton"—or vice versa? We don't know.

Not even the people at Nick Lyons Books know the answers to these questions—though NLB has now undertaken to bring all six of the Crompton nature books back into print.

In 1913 John Crompton (under that name or another) left England for Africa, where he joined the South African Mounted Police (or was it, as another source tells, the Rhodesian Mounted Police?) as a trooper. For six years he patrolled large zones of wild backcountry, supervised out-stations, and observed animals. Then he signed on as inspector with a shipping firm and was sent to the interior of China. Further encounters with exotic fauna. He spent his vacations on safari, back in Portuguese East Africa. Later he would express remorse over having shot elephants, and tell tales of the rats of Rhodesia, the roasted spiders that were a delicacy among the Matabele tribe, the jumping spiders that policed the walls of hotel rooms in Hong Kong. John Crompton got around. Finally, after wartime service in Iceland for the Royal Air Force, Crompton settled back in England, devoting himself quietly to the study and celebration of what are generally considered unsavory little beasts. He wrote his books. In them he showed the passion and gentle empathy of a J. Henri Fabre, crossed with the starchy English fairness of a character out of Ford Madox Ford.

Whoever this man was, he was unmistakably himself. The voice is distinct.

It is the sort of voice that can say: "'Dirty' and 'Repulsive,' followed closely by 'Beastly' and 'Ugly' are the adjectives I have heard most commonly applied to spiders. 'Beautiful,' never. Yet many spiders, particularly in hotter countries, have a richness of colouring that transcends that of butterflies. Unfortunately the colours cannot be preserved after death. Death seems to turn off a light inside."

It is a chatty, confiding voice, cranky at times, disarmingly forthright, and making no claim to scientific authority: "What then is the strength of the thread made in the spider's (internal) factory? Experts have gone into this matter and their verdict is that the tensile strength of spider thread is second only to that of fused quartz. Frankly I do not know what fused quartz is. It is certainly not in use in the home. So if we are content to ignore this little known commodity we may say that spider silk is the strongest stuff that exists."

On some points of biology, I think, Crompton's voice is downright unreliable. But never pompous or tedious. It seems to emanate not from a teacher or a scientist or even a painstaking naturalist but from a jovial and well-traveled English gentleman whom we would be glad of having sat next to at dinner or on a train. It is a voice that says: "A Mr. Wadey in Australia had a gold-fish pond and over this pond there was an outjutting piece of rock festooned with spider web. One morning in 1935 he saw much splashing there and found one of his gold-fish, two to three inches in length, entangled in the web. Going nearer he saw a large black spider on its back. The fish died. So did the spider, for Mr. Wadey had a kink in his make-up and preferred gold-fish to spiders."

The man to whom this voice belonged had a few kinks in his own make-up, no doubt, but definitely not that particular one. Who was John Crompton? He was a former policeman, an itinerant shipping inspector and big-game hunter, with a fine ear for stories and a good eye for detail and a transcendant love for wasps, ants, spiders.

A personal admission: I align myself with the craven Mr. Wadey of Australia in preferring, for almost all purposes, goldfish. Spiders are creatures of hideous multi-eyed countenance, ruthless habits, too many sets of legs, long fangs, and skulky demeanor, and I confess to you they make me jumpy. All species, all, are predatory. In many species (not just *Latrodectus mactans*, the American black widow) the females occasionally cannibalize their mates and their

5

children. They feed by sucking their victims empty of fluids, leaving death husks like squeezed-out oranges. For these reasons, and others far beyond the realm of consciousness, spiders tax my nerves and my tolerance and cause the floor of my stomach to rise like the deck of a boat.

Three days ago, for instance, I was gaping through plate glass at a monstrous tarantula, a Boone-and-Crocket specimen with a body as big as a hamster and legs as thick as Bic pens, and the terror I felt was deeper than if the animal had been a tiger or a cobra. My brain knew that a tarantula is virtually harmless to humans, but in my gut that didn't matter. Does anyone else out there share this neurosis? Does anyone else go woozy from one glance at a *photograph* of a black widow?

I suspect that many of you do.

Then why in God's name should we torment ourselves by reading a book titled *The Spider?*

Part of the answer is simple, and can best be delivered by analogy. Why do Hitchcock's films endure? What puts Stephen King on the bestseller list? What makes people pay money to ride on rollercoasters or to kayak down boat-eating rivers or to see a movie called *Friday the Thirteenth—Part Five?* Of course it's the inherent appeal of fear, the excruciating delight of being titillated by fright. Juices of hysteria go awash in the blood—and in a hypercivilized culture like ours, the flow of those juices is a rarity to be sought. The very subject of spiders—many legged, many eyed, ravenous, silent, furtive—has for me and perhaps for you a touch of that same dark and tangled potency.

But spiders also happen to be more surprising, more complicated, more terribly beautiful in their way—and certainly more graceful—than the creations of Hitchcock or King.

How graceful can a spider be? How complicated? How surprising? I could attempt here a cramped summary answer to those questions, citing maybe an example or two. But that would be foolish and unnecessary. Because a man who called himself John Crompton has written a whole book.

—DAVID QUAMMEN

PREFACE

COMING out of a theatre one may expect to hear some member of the audience remark to another that the play, though very good, was quite impossible; that such things could never happen in real life. It always seems to me that the lives of certain insects are more like plays than reality. And very good plays a lot of them are, particularly those staged by the bees, ants, and wasps. But of all the plays now running I am inclined to think that the one produced by spiders is the best. It has almost everything the modern audience wants; love interest, suspense, psychology, battle, murder, and sudden death. But here again one comes away with the impression that it is all very far-fetched; that such things could not possibly happen in real life.

There is a large cast—565 species in Britain and perhaps 100,000 in the world—but this is not altogether an advantage. In fact, this wealth of material which is such a joy to the systematist is apt to prove rather a headache to the beginner. It is not easy to memorise so many scientific names. And when (and if) he does, the beginner will find that another headache is on the way. For these names do not always remain the same but are apt to be changed and shuffled about.

All this sounds depressing, but there is a bright side. First, scientists assure us that the latest change (which has just been made) is likely to be the last, and that our common spiders will now keep their names for all time. Secondly, a beginner does not sit down and learn up the names of spiders, not, that is, if he wishes to keep sane. He gets to know a few of the better known or more interesting species and then gradually (if he wishes to) becomes acquainted with others.

The sorting out of spiders into main groups so that they can be more easily dealt with presents no difficulties. In fact the spiders have already sorted themselves out for us. Our forebears grouped them according to the way they made their living, just as we might group men into hunters, fishers, farmers, and the rest. This rough classification is in use to-day and most of the spider families (with a little pushing in some cases) can be put into one of five groups. These groups are, Web-Weavers, Wolf Spiders, Jumping Spiders, Crab Spiders, and Trap-Door Spiders.

Our knowledge of spiders—in this country at any rate—is due entirely to spare-time naturalists, men who labour, or laboured, for love; clergymen, schoolmasters, doctors, businessmen, and others. Amongst these men there is a kind of brotherhood; they have one aim only—the increase of knowledge. I myself am a layman writing for laymen in what is called a "popular" way. It might be thought therefore that our leading experts would be unable to feel much sympathy for such a book as this, yet all I have approached have offered me the fullest help whenever I needed it and shown the most kindly interest in my efforts. Since this attitude has been general it is somewhat invidious to mention names, but I must thank C. Warburton and W. S. Bristowe for permission to use their drawings, and G. H. Locket for specially making the sketch on page 193. Particularly do I thank that leading authority, W. S. Bristowe who (though there can be few busier men) has found time to go most carefully through my MS., helping me over difficult places, and giving me a great deal of information. I must also thank Mr. W. F. Phillips for his work in drawing Figures 1-10, 12-16, 18-21, and 23-24.

Finally I must ask for leniency from a certain section of readers. Nothing is more irritating than solemnly to be told something one knows already. On the other hand it is equally irritating to be expected to know what one does not know. Therefore, since I am bound to annoy someone whatever I do, the best way, I think, is to take a firm stand and begin where things do begin, at the beginning.

So now, over to spiders.

CHAPTER I

THE WEB WEAVERS

At Colophon in Lydia dwelt Idmon, a dyer in purple, and his daughter, Arachne, a weaver of fine fabrics and tapestry. Supreme in her art above mortals she had the temerity to challenge Athene, the daughter of Zeus and the Goddess of Female Arts and Industries. Goddesses would appear to be as jealous and temperamental as film stars, for the perfection of the tapestry Arachne wove so enraged Athene that she tore it to shreds. This preyed on the mind of the unhappy sempstress and she hanged herself. Smitten with remorse (or pretending to be, for there still seems a certain amount of spite in what she did) Athene changed the rope from which the dead girl hung into a web, and the girl herself she changed into a spider, a creature surpassing all others in the art Arachne practised.

That is why the family, or, to be scientifically precise, the class to which spiders belong, is called Arachnida. It is a large class and contains many fascinating animals including mites and scorpions, but since this chapter only deals with spiders and moreover only with the small percentage that weave webs, we will say no more about it.

To see a web, particularly one of the more elaborate kinds, is to make oneself wonder how on earth such things came about. We do not know the answer to this problem but it is interesting to speculate in a general way on the state of affairs that gave rise to webs, and to many other things as well.

On this planet of ours a state of perpetual war exists, a war fought entirely over the question of food. In war the side that fails to evolve weapons and tactics to meet the ever improving devices of the other side ceases to exist. Antelopes, for instance, to get their food, need travel no faster than about a mile an hour, but to cope with the attacks of the carnivorae they have had to learn to go much faster than that. This in its turn calls for increased speed and alertness from the carnivorae, for the aggressors in the war are in no less dangerous a position than the defenders. Endless instances could be given of this thrust and parry, these actions and counter actions. The snail grew a shell and no doubt smiled to itself as it pictured the fury of the thwarted birds. But the thrush learned how to smash that shell against a stone, and other birds will follow suit and the snail will have to work out something else, or join the ranks of the fallen. Others, including the ladybird, depend for protection on being nasty to eat and advertising the fact by conspicuous markings which are really notices saying, *Not to be Eaten—Horrid!* for it is no use possessing a nasty taste if you have to be chewed up before it is discovered. This scheme sounds good but those who practise it, if they are wise, will be busy already turning over other protective devices in their minds. For there is such a thing as an acquired taste and sooner or later creatures may decide that they *like* the taste of ladybirds and the warning colours will play the traitor and change the notice to *Your Favourite Dish*. The rabbit owes its success to having developed alert senses, speed and dodging power, a good underground shelter, and fecundity. None of its enemies in England or Australia has succeeded in outwitting these four devices, and the rabbit flourishes. But Africa possesses creatures very well able to outwit the rabbit. Its methods there are out of date, so there are no rabbits in Africa and none that are imported ever survive except possibly in places where man has destroyed its opponents.

All successful species therefore must have some adequate plan of offence, defence, or both, even if the plan is merely intensive reproduction. This necessity has given rise to many ingenious inventions, including the web of the spider.

Nor does the spider's ingenuity stop short at webs; it has worked out other schemes, so that in inventiveness it is probably second only to man.

And now it is time to examine these webs and some of the spiders that make them, dividing them for the sake of convenience into those found out of doors and those found in.

The Outdoor Weavers

The webs seen in the country, in the garden, outside houses and sheds, and in fact everywhere, are rather bewildering; there seem to be so many different kinds and so many that are crude and amateurish. Do not think however, as I know some people do, that the spider builds well or badly according to the mood she is in: each species builds on one fixed pattern, but the talents of the different species vary. Some webs are as crude as the efforts of a small girl to make a scarf before she has learned to knit and some are more delicate than the handiwork of the most expert sempstress. So, before we do anything else it will be advisable to sort out these webs and give a list of the *main* types starting with the ridiculous and going on to the sublime.

I. The first is a bluish-coloured blob found on palings, doors, window ledges, under stones, logs, the bark of trees. It is also seen in cellars and sheds, where it cannot be said to be out-of-doors, but spiders rarely keep to rules so we will qualify the heading of this section and call the subjects *mostly* outdoor weavers. This blue bit of matting is made by Ciniflo, and though the webs—if you can call them webs—are small, the makers themselves are usually rather large.

II. In bushes and under hedges you will often see a tangle of a different kind; a number of threads stretching here and there and crossing each other in all directions. This is the work of Theridion, the members of which tribe are mostly small, perky, and brightly-coloured little objects. These webs have always been regarded as primitive but recently webs of this type have been found to possess hidden and clever devices, as will be shown later.

III. In hedges and on shrubs or bracken you will not fail to identify the conspicuous hammock of Linyphia. The silk used is fine, so that the hammock looks rather like a misty cloud. There are threads stretching above and anchoring threads below. Linyphia takes her station just below the hammock.

IV. The none-too-clean handkerchief with a funnel-shaped hole in the centre or at one side laid out in gorse bushes, brambles, ditches, in the south of England is the work of Agelena, and is called a sheet web.

V. We ought to pause here, and then, to the sound of trumpets, announce Aranea, the master weaver, maker of the orb web. Set perpendicularly or slant-wise you cannot mistake the famous cart-wheel pattern.

Having got a vague idea of the more usual types of webs the time has come to study the actual making of one of them. We cannot deal with them all, so naturally we shall select the spider's supreme art, the orb web of Aranea, surely lineal descendant of Arachne herself.

When I first saw Aranea working I did so more or less under compulsion. A friend with one of those shaded watch-maker's lenses said to me, "You must see this!" just as I was leaving his house. I went up although conscious of a bus to catch. It was an immature spider making a web. Spiders are always doing this and I wondered why he wasted my time about it; just a small "insect" running here and there and dangling from time to time on threads. Then he handed me the lens and the picture changed. I saw not only a spider making its web, but a skilled craftsman engaged in an intricate piece of work. Except when joining or fastening lines (which only occupied a split second) this spider did everything at a run. It was not a flustered or excited run but a steady trot. It was rather like the trot of experienced naval seamen running with ropes.

I soon became aware of someone muttering by my side. It was my friend wanting his lens back. I gave it to him and waited impatiently for my turn to come again. Only dusk and the inability to see sent us away. I had found a new thrill, which has never diminished.

To give an idea of the magnitude of the spider's task I am going to set a man the same task, or rather the bare beginning of the same task. If this is being anthropomorphic then it is equally anthropomorphic to photograph an insect with a man's hand behind it so that you may judge the insect's size, or pose beside a salmon one has caught. If man's capabilities or defects help us to gauge the capabilities or defects of animals and make the picture clearer we *ought* to use him as a measure. I am always doing it. I cannot help it. For instance, if I hear that some outer frameworks of Aranea webs are (as some are) ten feet across I automatically ask myself what that represents, and this I do not really know until I have worked out how wide it would be if made by a man on the same scale. Taking the spider at half an inch in length and the man at five feet, I find that it would represent 400 yards for creatures of our size. With behaviour I use the same gauge. It is an unreliable gauge but it is the only gauge a man can use. Furthermore every one of us is an anthropomorphist. We could not understand one thing another animal does, however simple, without translating it—unconsciously—into our own sensations.

The first thing to be built in Aranea's web is the framework. This takes the form of a four-sided figure or, more rarely, a triangle. We will select St. Paul's Cathedral and Ludgate Hill for the site of the web the man will make. He will be seen in due course climbing up to the roof of a Ludgate Hill building. He is a good climber by the way, though he cannot climb anything precipitous unless he finds footholds—and he is an expert tight-rope walker. About his person are coils of rope ready to be paid out. He ties the end of his rope to one of the chimneys and clambers down again into the street and as soon as he has reached ground level proceeds at a run towards the cathedral, paying out rope as he goes. Still paying out rope he climbs the great edifice until he reaches the dome and here he hauls in the slack until the rope is taut, and fastens it somewhere at the top of the cathedral. In almost no time at all he has run down the other side of St. Paul's and climbed to the top of a shop away down the street. Here he finds another chimney and again hauls in his rope and makes fast.

We are being very kind to this man. We are letting him make the simplest of web foundations, the triangle. So all he has to do now is to clamber over obstructions and climb to his original chimney, pulling in and making fast the rope from across the way. He has been using stout rope because this is the framework of his web and with luck will last him a long time. But even so, one thickness is not enough; he goes (tight-rope walking) round his triangle twice more, joining on rope and making it of treble thickness, which for such a small affair he judges sufficient. That same day, he will have to decide in what quarter he desires to take up residence and will probably fix on some apartment in Holborn. He will insist of course on a telephone but he will install it himself. He will run a wire from his web to his bedroom and even when asleep the slightest vibration will inform him if a visitor has arrived.

The man has made the bare framework but has not started the snare. For the snare he will need a lot more expertness and agility than he has shown so far, ten times as much rope and several drums of glue. So we will, I think, dismiss him. He has served his purpose; we have an idea now of the vast scale of the web-weaving spider's work. No wonder it has to run.

One of the differences between the man we have just dismissed and the spider is that the latter does not carry her ropes ready prepared. She makes her rope as she goes along, for she has inside her a rope factory. We will not go over that factory in detail for it is very complicated, but we will mention a few of the chief features. There are silk glands and other machinery inside. Outside, at the end of her belly, are four or six teats, comparatively large in some species, barely noticeable in others. From these teats, and Aranea possesses six, comes a spurt of liquid which solidifies almost immediately in contact with air and forms silk. The spider can employ one or more or all of these teats at any time she wishes.

This sounds fairly simple. It is not so simple as it sounds. Avoiding technical terms—spools, spigots and the rest—I will try to straighten out the complexities. These six teats (called spinnerets), the size of a pin's head perhaps, are not like the end of a delivery hose as from a petrol pump; they are little hillocks from which poke out extremely tiny taps, in number six hundred. It still sounds simple. One imagines a garden syringe, one with a cap perforated with small holes through which water or anything else is forced at pressure. It is not like that, for each of those six hundred little taps is connected by an individual tube to a separate gland in the spider's body. And the spider can use what number of these tubes she wishes. She can also move her teats about and join threads together or send them out in separate threads or in a broad band, as when swathing struggling victims.

I did warn you it was going to be complicated, and if you wish to go into it fully I advise you to reach for a damp towel. I only give the barest outline. The glands, the six hundred of them, manufacture the silk and the liquid silk goes to the taps on the teats. But the glands manufacture different kinds of silk, seven, to be precise. All have their names, but we will not give them here. No spider possesses all seven, all have three, and Aranea has five.

One can imagine that Arachne, the daughter of Idmon, had at her fingers' ends every sort of material and thread to choose from; all sizes, textures, and strength. But possibly even she worried at times which to use and when. Whether Aranea gets confused I cannot say. I think she is pretty sure of herself by now, but with six hundred taps to think about and five different kinds of silk at her disposal (to be mixed or not) the making of an Aranea web must be a complex affair from the point of view of selection only.

In a moment we are going to watch her at work, but first we will have another look at the silk. If a woman buys silk thread she tests its strength. If the stuff breaks she does not like it. What then is the strength of the thread made in the spider's factory? Experts have gone into this matter and their verdict is that the tensile strength of spider thread is second only to that of fused quartz. Frankly I do not know what fused quartz is. It is certainly not in use in the home. So if we are content to ignore this little known commodity we may say that spider silk is the strongest stuff that exists. That is not the impression one gets when one's feather duster obliterates a web but if you watch a web in a gale you will find that it *is* strong. A large leaf will be held, though it struggles like a live thing in the shrieking wind to get away, drawing the web right out. A split second ought to see it tear a hole and whisk off. But the strands hold. Once in such a gale I saw a spider venture out and moving with care climb to the leaf and cut it out just as a sailor in a hurricane might cut away a sail for the safety of his ship.

And abroad, where spiders grow bigger, I have had my helmet torn from my head by a monstrous web.

Spider silk factories produce material for all uses and occasions: elastic silk, not so elastic silk, silk for foundation lines, silk for scaffolding, silk for roping victims, coloured silk, cocoon silk, silk for balloons, silk for kites and fluffed silk for stuffing cushions. That they do not produce silk for ladies' stockings as well is our own fault because we cannot make machinery delicate enough to cope with it. We shall deal with that later.

When the man with the rope made his foundation we treated him kindly in two ways. First, very few spiders manage to fit in a triangle, the more involved four-sided figure being generally necessary; and, second, we allowed the man to haul his rope along after him. A spider cannot do this, her line is more fragile than a rope; she has to keep it clear of obstructions and she does so by stretching out one of her fourth legs behind her and holding the silk aloft as she runs along. And there are other things. Suppose we had told this man to make his snare over the river Thames? That would have stumped him!

The spider, seeking a site for her web presumably studies the terrain. Perhaps, like our bird catchers, she wishes to get established in some insect air-line. Perhaps not. Anyway for some reason best known to herself she frequently makes her snare in extremely difficult situations, and one of the most difficult is over a stream.

She comes then to the stream, and raising her belly so that its extremity is as high aloft as she can get it, emits a thread of silk. There seems to be nothing at the end of this thread though certain observers claim to have noticed a terminal tuft of silk. Be that as it may, the thread rises in the wind like a boy's kite, and the spider pays out string. As with the boy, the more string there is the better flies the kite. She holds this string by the claws of one of her second pair of legs so that she can *feel* when her kite meets an obstruction—for her eyesight is poor. Then comes the obstruction in the shape of some branch or whatever it is, and the kite is held. This would spell disaster and tears for the boy, but it is just what the spider has been waiting for; her thread is fixed to some object up above and over the stream. She has her gangway now over the water.

Of course, once the stream is bridged the rest, for Aranea, is simple. She will make stronger ropes and fasten the ends anywhere she wishes. The kite method by the way is often used even when there are no obstacles to cross, in which case the kite is allowed to fly haphazard and settle anywhere it likes. The making of webs over streams *may* also be haphazard and accidental, but it is a wonderful spot for insects.

Aranea prefers to make her web almost entirely on foot, but

on occasions she will, if necessary descend from some upper base by air, dangling from rope which she pays out behind.

Enough of these preliminaries. Aranea is waiting to show us the manufacture of a snare. Although it goes on under our eyes I must warn you it is not easy to observe. It is like a man watching a woman knit. He *ought* to be able to tell you exactly how it is done—but rarely can. Also Aranea does not make her lines always in the same fixed order, though the *modus operandi* is fairly constant.

The species of Aranea we have selected to demonstrate to us is the well-known "Garden Spider," *Aranea diadema*.

The foundation, or framework, as we have said, is generally either a triangle or a four-sided figure. Incidentally it will not remain so long: extra supports will have to be added, slack taken in, etc., so that by the time the web is finished the outer framework will be a polygon.

We start (Fig. 1) with the framework already made. In nature it would be a trapezium but for the sake of simplicity we have made it a rectangle.

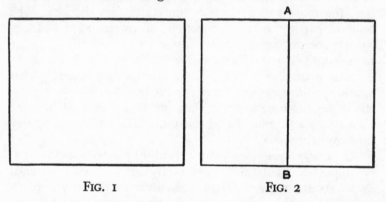

FIG. 1   FIG. 2

The spider runs to the point A (Fig. 2), attaches silk from her spinnerets, and drops on a line to B, where the thread is made fast. She does not really like this aerial method and from now on will make the whole of the web on foot.

From B she runs back half way along this newly made line to C (Fig. 3), and at that point attaches another thread. She is about to make the spokes, or radii, of the web, and C will be the centre. From C she makes her way to A, paying out loose rope behind her. At A she turns and goes along the foundation line to D, still trailing loose rope in a manner somewhat similar to that of a man running along a quay to a bollard, trailing a rope thrown from some ship about to berth. At D the loose dangling line is hauled in, tightened, and made fast. Three of the spokes of the web (A-C, C-B, and C-D) have now been completed. The dotted line shows the course of the spider when trailing loose rope.

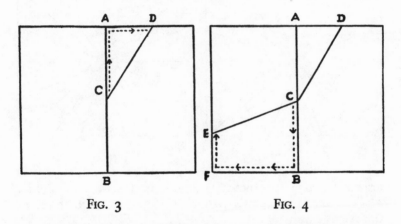

FIG. 3   FIG. 4

Back again along D-C to C, where another line is attached. The next spoke will stretch from C to E (Fig. 4), and to get to E (paying out loose rope, of course, and taking the greatest care that it does not get entangled with the other lines) the spider runs along the lines C-B, B-F, F-E. At E the line of the fourth spoke is hauled in and made fast.

From E she will make her way back to the centre by her last laid line, fasten another line there, and going via C-D fix it somewhere in the right-hand locality. And so on, laying one or more lines on one side and then one or more lines on the other side, keeping the strain balanced and if necessary adding extra stays to keep it so, until at last all the spokes are laid.

And so we come to the end of the making of the radii. The spokes are marvellously equidistant considering the irregular order in which they were made; not *exactly* equidistant but very nearly so in the majority of cases. We now have a picture rather like Fig. 5, though the sketch has been made simpler by reducing the number of spokes. We have

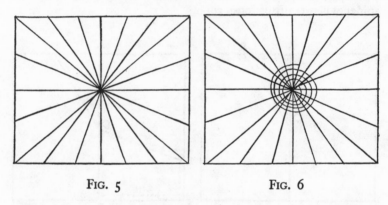

FIG. 5   FIG. 6

drawn twenty; the actual number in the web of *Aranea diadema* varies from twenty-five to thirty-five, with thirty as the average number.

Fig. 6 speaks for itself. The centre is strengthened by a few spiral lines.

And here the uninitiated observer may be disappointed. Starting at A (Fig. 7) and working even faster than before Aranea lays down a rough, wide-spaced spiral finishing at B.

Possibly the observer goes away. If he does, and decides to come back later he will find something like the state of affairs represented in Fig. 8.

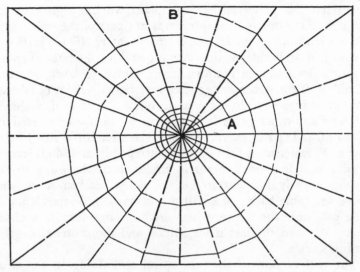

FIG. 7

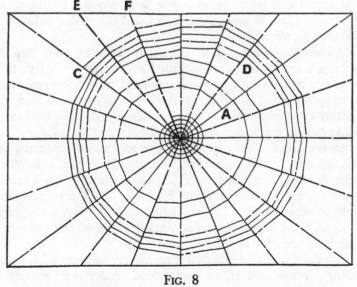

FIG. 8

What has happened ? To explain we must go back to Fig. 7. That amateurish spiral was not part of the web at all. It was scaffolding, made to be destroyed later. *We* use scaffolding when we build. So does Aranea, and for the same purpose —for a foothold; a platform from which to work, for the making of the web now becomes very tricky. A lot of labour has gone into it up to the present, but as a means of catching flies or any other game it is useless. So the spider started at C to make her real snare. From C she stretched a line to the spoke E, fastened it, then on to F, fastened it, and so on round and round in close concentric circles until she came to D, which merely happens to be the point reached when the observer came back. She will go on with those spirals until she gets near the centre, when she will stop, leaving a clear space between the last made spirals and the centre-strengthening spirals.

It will be noticed that the spiral scaffolding in the area over which she has worked has disappeared. She used it for a platform and rolled it up as she went along. By the time she comes close to the centre it will all have been rolled up and thrown away.

A change has come over Aranea in her latest task. She is moving more slowly and working more carefully. It would seem that her job has become more complicated. She pauses at every spoke and does things to the line. She has switched on to more elastic silk than she used before but it is not that that delays her, it is the fact that these lines must be made sticky. Those six hundred little pipes of hers are not *all* connected to silk factories; there is another factory inside her, a smaller concern altogether, that manufactures glue and has one or two discharge pipes of its own. So as she lays a line from one spoke to another (and in all she will have to lay down roughly 13,000 of these lines) Aranea anoints it at the same time with glue from the glue pipes.

She does more. Perhaps a line merely painted with glue would dry too quickly, or dust would render it inoperative, or perhaps glue arranged in little drops has more holding power. At any rate she arranges her glue in a number of minute droplets. Observers had known this for a long time and had studied the threads under the microscope and had found that the drops were arranged close together and all *exactly equidistant.* The spider's ability to arrange them so excited both admiration and puzzlement. Then the secret came out. If you put fluid on a violin or similar type of string and twang this string with your finger, the fluid, for some reason probably better known to you than to me, separates out into drops equally spaced. This is what Aranea does. Having laid her line between two spokes and smeared it with

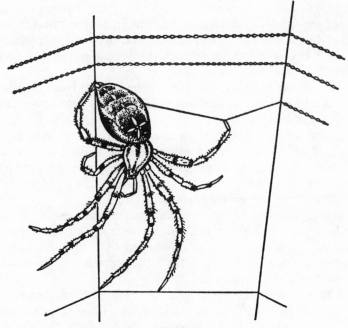

FIG. 9
Twanging the gummed spiral
After Warburton (*from Spiders—Cambridge University Press*)

glue she pulls it down with a claw of one of her hind feet and lets it snap back (Fig. 9).

How did the spider learn to do this? How did she hit upon a method which would have defeated me? When I ask people they smile tolerantly and say, "Oh, instinct." If you say "instinct" you have, apparently, explained everything. The building of the spider's web, the paralysing of its prey by the hunting wasp—instinct. Instinct, and therefore nothing wonderful at all. Yet these things had to start. I know we have to use it but I hate the word instinct. We say it with such smugness. To my mind, far from explaining anything it makes the problem infinitely more complicated than it was before.

And so Aranea moves from spoke to spoke, tying, glueing, twanging, and proceeding in concentric circles towards the hub. Short of the hub, and leaving the circular space known as the "free zone" she concludes the laying of the gummed snare.

Little more remains to be done. The hub has to be attended to and a telephone installed and possibly a few more stays and supports added. At the centre, the original point C, there is a tuft of silk, the result of all the fastenings that have been made. This is bitten away together with a further portion of the centre. The resulting hole is filled up (or not) according to the whim of the species. *Aranea diadema* fills up hers with a meshwork of irregular threads (Fig. 10).

Some, including *Meta segmentata*, the commonest of all the outdoor spiders, leave a hole in the centre; others make a platform of almost solid silk; and so on. From this and other signs the expert can tell which spider has made a web without seeing the spider at all.

What I called the "telephone," which is a good enough description for the moment, is a long line connecting the web with some retreat. It also serves as a bridge from the web to the retreat.

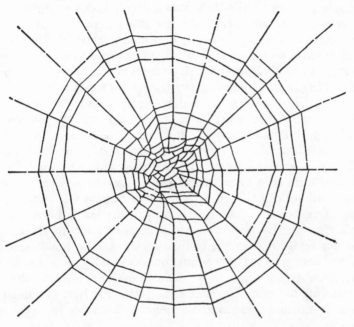

FIG. 10
Central portion of the completed web of *Aranea diadema*.

So there it is, the web of Aranea, a beautiful, almost invisible work of art. We admire it on dewy or frosty mornings because that is the only time we can see it but its lines then are coarsened and thickened, the delicacy has gone. It always seems a pity to me, studying one of these newly-made creations, when some clumsy daddy-long-legs or other oafish creature blunders into it and tears gaping holes. I know that the sempstress herself welcomes these vandals, but it is desecration nevertheless. It is as if an ill-bred urchin made holes in tapestry. That the urchin is going to be punished, and in the case in question punished very severely, does not lessen one's annoyance. The culprit, bound and trussed, is led off, but the hole he made remains. The tapestry is spoilt. And if you think that Aranea, is going to repair that hole you are very much mistaken. A creator, a supreme artist, does not lower herself to the extent of taking on darning. Clumsy unskilled workers like the house spiders may do it, not Aranea. She has a look at it. And then she goes away. During the day others come. There are more threshings about by foolish creatures who will not realise that they are in a snare from which escape is almost impossible. Soon there will be many holes and Aranea will take the whole thing out of its framework, and make a new one.

Sometimes she is very particular. I saw one individual discard a web and weave another after only one small hole had been made in the first. At other times she does the reverse and will suffer her web to be torn to threads without doing anything about it, but this is only when she is bloated out with food and has several roped-up prisoners awaiting slaughter in her dungeon. In the ordinary way Aranea builds a new snare once every twenty-four hours, making this snare at a given time, after dark, before dark, or before dawn, according to her species. For each species, like human builders, has, in normal circumstances, definite hours for this type of work.

The scaffolding mentioned before was necessary to give Aranea a bridge across the spokes from which to work ; also to enable her to avoid treading on her own limed threads. She *is* however able to tread on the lime without getting stuck, and hoist, as it were, with her own petard; indeed she often has to tread on it, especially when dealing with ensnared insects, but she prefers not to do so unnecessarily, just as a man will often avoid mud and puddles even though wearing gumboots. The reason she is not held fast like her victims once puzzled observers. Fabre, who has solved many problems, solved this one. The secret is that the spider's feet are covered with a film of oil; they exude oil like sweat. Fabre found that the end of a glass rod, when dry, stuck to the gummed line but did not stick when lightly smeared with oil. He also found that a leg freshly taken from a garden spider did not

stick unless it was left in contact with the line for a long time.
A freshly taken leg, however, washed in bisulphide of carbon
(which dissolves every trace of oil) stuck at once. Which seems
adequately to explain things.

The glue of the spider, like our "gum," is soluble in water,
and rain in any quantity washes it away. It is also acid. They
say you can taste the acid if you lick the spiral part. I must
admit I have licked the spiral parts and detected no taste. But
it *is* acid and I sometimes wonder if it does not contain a certain
amount of poison like our fly papers. The effect of this acid is
well illustrated by the experience of a certain sportsman, Mr.
Hart, in America. Mr. Hart was out shooting and his path
led him through some woods. Here he encountered numerous
spider webs of the sort that tore my helmet off in Africa. They
are not pleasant things to force one's way through, so Mr.
Hart put his shot-gun in front of him to break and ward off
the webs. Soon the barrels were festooned with trailing
threads, and four hours later he found that these strands—
especially where they had lain thickest—had destroyed the
"blueing" of the barrels.

I have protested against overuse of the word "instinct."
The making of the web, however, *is* now (apart possibly from
the selection of a site) entirely instinctive. Remote and clever
ancestors found out how to do it, not at once but by a series of
improvements, and possibly taught the art to their children
just as the carnivorae teach their children to hunt. That
spiders to-day, after their children have achieved a certain age,
only regard them as something to eat has no bearing on the
question. Because an animal behaves in a certain way now it
does not follow that it behaved in the same way a million
years ago. Indeed the reverse is the case, for nothing stands
still. Even now the mother spider absolutely dotes on her
very young. That doting fondness may have been carried to
a much later stage in ancestors, so that parent spiders then *may*
have taught their young to weave. They may have been more
social too. At least families may have lived together. Then

competition came in. Spiders began to cover the earth; food became short. The mother found that her own young were taking food *she* might have had and which she needed. She chased them off. Later on in the scale of time she found them good for food. And so on until to-day each spider lives alone and the young take good care to leave their mother before the present short period of love has ended. The more primitive types of present-day spiders are however very similar in appearance to their remote ancestors of the carboniferous period, so that there are no scientific grounds for supposing that the habits of spiders generally have greatly changed.

We know that the ability to make a web is inborn in the spider, chiefly because the babies make webs also—and adorable little webs they are ; perfect miniatures no larger than a postage stamp and correct in almost every detail, though not possessing all the features of the web of the adult. Watching the making of them under a lens is more fascinating than watching the work of their mothers; the field is so small that it is easier to keep it under observation.

The young of most species display asexual traits; girls and boys have similar voices, girls will climb trees and boys may play with dolls. So it is not surprising to learn that immature male spiders make little webs almost as good, at first, as those of their sisters, but when they become adult they cast away, together with their last skin, what they doubtless consider childish things. They are adult only after the final moult and then all ability to weave leaves them. They become purely rovers, lascivious roués, following and accosting females. We will waste however no sympathy on the female on this account for she is more than able to look after herself.

To return to Aranea. The web made, she fashions herself a retreat, a sort of bedroom near the end of the telephone wire. It is a horrible bedroom really for it is used as a slaughterhouse as well. Insects not powerful enough to resist her she takes there direct and sucks their blood. The larger ones, those she cannot control, she ropes up whilst on the web and either kills them on the spot or takes them thus lassoed to the bedroom. If surfeited she will not kill them yet but keep them awhile. She rarely keeps them long for she feeds only on blood and prefers victims in which the generous fluid pulses strongly —not half-starved, half-dried wretches. She is more of an artist in slaughter than the others. She is a butcher more like our own, and does not engage in rough and tumbles with her captives, preferring to have dealings with animals only after they have been made helpless.

Let us see her deal with a victim, and let us take a small grasshopper. This impetuous creature would do well to take to heart the motto, "Look before you leap," but that is the last thing he ever does and as a consequence lands himself in many undesirable places including spiders' webs. In many of these he has a sporting chance but none on the limed threads of Aranea—provided of course that Aranea does not delay *too* long. The spider runs out and her first act is to inspect the struggling visitor. He has spurred hind legs, more powerful for his size than those of a kangeroo, and a mouth like a rat-trap. The portly proprietress of the web gives him a calm scrutiny and two thoughts probably occur to her. (1) He is not a wasp or a bee, and (2) he is a powerful kicker that will soon make havoc of her property and—glue or no glue—get free unless action is taken. She turns the end of her belly towards him and those protruding udders, the spinnerets, gush out a milky cascade of silk. The whole of them work together producing, not lines suitable for webs but a broad swathe like a linen bandage. Her hind legs gather this flowing stream and fling it over the plunging beast behind. Immediately afterwards, well-directed kicks from these same hind legs set the grasshopper rotating between the elastic threads that hold it, like a carcass on a spit. He revolves, and with each revolution is enswathed with another layer of silken bandage.

Soon he hangs, roped up, straining at his bonds, ready for the knife.

His butcher however does not always use her knife to kill. It is blood she wants, not meat. Either on the spot or in her lair, after she has dragged him there by a rope attached to her spinnerets, she pierces his body with her fangs.

Gradually the beast becomes torpid as if in death. But he is by no means dead; he is numbed, anaesthetised. Take him away now—disregarding the indignation of the butcher—and he will recover. In a day or so, if you remove the bandages, he will be able to jump as well and foolishly as before. This is not to say that he is as good a grasshopper as he was. He is not: he will refuse all food and in about two days will be dead.

When the grasshopper is trussed Aranea will have an orgy, and her fat stomach will have swollen considerably in a few hours. Incidentally she is on velvet here. The stomach of most creatures has its limitations. Our own, for instance, is strictly limited as we often know to our cost, but the spider's stomach is anatomically unconfined and can swell and swell without doing her the slightest harm or causing her discomfort. One envies her, for not only can she gorge beyond our wildest dreams but she can fast. A fast of a couple of days distresses us but the spider can go without food for a year and a half.

The orgy will last about 18 hours. When Aranea has finished, the corpse, if tossed into the air, offers no more resistance than a feather.

Victims call for different methods according to their size and strength. Small creatures are treated with scant respect and merely eaten on the spot without being bound up at all. A bee, and especially a wasp, is regarded with a considerable amount of doubt. Aranea goes nearer, hesitates, runs away, comes back. On the whole one gets the impression that she would have preferred them to stay away. The wasp (and I have put many of them into various types of webs) is either cut out of the web and set free by the spider herself, or gets out by his own efforts after long struggles. About the bee I can say nothing. I do not put bees into spiders' webs and if I find one caught I release it. Every single bee is a valuable asset to mankind. I have, however, found many carcases of bees roped up and have come to the conclusion that normally only a young, fresh, unladen bee can escape Aranea and her scientific snare. Bees full of honey, loaded with pollen, old bees, tired bees, have little hope. And Aranea treats even such with respect, for the bee's sting is the most powerful weapon that any insect possesses.

McCook in America witnessed the capture of a large honey bee by an Aranea. The ending in this case was unusual. The spider got her first deadly rope round the struggling creature and then began to swathe it round and round and round. She was taking no chances and when she had finished the bee looked more like a mummy than anything else. The spider then attached her long hauling ropes and got ready to pull the prize to the dining-room. Meanwhile the bee, though apparently in hopeless case, began to struggle hard again and in these struggles managed to get her head out of the kind of sack that enclosed her. She then, by degrees, squeezed her body out like an insect emerging from its cocoon.

One would have thought that after such a dreadful experience the bee's first idea would have been to get away. But not at all; she was in a state of fury at the treatment she had received and was determined that someone should suffer for it. But instead of attacking the spider (who was still unaware of what had occurred) she went for the sack from which she had escaped and plunged her sting into it several times. Even this did not satisfy her and catching sight of McCook she went for him, buzzing angrily round his face. Fortunately, both for McCook and herself, the bee decided against stern measures and flew to some blossom from which she drank deeply after her trying adventures. At last the spider, surprised at the lightness of the load she was hauling, ran back to her victim's shroud and stared unbelievingly at the empty bindings. Only when she had examined them from every side and angle did she accept the situation and resign herself to the fact that her prey was gone.

The wasp is lithe, active, a fighter, and a stayer with apparently inexhaustible vitality, so one need not wonder that in his case the spider hesitates. The wasp flies a black and yellow ensign that carries dread to the insect world. It is what the skull and crossbones were to seafaring folk many years ago. Such respect do these colours inspire that a host of perfectly harmless insects have imitated them in the hope of putting to flight those who normally would eat them. It is as if rabbits were to paint their coats with the markings of the wild cat. But wasps, like ourselves, grow old and feeble, and sometimes, too, get drunk. It is these tired elderly wasps and those drunk on fruit-juices that certain spiders overpower and thus they get credit for being able to tackle wasps in general.

Aranea's web is not merely a game trap; it is a safe retreat from many enemies—and a residence. When you walk along a country road with webs in the hedges on either side, you are not walking in an unpopulated area. You are passing between rows of villas just as if you were in some London suburb. And if you knock gently at any of these villas the mistress will appear to enquire your business. Do not, by the way, ask to see the *master* of the house. He is not "in" and he is not the master.

Equally with us the spider regards her home with affection, and with more reason, for she drew up the plans and built it herself. But we ourselves sometimes covet the homes of others. Our wives especially are jealous of other wives who have nicer houses. Now assuming that Mrs. Smith of "The Laurels" were larger and stronger than Mrs. Jones of "The Birches" she could easily enter the more commodious house of Mrs. Jones and kill Mrs. Jones and take it over. Only one thing stops her (according to our theorists if not our theologians) and that is the policeman. In Spiderland there are no policemen —though heaven knows they are needed badly enough—and there is nothing to prevent one lady taking over another lady's house. Therefore, spiders being what they are, one might expect continual battle in these rows of villas, for some webs are large and in good order, and others are small and torn, and the owners of the better ones are not always the strongest. But nothing of the sort happens—at least so far as has been observed. Each spider seems content with her own web, so long as it is a web and the foundation lines remain intact.

And yet the spider has no respect for property (other people's property), as Fabre and others have shown. Fabre in particular studied this matter with his usual thoroughness. Having found that a spider (whom we will call Mrs. Smith) though a big, powerful creature, kept to her own house and never apparently coveted those of others, he decided to see what happened if she were *made* to enter the house of another. He therefore took her away from her own home and put her into a strange one.

Mrs. Smith saw the house of Mrs. Jones into which she had been introduced and found it good. Then she saw Mrs. Jones coming down the stairs breathing rather quickly and asking what she wanted. The well-built Mrs. Smith advanced without a word and soon the two matrons were struggling on the stairs in one of those all-out affairs usual when ladies fight.

Alas, just though her quarrel was, Mrs. Jones was not armed sufficiently to contend with Mrs. Smith and soon that ponderous female was standing over her, and shortly afterwards tying her up.

It *was* a good house and Mrs. Smith took up residence forthwith, her title deeds all in order—the most rightful title deeds that exist, even to-day, MIGHT.

And what of Mrs. Jones? Mrs. Smith ate her.

Now Mesdames Smith and Jones were spiders of the same species. Fabre says that Mrs. Smith, placed on the same type of web as her own, thought it *was* her own home—which is nonsense. Fabre thinks that all insects walk, as it were, in their sleep, or, to vary the metaphor, are puppets jerked about and made to appear alive by Instinct. Mrs. Smith knew every inch of her own web, every strut and stay and guy rope; every thread of it. So of course she realised she was on another lady's property, but, since she now lacked one of her own she decided to take it. Had she not fought for it? Do *we* after fighting for territory and winning, give it up ? Well, we do, yes, *some* of us, but we get no respect for doing it. We are merely called weak. The spider does not fall into *that* error.

In order to prove up to the hilt his contention that spiders do not recognise their own webs Fabre made another experiment, this time with a species he called the Banded Epeira. ("Epeira," by the way is the former name of "Aranea." The two are just the same.) His experiment was a very simple one; he merely transferred these two spiders, putting one on the web of the other, and vice versa. Both stayed there and carried on their business. So Fabre argues they thought they *were* on their own webs. Of course what a spider really does think is impossible to say, but web-weaving spiders are almost blind, ruling their actions by the sense of touch. Had they left the strange webs to try and find their own they could never have done so. So they were well advised to stay where they were even though the unaccustomed positions of the threads must have disconcerted them at first.

McCook's experiments show that spiders *do* know their webs and remember every part of them. He took an Aranea from its web and put it in a jar where he kept it for several days. He then returned it to its own web. It was immediately at home, knew where its trap line was and darted down it and into its cabin immediately. Another experiment with another Aranea gave the same result.

Every species of the superb Aranea craftswomen works on
a different pattern. Some make their spirals zigzag, some
leave two cones completely free. And so on. Fabre now
made the experiment of exchanging Araneas of different
species. So on the web of a Banded Epeira he put a Silky
Epeira, and on the web of the Silky Epeira was placed the
Banded Epeira. The Silky Epeira has a web with very close
spirals; the Banded makes large spaces in between. Both
spiders remained where they had been put: each, as it were,
took over the web of the other.

One would have thought this definite proof that the spider
simply makes the best of circumstances. A spider cannot be
all that silly! Yet Fabre sums up as if there were no doubt at
all on the matter. "The Spider therefore is incapable of
recognising her web. She takes another's work for hers, even
when it is produced by a stranger to her race."

The experiments continue. A Banded Epeira is introduced
to the web of a Silky Epeira while the Silky Epeira is in residence. The result is similar to the Smith-Jones affair, the
proprietress, poor soul, being overcome after a grim struggle,
bound, and eaten. In Spiderland the vanquished is always
eaten. Horrible ! Yes, but even to-day *Homo sapiens* does the
same thing. So can we who are of the same species, *sapiens*,
as the cannibals, afford to shudder at the doings of the spider?
Take away all the butchers' shops and their contents and who
knows what you or I might do!

Fabre's summary after the experiment we are about to
tackle is in direct opposition to his previous conclusions.
On to the web of what he calls the "Cross Spider," which is
our old friend Aranea, or Epeira, diadema, he placed a Banded
Epeira. The Cross Spider (we will continue to use his name)
was in her cabin holding the end of the long thread connected
to the web centre. Something about the vibrations alarmed
the Cross Spider for she never ventured from her cabin. Had
it been a struggling insect she would have run across the
"telegraph wire" to the web immediately.

Meanwhile the Banded Epeira was not behaving at all in the way she did with her silky relative. She did not go to the centre to take possession after, if need be, slaying the owner: she stood like a cat in a puddle, picking up first one foot and then another. The reason soon became obvious, for when she began to walk she seemed to have difficulty in pulling her feet from the limed spirals. Evidently the glue made by Diadema is stickier than that made by the Banded one. Either that or it is a different kind of stickiness and of a type with which Banded cannot cope. Indeed she seemed in danger of being "caught" herself and perhaps Diadema was waiting for such a desirable event.

Some Spiders unfortunately are semi-nocturnal, like cats, so that their more interesting activities are often hidden from us. Nevertheless the end of this drama did not occur in complete darkness and Fabre was able to see it. Emboldened by the setting of the sun the Cross Spider came along the telegraph wire to the web in order to have things out with the other. The Banded Epeira, scared stiff at her sudden appearance, fell right off the web and scuttled into the undergrowth.

Fabre now sums up. Why did they not fight? Because, he says, the limed threads were of a different degree of stickiness from those of the Banded Epeira and because the latter " would have to contend with an adversary *ensconced in a stronghold whose ambushes are unknown to the assailant.*" The italics are mine.

But these slight inconsistencies are immaterial. It is the experiment that counts and not the inference drawn. Let us examine some more performed by the same painstaking man. The "telegraph wire" runs from the centre of the web (the nucleus of all the vibrations) to a niche some distance away. This niche, which is merely a crevice, or some leaves bound together, is situated in various positions; on the ground, or in brambles on the same plane as the web, or above the web, and here (when she is not at the centre) Aranea sits holding the line. It is usually the younger spiders that stand at the centre on the *qui vive*; the older ones prefer to go to sleep in their cabins. And quite rightly. What is the use of installing an alarm bell if you are going to keep watch as well?

These spiders remind me strongly of Brighton pier. Here, on certain days, lined along the edge, will be found fishers of all ages, their lines stretching from rods into the sea below. Catches (so far as my observations go) occur but rarely, yet some, usually the younger members, stand tensely holding their rods. Others, the more elderly and mature, sit on chairs asleep or comatose, a bell attached to the ends of their propped-up rods, which bell rings by the vibrations of any fish which may chance to take their bait.

It was with these elderly sleepers that Fabre experimented. In some cases, with some species, the telegraph wire stretched as far as nine feet. Fabre first asphyxiated a live locust with carbon disulphide. He then placed it very gently on the limed portion of the web of a Banded Epeira. The spider took no notice. Fabre then agitated the body of the locust with a long straw, and Aranea immediately came rushing along the line. She went on to the web and straight to the locust whom she roped up, quiescent though he was.

A small bundle made of red wool was tried next, and with the same result at first. Until the bundle was agitated no spider came; when agitated the spider came at once. What followed shows us how dangerous it is to jump to conclusions after one experiment—especially if the subject is a spider. The first Aranea experimented with actually roped up the quivering ball of wool. But Fabre, going on with this same experiment many times elsewhere found that among the Aranea females—as among our own—there are the wise and the foolish. Some roped it up immediately; others explored it, felt it with their palps and their legs and, wasting no precious silk on it, pushed it scornfully from the web—which proves, I think, that spiders are not automata.

Fabre's next idea was to cut the telegraph wire and see

how this affected communication with the web. But first he must test his subject's normal reaction; make sure in other words that everything was functioning. So he placed a live locust on the web. The locust, caught on the glue, kicked and plunged, and the spider ran at full speed across the tight-rope to the web. The locust was scientifically bound and then hauled by a rope to Aranea's lair. Several days were allowed to elapse and then another locust was placed in the web—but first, and very carefully, causing no tremor, the telegraph wire was cut. The locust struggled as did the other and the web was violently agitated, but the spider in her cabin paid not the slightest notice. Of course the bridge had been destroyed and transport by that route was at an end, but there were a multitude of by-passes: the ends of the web were fastened to twigs innumerable, struts and stays stretched everywhere. Aranea could have got to her snare by any of these routes in very little more time than by the bridge. But she simply was not interested. She stayed where she was, lost in profoundest meditation. Obviously she did not *know* that she had caught a locust.

But after an hour (luckily for the experiment the locust did not break loose) Aranea tumbled to the fact that there was something wrong. She tested the end of the wire she held and found it slack. Immediately she rushed to the web (going without hesitation by one of the by-passes) and arriving there, perceived the locust who in no time at all found himself pinioned. She then left him, to inspect the wire, found it broken and mended it, or rather made a new one. Only when this was done did she return to her guest and lead him over the new bridge to have an interview with him in the privacy of her living-room.

Fabre was a thorough man. Where you and I would let two or three experiments suffice, he made scores. Naturally therefore he made the same experiment on many different species of Aranea and with many types of game. There is no need to follow him; the matter is proved to the hilt. Aranea can see only at very close quarters and relies almost entirely on her sense of touch.

Leaving Aranea, it will be remembered that the maker of the fourth web on our list, the "sheet" web was a spider called Agelena. We are not going to study the making of this web, but we are going to have a look at it and also interview the spider herself. Actually though not possessing Aranea's weaving skill she has a much nicer character, being a devoted mother and an exemplary wife—as exemplary, that is, as you will ever get wives to be in Spiderland.

There is only one Agelena and her full name is *Agelena labyrinthica*. She is a big spider, three-quarters of an inch long, and wears a kind of sports costume, brown with a white herring-bone design down the back. (*Aranea diadema*, by the way, like some medieval knight, wears a surcoat with a large white Maltese cross, but her conduct is far from knightly and her behaviour to the weaker sex disgraceful.)

Agelena's web is entirely different in principle from Aranea's and we must forget all about Aranea's web when we are looking at it. It is however quite an efficient snare in its way though it necessitates the owner's taking considerable risks with the larger types of prey, risks that Aranea would never dream of taking.

The web is a fairly common object in the south of England, a small sheet spread out over herbage and looking very conspicuous, especially when the early morning dew is on it. The fabric at the centre is dense and satin-like but the texture becomes thinner towards the edges which are secured by guy ropes stretching in every conceivable direction: upwards, downwards, obliquewards, some taut, some slack. She would appear to have no idea of strains and stresses but to go on the theory that the more supports you have the better. Were she to design a tent and put it up, you would not be able to get near that tent owing to the barrage of ropes that would stretch from it.

In the dense, satin-like centre is a funnel, broad at the top narrow at the bottom, somewhat after the fashion of a small child's fishing net. The funnel descends eight inches into a dark retreat where Agelena has her lair. The huntress, however, is often the hunted, and Agelena does not make the mistake of the rabbit that cowers in some inner recess when the ferret goes down after it; her lair is open at the base and she can dash out and get to other cover if an enemy seeks her there. Incidentally there is nothing very dangerous to the enemy in walking over the web. It is laborious, but at the centre the surface is almost as solid as a linen sheet, and Agelena knows nothing of the diabolical art of gluing.

Where then does the snare come in? What is the use of a web, a sort of platform, on which things can walk? The snare proper lies in the multitudinous guy ropes; the crazy rigging above the web. When something that flies or jumps, such as our friend the grasshopper, blunders into this barrage it gets temporarily held up. It struggles, plunges, twists and turns and then gets free. But these struggles have entwined bits of thread about its person; stuff it will get rid of soon, but at the moment its movements are hampered and it falls. It falls of course on to the platform where Agelena, who has been watching, is waiting. She wastes no time. The grasshopper is not scientifically bound; it will be free in a moment. There is another reason why it is advisable to act quickly; the grasshopper is upset, its heart is thumping after the struggle, and it has not yet recovered what wits it has. So the spider, risking injury, fastens on to one of the grasshopper's kicking thighs and sinks in her fangs. After that the grasshopper soon lies more or less quiet and the danger is over.

The hunting wasp injects poison into the nerve centres of her prey with such surgical knowledge that (normally) complete and perpetual paralysis ensues. But her prey is intended for very delicate children whose meat must remain alive for a lengthy period, during which time it must not move. The spider knows nothing about nerve centres and cares less. Nor does she care if her injection causes death. So she bites any-where—in the case of the grasshopper usually in the thigh where the skin is thin.

If at all hungry (and she generally is) Agelena does not withdraw her fangs but immediately commences to suck the blood. It is a lengthy process and monotonous to watch; she remains glued there and motionless for hours. When that particular joint is finished she goes on to the next and sucks the blood from that one also. And so on to every part until the grasshopper is merely a husk with as much blood in it as a blown egg has meat.

The body is now contemptuously thrown off the web. It may be caught in some loose silk in the process, in which case it hangs there like one of those dried-up bodies seen outside gamekeepers' cottages.

If things go well that day other game is caught and dealt with in the same manner and the proprietress's paunch becomes enormous—though not approaching the balloon-like dimen-sions of Aranea when *she* has had a good day. But there is a limit even to a female spider's appetite and the time comes when she can drink no more blood. In this case the bite is admin-istered and the prisoner hung up paralysed waiting until its captor requires more nourishment. Sometimes she may only manage to get through one leg: the treated leg is then (though not always) detached and the remaining joint hung up.

Small game is pounced on and taken straight to the lair. Difficult subjects are bitten and often dragged when dying to the retreat. Agelena's methods of course vary and much depends on where the prey falls. If near the edge of the platform and therefore in danger of escaping, silk may be trailed round it in a rough and ready way, or considerable risk may be taken to drag it forcibly to a safer place before biting it. The dice of course are loaded in the spider's favour for she is able to move unhampered about the web. Bristowe in a neat analogy compares the position of an insect trying to escape from Agelena's web to that of a man trying to run through thick, soft snow pursued by an enemy on skis—which is the sort of thing that happens to one in nightmares.

I said that Agelena was an exemplary wife and a doting mother. She is an exemplary wife because she allows her husband to live with her on the web or even in a cage without killing him, conduct which Aranea would regard as ridiculous and calculated to give husbands ideas beyond their stations. A husband's place, Aranea argues, is—after he has done his duty—in the digestive tract of his wife. I must admit that I once found a dead husband in a cage that had for some time happily housed an Agelena and her mate, but lacking further evidence I prefer no charge, even though the husband was in a somewhat dry, sucked-out condition, a mere husk of his former self.

Whether or not Agelena is *always* patient with her consorts, there is no question about her love for her young—even though she never sees them. We shall go into the question of husbands and mating in another chapter and confine ourselves now to Agelena's preparations for her children.

We have of course long before this marked down a web and become on nodding terms with the owner. We visit her almost every day and knock on the sheet. She comes running out eagerly, and seeing us at once goes back to take up her position in the funnel again, showing no signs of annoyance. Then, one morning in August, when we knock, no spider answers us. The web is there and in good order but no form can be seen in the semi-darkness of the retreat. We are upset. Some assassin, we fear, has entered the poor creature's abode and done away with her.

Well, some assassin may have done, of course, but more probably Agelena has left her home of her own free will, never to return. You may do what you wish with the web. No one will care. It will never be used again. It will still catch grasshoppers but the grasshoppers will have ample time to get away. Nor is it any use searching the ground underneath. She is not there. She has gone some distance from that glaring advertisement of a web and under some bush or bramble is making a nursery. It is a silken bag and soon she will sew leaves round it so that you and I—and others even more undesirable—may not be able to find it.

Inside this bundle of leaves things are very complicated. There is an outer covering of tough silk which encloses, not a mass of eggs, but galleries supported by hard white silk pillars and a sealed chamber containing silk cushions of most delicate texture. This inner chamber is enclosed by three separate coverings; first white silk, then silk mixed with sand that withstands the pressure of the fingers, then white silk again. In it, on the cushions, lie the eggs, about a hundred of them, large considering the size of the spider—about $1\frac{1}{2}$ millimetres across.

It is impossible under natural conditions to see what goes on, but spiders in cages will give those who have the patience, and are prepared to stay up all night, the information they require. Many observers, including Fabre and Warburton, have written full accounts. In captivity Agelena sews no outer covering of leaves and the cocoon is seen to be a large ovoid of opalescent white. Nor in captivity does she construct the sand-silk cement shell for the inner chamber even if you supply her with sand.

That inner, cushioned chamber is now the apple of the mother's eye and she will protect it fearlessly against anything, including one's pencil. She watches over it and parades round the galleries like a soldier on guard duty. She has a few threads outside and occasionally catches game, which she eats, and those in captivity accept what food is given them. Other mothers may mount guard over their cocoons with such determination that they refuse all food, but not Agelena, and the reason for this is that her work is not finished. She has already used a lot of silk but she needs more to strengthen the walls on which she continues to work for a month after the eggs are laid. And to make silk she must have food.

In September the mother hears from the inner sanctuary the sounds of her little ones emerging. Though continuing to strengthen the walls she is eating less. Probably under natural conditions she eats nothing and even in captivity she refuses all but a small portion of what is offered. Spiders can starve for a long time but not when bled of a vast amount of silk and a clutch of eggs. Soon we see the mother producing no silk and eating nothing. She is thin and withered, and in late October she clutches the inner shell as in an embrace and dies, holding it fast to her.

In spring the little ones, having passed the winter in cushioned comfort, break from their prison and brushing by the withered body of their mother swarm outside. Like boys out from school they rush along, a yelling mob. One cannot hear them yell, I grant, but one somehow feels that they are doing so. Soon, like schoolboys also, they are climbing up every post and tall edifice they can find, and soon they have spread balloons and are going skywards, tiny aeronauts bound who knows where? This final feat the schoolboy cannot emulate, much as he would like to. The subject of ballooning will be dealt with in a later chapter.

Agelena died. She died of starvation, but we will waste no tears on her for she would probably have died in any case, having come to the end of her allotted span. Whether she would have died without the terrific strain imposed on her by the making of that large cocoon and the laying of eggs it is impossible to say because even in captivity and without the advantage of a husband she insists on making the cocoon and on laying eggs. True, on rare occasions she has the intelligence to realise that the eggs are infertile and to eat them, but the damage has been done by then and she is drained out.

We have seen the last days of Agelena and it is necessary

in order to round off their stories to do the same in respect of Aranea. The names Agelena and Aranea are so similar that they are possibly causing the reader some confusion. No novelist would give his characters names so much alike. I regret this but I cannot help it. I should much prefer to use Aranea's old name, Epeira, but one has to keep up with the times. You must blame the systematists and not me.

From such an expert weaver as Aranea we might expect something very special in the way of a cocoon. And we get it. In its making her silk factory produces silk of various colours, red, white, brown, black, and turns out (under the weaver's manipulation and control) fabrics of varying kinds: silken sheets, porous felt, waterproof cardboard, eiderdowns, pillows, and satin.

Now before starting this cocoon at all Aranea has used a lot of silk. Times out of number, over a hundred times perhaps, she has renewed her web, but this has used less silk than the swathes she is continually turning out to bind victims. As we have said, the making of silk is an exhausting process. The factory has an output of just so much at a time. When that comes to an end, raw material in the shape of food and old silk (old silk is useless by itself) must be taken in. Then the works get busy again but it is some little time before the finished product is ready for delivery, *and* when working at high pressure over long periods the machinery itself gets worn out.

So in autumn when the time comes for Aranea to make her cocoon and lay her eggs the machinery of her silk factory is showing signs of wear. Work on the cocoon begins and the machinery is set to work at the highest possible pressure. Several stoppages occur owing to lack of raw material but at last that intricate and wonderful cocoon, the size of a pigeon's egg or larger, is finished—and so is the machinery and the spider as well. After going to this terrific effort there is no more strength left in her and the engines are fit only for the scrap heap. It is useless now for her to go back to her web.

The silk factory has gone out of business and she has no rope to bind prisoners or make a new snare.

Having made that super nursery, insulated, waterproof, and furnished with the richest silks, satins, teazled floss and blankets, the mother takes no more interest in her eggs or young. Unlike Agelena she will never hear the stirring of tiny bodies in the sacred inner crèche. Nor would she be interested if she did. As far as she is concerned the end has come. That once portly matron is a withered hag and soon dies.

A word about cocoons in general. All spiders make them as nurseries for their young, but it is impossible to sort them out here—even if they were known. Almost every species makes a different kind. Cocoons are of every conceivable shape and size; some simple, some complicated, some hard, some soft, some beautiful, some not, and they are found in every conceivable situation; hanging from threads, from twigs or grasses, under stones or bark, in wall crevices and corners, on branches like Christmas tree candles, in window frames, in keyholes, under mattresses. One common species lays only two eggs in a cocoon, Agelena lays 100, *Aranea diadema* lays 500, and some American species lay over 2000. Again, some mothers are interested in their eggs and young, some not. And so on.

A detailed description of the making of a cocoon would be tedious both to write and read, but to *see* one being made, in a cage or elsewhere, is one of the most fascinating sights I know.

Ciniflo, Theridion, and Linyphia, the makers of the first three types of web on the list, comprise many species; so many that to study them would merely involve us in a long list such as can be found in almost any book on classification.

Aranea, like Agelena, and many of the outdoor weavers, lives only one year, but no psalmist has measured out the span

of life of spiders generally. Some, like the house spiders, live
for five years, and others, of the trap-door group, can live
for twenty-five.

The House Spiders

A friend of mine (the same friend who first drew me to
spiders by making me watch one through his lens) and myself
once went to tea at a lady's house. After tea we went into the
garden to admire the fruit trees, flowers, and vegetables. But
whilst brooding over the herbaceous border I noticed that my
friend's eyes were rarely on the flora pointed out but were
roving over the wooden paling behind, and that later, while
affecting to admire the runner beans, he was studying the
intersections of the poles which had proved an admirable site
for the makers of sundry webs. All pretence was soon abandoned and our bewildered hostess trailed after us on a spider
hunt, and it was her turn to affect to take an interest in what
was pointed out.

A perfunctory remark of hers concerning indoor spiders
made my over-keen friend lead her quickly to her garage. The
garage was built on to, and a part of, the house and was as
clean as a new pin and our hostess, with something icy in
her voice, told him that he would not find any spiders there.
But he did, and a big one, in a corner. He caught it too, and
showed it to her, and commented on the markings and distribution of *Tegenaria atrica*. He then replaced it in the corner
with care.

"You're not going to leave it there!" cried our hostess
indignantly.

He said he was, but a chill air seemed to have arisen and
even he realised that the time had come to stop hunting for,
and talking about, spiders, and that in fact we ought to go.

This, I think, illustrates the attitude of nearly every mistress
of a house. Spiders, since for some reason they have to exist,
had better take care to do so out of doors. And the same

applies to spider hunters—with one reservation. Spider hunters can search for spiders inside the house if, when they find one, they kill it or throw it out into the garden. For women have declared war on spiders notwithstanding the fact that the spider's one ambition in the house is to destroy flies and other pests. Mistresses and maids, young and old, plain and pretty, give no quarter to the house spider. And yet, although the war is fought inside ladies' strongholds, even in their boudoirs, the house spider survives.

It must therefore have courage and pertinacity. Or is it merely stupid? We should not admire a man who set up house in a lion's den nor feel particularly sorry for him when he was killed. We should merely wonder why he went there at all. But when the spider first decided to invade human habitations there was little danger attached to it, for the females of those days, sitting in their smoky caves, were not so particular as their present day descendants about a few blemishes on the walls or ceiling. Indeed, spiders probably got the impression that women were quite nice to live with, an impression they have since had to readjust.

But even with women as they are to-day, the invasion is not so stupid as it might seem. The spider is cunning in discovering niches overlooked by duster and broom. It simply amounts to the fact that the spider has agreed to pay a stiff price (as most of us have to now) for inside accommodation. And there are advantages. The outdoor spider has a lot of trials and troubles that never touch the house spider. Gales and rain may destroy its web, and a host of enemies fiercer by far than women may destroy the spider itself. It works out, I suppose, about fifty-fifty. Inside or out there is no peace for the spider.

The House Spider is called Tegenaria and is of the same family (Agelenidae) as our old outdoor friend Agelena. The whole family is distinguished by having the two outside spinnerets extremely long, but that fact belongs to classification, a subject I am doing my best in this book to avoid. There are many kinds of spider you *may* see in a house but Tegenaria is the House Spider proper. There are four of these unpopular creatures and we will have them parade before us. First comes *Tegenaria domestica*. The female is nearly half an inch long. As she scuttles away she appears to be just an ordinary rather dingy spider and she certainly has no claims to beauty. But closely studied, she has a subdued colour scheme that is not displeasing. Her legs and upper part are a brightish brown and her abdomen is a greenish yellow covered with black spots. And if you see any normal-sized spider about the house of this size it is almost certain to be Domestica.

Like the other house spiders she nearly always weaves a triangular web in a corner of the room. There is no beauty in this web; it is just a mass of threads. And it becomes more and more a mass of threads as time goes on and if Fate in the shape of broom or duster permits. In the corner is a dense little tube where Domestica lives. This tube is sometimes higher up—well above the web. In the unequal struggle, the web has not a great expectation of life but Domestica fares better in sheds and garages where man, the less dangerous of the species, is in control.

And Domestica has another trick up her sleeve. What the eye does not see the heart does not grieve about. Many an apparently spotless drawing room is a whited sepulchre. Visitors do not look behind picture frames. And what of the library? How often are the books taken out and the space behind dusted? In such sites Domestica flourishes and builds an entirely different kind of web. Indeed you can hardly call it a web at all; it is just a mess: threads anywhere and everywhere. In that restricted space of course any work of art would be impossible—and you certainly do not get one. Her main web—the one in the corner—is not altogether without merit; at least there is some sort of a plan about it. We might perhaps study it for a moment before continuing with the stuff behind the picture frame.

Aranea, as you know, manufactured all kinds of silk.

Tegenaria can produce only one kind, and silk only of one thickness. Nor can she manufacture glue. This main web of hers, given a chance, becomes so thick that it is almost solid and forms not a snare at all, but a platform from which the spider operates, and here we see her resemblance to her kinswoman, Agelena. It is the few threads above this platform that constitute the snare. A fly going into this snare is rather like a man walking in the country who finds himself in a clump of brambles. He ploughs through and gets free at last. So, given time, would the fly. But the alarm bell has rung. Tegenaria hastens on to her platform and from her platform grabs the struggling insect.

To return to the picture-frame and the library. There is no method here. Behind the picture frames and behind the books she goes backwards and forwards, backwards and forwards, upways, downways, anyways, in the narrow space, spinning all the time her crude unaltering silk. The result is a tangled mass like cotton wool.

She works only at night. She seems to consider her art a secret; something not to be given away. Very hush-hush. Really, I don't think she need worry. I doubt if any other spider would wish to copy her aimless design behind the picture. She goes on and on and on. As one critic said, she never knows when to stop. At first sight however *Tegenaria domestica* has one advantage over the supreme Aranea. She can mend. If you make a hole in what she chooses to call her web she mends it. Next day there is a shining new patch there. Really this is not so creditable as it sounds. It is just that she weaves threads in any space at her disposal and automatically fills in the hole.

Detective writers might do worse than study spiders. They could provide many plots. Here is one connected with Domestica. The scene is the library where the villain is suspected of having hidden a last will that disinherited him. Holmes and Watson are present and it is suggested that the will has been placed in one of the books. But Watson points out that every book is covered behind with thick matted web showing that none have been recently removed. Holmes smiles. "On the contrary, my dear Watson," he says, "the indications are not as you suggest. Perceive the lighter colour of the webbing behind this particular volume. *Tegenaria domestica* as you possibly know spins incessantly and soon fills up any rupture in its handiwork. But the new thread is white. Unless I am much mistaken it is in this very book that we shall find the missing document. . . ."

I suppose the barrage behind the picture catches game. Indeed I know it does for I have seen flies in it. They too seek shelter away from "flit" and dusters. But if the spider has been in residence a long time so thick becomes the accumulated threading that one would imagine it would keep flies out rather than capture them. But flies are silly things—so they say; I have never found them silly myself. They are one of the world's most successful forms of life and one of mankind's greatest curses.

The second of the quartet is *Tegenaria parietina*, and when we meet her we meet the largest of the British spiders. To those who dislike spiders she is a nightmare. She is nearly an inch in body length only, and if you take her long and hairy legs into account she measures four inches across.

This huge creature has a habit of scuttling suddenly across the floor. One of her ancestors once did so across the floor of Cardinal Wolsey's room at Hampton Court and gave that proud prelate such a shock that he barely recovered from it. That is why this spider is known as "The Cardinal."

She terrifies others too. A lady once wrote to me from Devon about an article in a magazine. She said :

" . . . I am one of those people who have a real horror of spiders. I want to know what are those huge black ones with big bodies and hairy thick legs that simply run like hares all over the floors? I've lived in two houses built in a field (this is one) and life in the evenings this time of year is a nightmare. You see one racing across and the only thing to do is to get up and run. . . ."

This spider of course was either Parietina or its close relative Atrica. Whichever it was it was not black but might have appeared so by lamplight especially since all the examination it got was one horrified glance.

This spider also confines itself to houses though it is a marvel with its great size how it manages to elude and hide from its pursuers. Its web is like that of Domestica.

Tegenaria atrica is similar to Parietina both in size and appearance and it is hard to tell the difference. Atrica however is slightly smaller and has shorter legs. It is much more common than Parietina. Indeed Parietina is particular about her address and only stays in what she considers the best localities. Atrica is not entirely a house spider. You will find her out of doors and in greenhouses (where all spiders ought to be very welcome). By the way, if you wish to tell the difference between the Cardinal (Parietina) and Atrica and do not wish to go to too much trouble about it, note the legs. The legs of the Cardinal have numerous dark bands round them. And at a quick glance her body looks darker. And if it *is* a Cardinal you identify, feel suitably honoured, for as I said the Cardinal is particular where she lives.

Tegenaria larva is hardly distinguishable from *Tegenaria atrica*. Scientists have found minute differences, but even scientists cannot distinguish between them until they are adult. Larva is an imported spider. We import a lot of spiders. They come over in cases of fruit and other commodities. Even the "bird-eating" spider has more than once visited these shores in bunches of bananas. Spiders are admirably equipped for making such journeys; they can go without food for long periods and solitude does not trouble them. The bee and the wasp perish from sheer nostalgia and homesickness if separated for any time from their friends, but not the spider; she likes it. For some reason Larva has selected Southport as *the* place, in which to live and so far as is known lives nowhere else in Britain. I dare say she is right. Southport, I believe, is a nice place. She is found, however, in Ireland (the country that once boasted it had no spiders). Indeed, in Ireland the very common *T. atrica* is unknown and *T. larva* takes its place. So unless you are a native of Southport or Ireland you need not worry about *Tegenaria larva*.

In the preface I told readers that the names of spiders had been periodically changed and warned them against getting confused on that account. This is well illustrated by *Tegenaria domestica* the first of the house spiders we investigated. Up to about 1900 it was known as *Tegenaria civilis*. Its name was then changed to *Tegenaria derhamii*, and in the late 1930's was changed yet again to *Tegenaria domestica*, the name it holds to-day. That is confusing enough, but to make things harder our friend The Cardinal used to be known, not as *Tegenaria parietina*, but as *Tegenaria domestica*.

So when you read works on spiders or look up illustrations of species you must first study the date of the publication or you may get led seriously astray. For instance, the finest coloured illustrations of spiders are to be found in Blackwall's *Spiders of Great Britain*. But if you look up *Tegenaria domestica* there you will find a huge monster that is, in fact, Parietina and not the modern Domestica at all. And so on in many other cases. Even experts admit that they get confused. But, as I have said, there is a hope that the names of spiders will now stay put.

Incidentally I may add that these name changes are not made merely for fun. There has to be a reason and any alteration has to comply with the laws of an International Commission. The reason for a change may be that a few spiders have been wrongly classified, but more commonly it is due to a rather unfortunate but unavoidable law, the Law of Priority. In 1758 the great Linnaeus founded the binomial system of names and all zoologists agreed not to recognise names given before that date. Afterwards came the law of priority which ordained that only the *first* man to find a new species had the right to christen it. Naturally, collectors are very pleased when they find a new spider, even if it needs a microscope (and it usually does) to find out if it is new or not, and value the privilege of naming it. They rarely, it must be added, give it their own name like rose growers, who make the tabs on rose plants look like a collection of visiting cards! They just like to be the ones to name it. The trouble is that two or more men may find the same species in different places and at different times. Thus, in 1890 a British collector found and named an apparently new spider in Britain. Then, forty years later, Bristowe found that the same spider had been described in a collection made in Majorca by a German about the year 1880. So priority had to be admitted and the German's name adopted instead of the name the spider had by then held so long.

The recent change of names is due to a somewhat different cause. It was agreed, as mentioned above, that no names of animals given before 1758 should be recognised, but so far as spiders were concerned this was not considered fair to a distinguished pioneer named Clerck who wrote a book in 1757. Scientists got up in arms about it, but the International Commission refused to make a change. In 1948 scientists, headed by a Frenchman, M. Bonnet, again took up arms and presented a petition signed by 98 per cent of the arachnologists. This time the International Commission relented and made an exception to their rule, and Clerck's nomenclature has been accepted.

The house spiders have been classified by observers as (1) those that live wholly indoors, (2) those that live mostly indoors, and (3) those that live equally indoors and out. Domestica comes into the first class but this classification cannot be *quite* correct for Domestica has to *get* to the houses she so pertinaciously occupies. If you build a house a mile from any other residence Domestica will soon be there. Therefore she travelled a mile in the open to get to it. Either that or she was transported with the furniture. But if you leave the house vacant for awhile you will find her there before the furniture.

This fact did not escape the notice of the earlier observers and in it they found, as they thought, a definite proof of their contention that all lower life is bred spontaneously from dust or filth.

The house spiders *do* at times invade the webs of others, and when one of them does so she does not first go around looking for webs possessed by spiders smaller than herself. So the result of the invasion is never anything one can safely bet on. It works out possibly at fifty-fifty; sometimes the owner is killed and sometimes the invader. Such rashness however is probably due not to bravery but to defective eyesight. The invader is not able to judge the size and power of an opponent until they are at close quarters when it is too late to make apologies.

Possibly I was wrong in saying that the result of the fights is fifty-fifty. Probably it is more like 70-30 in favour of the attacker, and for this reason: the house spiders spin incessantly and unnecessarily. This uses silk. (Aranea uses still more but never unnecessarily.) So after possibly four years the house spider's internal silk-making arrangements break down. This means that she can make no more webs, and without webs she cannot live. So she invades the territory of another, and being older, and therefore stronger and bigger, probably wins.

It is interesting and not a little sad to note in the Natural History books of the last century the attitude of writers towards the habits of the house spider and the virtuous horror they express—in long moralising passages—on the spider's motto that might is right and that property is sacred only to those who have the strength to defend it. And one sighs still more at their smug satisfaction when they take for granted that man has long passed that atavistic stage. Alas, the twentieth century has wiped this smugness from us. Indeed mankind could now teach the spider a lot more than it knows already.

Some Unorthodox Snares

Now that we have an idea of the more normal types of snare we might as well examine a few unusual devices evolved by spiders both here and abroad. For spiders, rightly or wrongly, never seem satisfied with the *status quo* and are always trying out new things.

If you live in one of the southern counties of England you may one night chance to see a yellow and black spider with long, thin legs moving slowly on the floor or on the wall. Used as you are to the quick rushes and alert movements of house-spiders the lethargy of this particular specimen will probably surprise you. It seems tired, indifferent.

Its name is Scytodes, and since there is only one species in Britain we will not worry about its other name. Should it happen to approach a fly, watch carefully for you are about to witness yet another of the many artifices used by spiders to capture game. And Scytodes has evidently patented this method, for here or abroad it is used by no other family. As a matter of fact I do not recommend you just to watch it in the hope that it may encounter some suitable victim. If you do you will probably stay up all night and then see nothing. The best way is to catch it and put it in a glass jar together with a fly.

Anyway, whether you see the performance or not, when some little distance from a fly, the spider's slow movements come to a stop. The fly, pretending to clean its face, has an ironic eye directed on the approaching form. It knows all about slow approaches. It has met them before in the gradually nearing human hand, and elsewhere. It is looking now for a sudden dart and is ready for it; indeed hoping for it. Conceited to a degree, flies welcome any opportunity to display their dodging powers.

Before the war there was an inn in Devonshire that I used

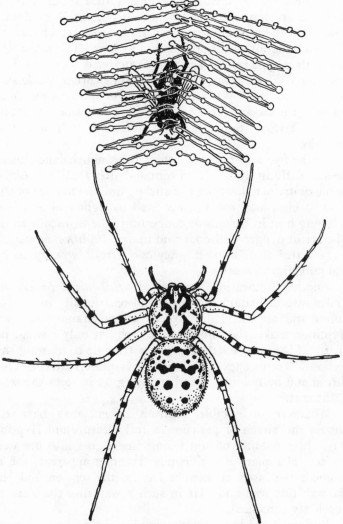

FIG. 11
Scytodes spitting gum over a fly
After Bristowe (*from* Spiders—*King Penguin Books*)

to frequent. The patrons were mostly tobacco chewers, and ever and anon in the midst of a rich burr of West Country talk one of them would turn his head and spit out what seemed to me to amount to almost a cupful of juice. The action occupied only a split second and never interfered with speech, yet frequently the spittoon would be in some corner, yards away. However far away it was, the stream of nicotine would sail through the air and land with unerring precision almost into its exact centre. Such an expert spitter, though more so, is Scytodes.

So the fly, waiting with ostentatious nonchalance, merely feels something light fall on him and after that finds himself in the centre of a downpour of sticky rain. Scytodes is spitting gum at him, and, moving her head to right and left, is enveloping him in threads of congealing glue from side to side. The artful dodger will dodge no more. He has met someone more artful than himself. Scytodes strolls wearily to him and puts him to death.

Another innovation is provided by *Hyptiotes paradoxus*, a spider rare in Britain though found occasionally in the New Forest and on Box Hill. We all know Aranea's orb web; Hyptiotes makes the same kind of web but only a small part of it. This part takes the form of a triangle containing three sections. To the apex of the triangle Hyptiotes attaches a long thread and by holding it and straining on it keeps the whole outfit taut.

Whatever undesirable qualities spiders may have they possess the virtue of patience in full measure and Hyptiotes stays there holding on until some insect goes into her weird device. Her plan of action now becomes apparent, for the moment the insect strikes she lets go the tension and jerks the web this way and that in such a way that the visitor is hopelessly enmeshed.

You must not however imagine her sitting on the ground and holding on to the string like a boy with a kite. She makes things more complicated by making two threads, one from the web and the other from some opposite support, and by forming with her own body a link between these two separate threads. And this is very clever of her for it gives the trap double leverage and elasticity.

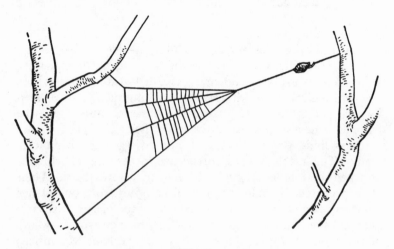

FIG. 12
The sprung web of Hyptiotes

The drawback to the scheme, if one discounts the patience required and the muscle strain involved, is that the snare is good for one head of game only. After a single capture a new web must be made.

In Brazil there is a common garden spider and at one time—I cannot tell you the date—naturalists were mystified because they could never find its web. Finally a boy, the son of a Dr. Goeldi, offered to keep watch on one of these spiders for a day and a night. It sounds an almost impossible task, but the boy did it, and discovered that the spider did not make its web until the small hours of the morning when it did good business with gnats and other things that go around about that time. When the sun rose the spider detached her web from its supports, folded it up, and putting it over her shoulder went away to her retreat where the enmeshed insects were carefully taken out and eaten.

Australia provides our next exhibit, a spider whose second name is Magnificus (her first, if you want it, is Dicrostichus), a lovely creature resplendent in cream, salmon, and white. Her operations, says Mr. Heber A. Longman, can be seen by any patient observer. And the observer must needs be patient, almost as patient as the spider herself.

Dusk finds Magnificus seated on a twig getting her tackle ready. This tackle is a silk thread two inches long to which is attached a globule of gum, the size of a pin's head. When all is prepared M. holds the thread hanging from one of her front legs and waits. Sooner or later a moth appears fluttering here and there in the erratic manner of these creatures. Many of the night-flying moths visit flowers. Perhaps Magnificus in her gorgeous costume *looks* like a flower, but observers think that it is more likely that she *smells* like one. For certain spiders emit the scent of flowers. Whatever the reason, a moth is certain to arrive that seems drawn towards Magnificus. It flutters towards her, goes back, flutters up again.

Up to the present Magnificus has made no movement but now she lifts her weighted line and begins to whirl it round her head. The moth comes and goes and at last ventures within lassooing distance. The thread is thrown; the globule sticks; the moth is caught. But it is not yet landed. Any salmon or trout fisher knows what happens now and may possibly envy Magnificus in the sport she is going to have. The elasticity of her line resembles the elasticity of the fisher's split-cane rod. The alarmed moth dashes off (and probably often breaks the line), is drawn in, goes off again, and finally, tiring, is gaffed by the fangs of the spider.

It was about 1921 that the hunting methods of Magnificus came to light and two years later Dr. Akerman found a very similar spider in South Africa. It is called after his name, *Cladomelea akermani*. I do not think he ever saw this spider catch anything, but the same might be said of many of *our* fishers. Cladomelea also whirls her line, globule on end, round her head, and does so for about fifteen minutes without stopping. After that she draws the line in and bites off the globule and puts on a new one. In fishing parlance she is changing her "fly," for no doubt the globule gets dry and loses its efficiency after fifteen minutes of this treatment.

Mennecus unifas and *Dinopis bicornis* of Australia make small adhesive webs about the size of postage stamps and keep these webs ready between leaves or grass. They are the Retiarii of the spider amphitheatre and when some game, usually a moth, approaches they pick up their nets and get them ready. At the right distance the net is flung and the moth comes plunging down and is quickly put to death.

Earlier on, in the list of the five main types of web, we mentioned those of Theridion and Linyphia. Linyphia's web, you will remember, possesses a hammock, or platform, but that of Theridion is just a number of threads going in all directions.

It was therefore always supposed that the web of Theridion was cruder than that of Linyphia; that Linyphia in fact was at a higher stage of evolutionary development than Theridion. And this may be so with many of the species but it has recently come to light that the webs of at least two members of the Theridion family (Teutana and Stearodea, both British), though at first sight as haphazard as any of the others, are really made on an extremely clever, ingenious, and (or so it

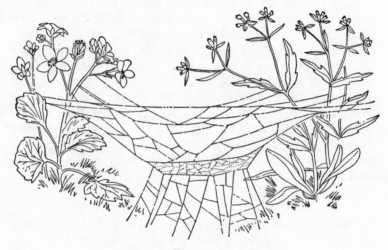

FIG. 13
The hammock web of Linyphia

would seem) well-thought-out principle. The discovery was
made by Wiehle in 1927 and was later confirmed by Nielsin
and Bristowe.

This web (made by both Teutana and Stearodea) appears,
like the rest, to have no plan and no platform. But looking
carefully there *is* a sort of platform; at least, the threads are
somewhat thicker about the centre. They are rather like the
bare joists of a first storey in the framework of an uncompleted
house. From these widely spaced joists taut vertical threads
run to the ground. On examination these threads (1) break
very easily, and (2) are anointed with glue at their lower ends,
near the ground.

There you have the lay-out; and is the spider's imagination
better than yours, or do you see exactly how this trap works?

A beetle, or some other pedestrian, comes along, and
touching one of the bottom strands finds itself stuck. It
struggles and the strand breaks. Being in the first instance

like stretched elastic the strand snaps back and holds the insect suspended in air. The alarmed insect struggles still more violently and swings about and this brings it into contact with other gummed threads close by. They break off too and soon the insect is hanging, a hopeless captive.

Meanwhile the spider has been watching from above and when the time is ripe goes to whatever joist supports one of the threads from which the insect hangs. This thread she pulls up and with it the captive, just as a sea fisher from a boat pulls up a dab. With large prey it may be necessary for her to descend and give an anaesthetic bite before hauling. In either case the prey is taken to some quiet niche and eaten at leisure.

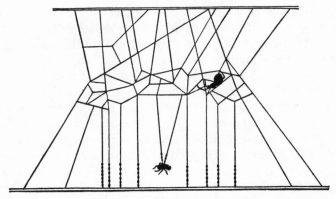

FIG. 14
Theridion's trap for pedestrians
After Bristowe (*from* The Comity of Spiders—*The Ray Society*)

Silk

Silk is a luxury for us; for the spider it is a necessity. The spider's life is bound and tied up with silk. It is born in it, lays its eggs in it, keeps its young in it, gets its food by it, makes houses, submarine chambers, sailing boats, and aeroplanes out of it, uses it for mortar, paper, cardboard, rope, string, and sewing thread.

The silkworm uses silk for pupation only. The silkworm is difficult to rear, gets diseases, needs heat, needs special food for which there is no substitute, and dies if called upon to fast for even a negligible period. So why do we bother with silkworms? Why do we not use the more plentiful, more beautiful, and stronger silk of the spider? True, it takes 50,000 spiders to produce one pound of silk, but they are easily fed. They only need flies and it is not difficult to breed flies —indeed, it is more difficult not to. A never-ending supply of them could be reared and automatically released amongst the spiders.

Well, it has been done, for in 1710 a Frenchman, Monsieur Bon, made some stockings and mittens from spider silk. And he was not the first: in the *Atlantic Monthly* for June 1858 we read that the Emperor Aurengzebe of Hindostan once reproved his daughter for the indelicacy of her costume although she was wearing seven thicknesses of spider silk.

What is the snag? For evidently there *is* a snag; otherwise ladies would all be demanding spider silk to wear on best occasions. As it happens there are two snags. In the first experiment several thousand spiders were kept in cages containing 50 to 100 spiders each. Flies were at their disposal and yet, in but a short time, each cage was found to contain one, or possibly two spiders. The cannibal nature of the subject had been overlooked and the idea was abandoned, for it would hardly be a paying proposition to keep several thousand spiders in separate cages.

The first snag therefore was entirely the fault of the spider; the second is ours. Mankind is inventive, too much so perhaps, but he has not yet been able to invent machinery capable of dealing with material as fine as spider thread. The coarsest spider silk is found in the cocoon but even so the silkworm's thread is five times as coarse as that of the coarsest spider cocoon. Monsieur Bon, when he made his stockings, frequently tore the thread, and torn thread reduces the lustre of the finished material.

Private investigators however still played with the idea. The Abbé Raymond de Termeyer found that silk can be drawn direct from a spider on to a spool, and he made silk by this method between 1762 and 1796. Once, he drew off silk from a spider and from a silkworm side by side and was amazed to find how much more beautiful was the spider silk. It was, he said, more like a mirror or polished metal than silk.

Wilder did the same thing in 1863. Having secured his spider he reeled off from her 150 yards of thread in one and a quarter hours. It seemed as easy as milking a cow but he found that his other subjects were not so complaisant as the first.

The large tropical spiders yield the best and their thread is thicker. But these methods cannot be used commercially, so I fear that we will never see the beauty of shapely calves and ankles enhanced by the metallic sheen of arachnidian silk.

CHAPTER 2

THE WOLF SPIDERS

The other day I met an undergraduate of London University. There is of course no reason why an undergraduate of London University should know any more about spiders than anyone else, but he informed me that all spiders made three webs, and three webs only. After that they made no more. I did not ask him what happened to the spider after the third web had gone—which might well happen in less than three days— but I did question his use of the words "all spiders." We had met casually and I was acting merely as listener. With this young man there was no chance of acting in any other way. He told me that *all* spiders wove webs. So, with the University of London behind me, I feel now that I need not apologise *too* much for going into things from the beginning and pedantically giving information that might be expected to be known by all.

Wolf spiders make no webs. They have no idea of web-making. Nor have any of the groups of spiders that follow except some foreign species of the trap-door group.

Wolf spiders in Britain belong to the families Lycosidae and Pisauridae and there is nothing much about them in general appearance to distinguish them from the web-weavers. Pisauridae only possesses two species here, so it is Lycosa with which we are chiefly concerned. These are the spiders you may see running about on the ground in the vegetable garden and (though they are not then so conspicuous) in woods and meadows.

The web-weaver, having patented a clever device, can now

sit back and collect the dividends; the wolf spider, unable
to think out anything in the way of a snare, has to pay the
penalty by leading a hard, strenuous, and dangerous life. It
has to get its prey by the crude method of running it down,
like the wolf or the wild dog. That, of course, is why it is
called a wolf spider, though in its hunting ways it resembles
a cheetah more than a wolf.

Mankind, like the web-weaver, sneers at this method. It
is primitive. And it is lucky for him that he does not have
to practise it. Consider yourself how you would fare if your
only food were to consist of creatures you caught by running
after them. It would bring home to you the progress made
by animals in counteraction against aggressors, just as it was
brought home to me in Africa; for once, when on trek, I
pitched my camp at midday and went out shooting with four
rounds of ammunition. I went along a river bed, crossed
it, and returned, having shot off my four rounds, along
the opposite bank, thinking that the river would inevitably
lead me back to camp. And so it would have done had I not
struck a tributary which curved away from the main bed and
took me in the wrong direction for several hours, finally
disappearing altogether. The result was that I was lost,
without ammunition, for two days before striking the camp
of a prospector, and during that period, for some reason connected with the irony of fate, I saw more game, large and small,
fur and feather, than I had ever seen before. *And* I was very
hungry and it struck me forcibly how helpless man is without
his inventions; how unfitted to take part in the battle for life
on his own.

The web-weaver is in a similar position. Without her
invention she would be too blind and slow to catch game.
But the wolf spider is keen-sighted and swift.

Some of the wolf spiders are long-lived, reaching an age of
six or seven years, though nearly all the British species live
for one, or, at the most, two years. The small ones are vaga-
bonds, running here and there and taking shelter under stones

and in crevices, but when they get older many begin to think of settling down and build shafts into the earth, which they occupy. These shafts get broader as the occupant becomes older and stouter, and the final home of a full-grown wolf spider can be quite a formidable affair; a castle with a parapet raised above the surface of the ground in which the owner lives like a baron of old.

A wolf spider that has gained more notoriety for itself than most is the Tarantula. It gets its name from the Italian city of Taranto in Apulia, on the outskirts of which it was once very numerous. Its scientific name is *Lycosa tarantula*. Now this Italian tarantula was, and still is, regarded as one of the most dangerous of customers. Only the other day a friend of mine, who had lived in India, asked, " *Is* there any cure for the bite of a tarantula?"—which shows how long these fables take to kill! When I told him the truth he smiled to himself and spoke no more about it, and I perceived that I had lost for ever any standing I might have with him as an authority on spiders.

The story of the tarantula has roots that are far-reaching. The belief was that if a tarantula bites you death follows, preceded by a state of melancholy called tarentism. If you wish to avoid death you must take action during this state of tarentism and the only cure is music. Not *any* music; you must get the right tune and the tune varies according to the patient's temperament.

This is what happens when the right steps are taken: the physician leads his patient (the unfortunate man or woman who has been bitten by a tarantula), dressed in flowing robes, into a large room where an orchestra is already stationed. The physician himself directs the orchestra and numerous dance measures ensue. But the patient remains sunk in despair. Then at last comes the right tune and the patient gets up, a wild look in his—or her—eyes and begins to dance in an uncontrolled way, shrieking frequently the while. Finally, dripping with perspiration, she (for it is generally a woman) sinks back into her seat, sleeps, and awakens cured.

One might have thought that it was the perspiration that had cured her if only one could bring oneself to believe that the bite of the tarantula had done her the slightest harm. For normally the only effect of a bite from a tarantula is a slight irritation.

But how did the tarantula gain its notoriety in the first place? There is no smoke, they say, without fire. In such a short space of time the bite cannot have become less deadly, nor can man have developed resistance to it. Therefore it never was deadly. Savory, I think, puts us on the right track. Long ago, near Taranto, Bacchanalian rites flourished. It was a popular form of entertainment and profitable to the promoters, and the priestesses of the rites dressed, and acted, much as the victims of the bite of the tarantula. Then the authorities decided to stamp out these orgies, which were merely an excuse for a sexual debauch. The stage-managers did not want their shows closed down so they cast around for an excuse and found it in the person of a local spider. That the myth continues to the present day is due largely to our ignorance of spiders.

There *are* spiders in certain parts of the world that give nasty bites—we shall deal with them in a moment. There are large foreign spiders too, and any traveller bitten by one is liable to call it a tarantula. I myself have had a centipede (of a species whose bite *is* dangerous and may cause death) pointed out to me as a tarantula. Indeed, many do not know that a tarantula is a spider, and a small one at that.

Nevertheless, no spider's bite should be passed over too lightly. Poison is injected. Mankind happens to have a strong natural resistance to this poison, but with some other animals it is lethal. The genus to be feared is LATRODECTUS. This genus does not live in England, though its family (which boasts the notorious Black Widow among its members), Theridiidae, is numerous with us. They are web-weavers and we have mentioned them in the last chapter. Strangely enough those representatives of the family that we possess are comparatively amiable, and their husbands live with them in as much safety as can ever be found in the vicinity of a female spider.

But Latrodectus is a different proposition and is almost the only spider that need be feared by the larger animals. She kills and eats tarantulas and scorpions, and horses and camels are put out of action by a single bite. In 1903 a camel bitten on the lip by a species of Latrodectus died in a few hours. Strangely, sheep and pigs are unaffected by her bite. A scientist named Reese once made extracts from the poison glands of Latrodectus and injected them into a cat, with the result that the cat died quickly. This same extract, not injected but in sugar pills, was swallowed by an experimentalist named Kellog, and the symptoms that followed were, he tells us, pains, a depressed heart beat, and constipation—a curious mixture.

Another spider that must go on the dangerous list is a funnel web spider from Australia, *Atrax robustus*, one of which according to McKeown bit a two-year-old boy in 1927. The boy died in one and a half hours. Between 1927 and 1933 there were three more deaths: a girl of five, who died in one and a quarter hours, a woman of 26, who died in 13 hours, and a woman of 47, who died in 11 hours. Against this are three known cases of people bitten by this spider who recovered.

However, these lists of deaths (like most statistics) are misleading. We are all of us greatly intrigued by murder and by murderers. The more popular newspapers know this and give any murder their full attention. They are always in search of a murderer. So when people die from the bite of a spider the deaths are advertised: the people *not* killed by the same type of bite are of no interest to anyone, especially the newspapers, and are ignored, however numerous they may be. The Black Widow of America (*Latrodectus mactans*) is probably the most dangerous of all the spiders. A whole book has been written about her. Let us boil down the evidence and accept the careful Cumstock's summing up. He says the symptoms following a bite consist of severe abdominal pains, a rise in blood pressure, perspiration, and nausea. The symptoms disappear in 24 hours. "There is no accurate estimation of the number of deaths but the percentage is certainly very small."

I must mention one more spider whose bite is poisonous if only to bring in its name. When scientists spread themselves in the matter of names they do it thoroughly. This was an Argentine spider called Podadore until scientists gave it the name of *Glyptocranum gasteracanthoides*. Well, *Glyptocranum gasteracanthoides* lives in vines and occasionally bites vine workers in the hand or foot causing a wound that becomes inflamed and takes from six to ten days to heal—a very unusual length of time for a spider bite.

But the reports of observers on the effects of the bites of the general run of spiders on human beings grow monotonous. And these reports provide nothing from which we can draw conclusions. Thus we read of a man bitten by a spider without any effect whilst his sister bitten by the same spider had a painful swelling that lasted several hours. Again, of a spider raising weals on a man's wrist but barely causing a mark on the wrist of a woman although it had bitten the woman first and given her most of its poison. And so on. The best thing to do if you *are* bitten by a spider is to take no notice of it. But if you are one of those who think that external applications are the slightest use for the bites of insects in general do not use a blue bag or similar application, for the poison of the spider is alkaline.

The smaller vertebrates however would do well to avoid the bite of *any* spider. Doleshall of America tells us how two large Mygalidae spiders when shut up with small birds used to bite them when the chance offered, and the birds died in a few minutes.

This is not the right chapter for them, but whilst on the subject of unusual prey we must mention the Nephila, the foreign weavers of huge orb webs, common in Australia and America. In its web small birds are caught and held. (A starling *has* been known to be captured.) These birds are killed by the spider,though whether they are used as food is not really known. Most of the authorities hold that they are killed to prevent too much damage to the web, and that they are then left where they are. But McKeown tells a story of a spider he once *saw* feasting on the neck of a bird caught in its web, sucking at the base of its skull and squeezing the flesh to get the blood, and later on noticed an increase in the spider's rotundity. It is difficult to discover the truth. Normally one only finds the bodies or skeletons of birds in these webs. One rarely sees one actually caught, and if one did one's overpowering impulse would be to release it. Probably in the majority of cases Nephila is merely annoyed when some finch blunders into her web making havoc of it, and she kills it as quickly as possible to prevent further damage. But an occasional spider, or one very hungry, *may* suck some of the blood.

A mouse in a house was once caught in a spider's web. It happened in America and the spider was not a big one. Indeed its body was described as being no larger than a pea. Anyway the mouse, a small one was caught, and held. All its struggles on the floor were insufficient to break the strands. And gradually the spider drew it up so that, after many hours, first its hind feet, then its forefeet, and then the mouse itself was hanging above the floor. The excited spider now attacked, running down to the mouse and biting it at the base of the tail. It made many bites, running away after each bite, and finally, though not for a long time, the mouse hung motionless and dead. It must not be gathered from this, however, that a spider web is a good mouse-trap, for I think it is the only recorded instance of a spider catching and killing a mouse.

Returning to the real tarantula, I think we shall have to visit Fabre again to get an idea of the effect of its bite on the

smaller creatures. Fabre died, an old man, in 1915, and there
have been many experiments since that time. But Fabre's
experiments have a continuance, a "leading on" quality that is
particularly satisfying and instructive.

Fabre's study must have been worth seeing. Nowadays a
scientist's study is rarely sacred territory. Wives and char-
women with brooms, hoovers, and tins of polish invade it
from time to time, causing havoc and destruction. Scribbled
important notes are put with the dust from the carpet into the
kitchen fire. Written sheets are put neatly together entailing
hours of work to sort them back again. And spiders in jars
—captive and helpless before their hereditary enemy—what
happens to them? Yet Fabre had his women so much under
control that he could keep dead birds in paper bags in different
stages of decomposition for a year or more on his study table.
And heaven knows what menageries and cages there must
have been besides.

His experiments into the bite of the tarantula were made
with a spider called *Lycosa narbonnensis*, which he called sometimes the Narbonne Lycosa and sometimes the Black-Bellied
Tarantula. It is common in certain parts of France, and is
almost identical in size and habits with the real tarantula,
Lycosa tarantula. Fabre tried the effect of its bite on the
Carpenter Bee. For this purpose he selected a huge species of
bee named *Xylocopa violacea*. Taking the Black-Bellied Tarantula
by its thorax between his forceps he made it bite the Carpenter
Bee in the neck. The neck is a deadly mark with most creatures,
and the Carpenter Bee died immediately.

Things were arranged with the next unfortunate so that it
was bitten in the abdomen and after this treatment it was
put into a bottle. Apparently it was none the worse, for it
buzzed about in the usual angry way of bees when imprisoned.
But soon it showed signs of distress and within half an hour
was lying motionless on its back. Occasional slight movements of the legs and a faint pulsing of the belly were the
only signs that life still remained. This carpenter bee died

(as did a number of others treated in the same way) the next day.

In natural circumstances however the carpenter bee is always bitten in the neck by the spider. It has to be, for, as we have seen, if bitten anywhere else it is as active as it was before, for half an hour. And not only active, but angry. In addition, it carries a particularly dangerous sting, so that the spider that is unable to kill it immediately had much better leave it alone altogether. In some of these experiments when Fabre was trying to make the tarantula bite the bee in the abdomen the bee got in first with its sting and it was the spider that died.

But in the ordinary way the spider never has dealings with the carpenter bee unless it sees a chance of a quick bite in the neck.

With unarmed creatures the tarantula avoids the neck bite probably because it produces death too quickly. Fabre made the same experiments with grasshoppers of various kinds, small grasshoppers and grasshoppers as large as one's finger; tough, powerful creatures. When bitten in the neck the result was the same—immediate death. When bitten elsewhere the result was also the same in the long run but the coarser organism of these creatures resisted the poison more strongly. Their strength however was but labour and sorrow. A grasshopper bitten in the stomach clung for 15 hours to the glass side of its jar prison (a feat requiring strength) before it dropped, thus showing 30 times the resistance of the carpenter bee. A large number of other insects were tested and showed varying degrees of resistance. All however, if bitten anywhere at all by the spider, died. There was no reprieve for any of them.

Following the master we have seen the dire effects of the bite of the Black-Bellied Tarantula on insects. What about other creatures? Fabre's first subject was a sparrow; a fully fledged sparrow just about to leave the nest. He made the spider bite it in the leg. The experiment is better described in his own words:

"A drop of blood flows; the wounded spot is surrounded by a reddish circle, changing to purple. The bird almost immediately loses the use of its leg, which drags, with the toes doubled in. It hops upon the other. Apart from this the patient does not seem to trouble much about his hurt; his appetite is good. My daughter feeds him on flies, bread-crumbs, apricot pulp. He is sure to get well, he will recover his strength; the poor victim of the curiosity of science will be restored to liberty. This is the wish, the intention of us all. Twelve hours later the hope of a cure increases; the invalid takes nourishment readily; he clamours for it if we keep him waiting. But the leg still drags. I set this down to a temporary paralysis which will soon disappear. Two days after he refuses his food. Wrapping himself in his stoicism and his rumpled feathers, the sparrow hunches into a ball, now motionless, now twitching. My girls take him in the hollow of their hands and warm him with their breath. The spasms become more frequent. A gasp proclaims that all is over. The bird is dead.

"There was a certain coolness among us at the evening meal. I read mute reproaches, because of my experiment, in the eyes of my home circle; I read an unspoken accusation of cruelty all round me. The death of the unfortunate sparrow had saddened the whole family. I myself was not without some remorse of conscience: the poor result achieved seemed to me too dearly bought. I am not made of the stuff of those who, without turning a hair, rip up live dogs to find out nothing in particular."

A mole comes next. It had been ravaging Fabre's lettuce plot, so there was some excuse for him. Again he must tell the tale.

"Nevertheless I had the courage to start afresh, this time on a mole. There was a danger lest my captive, with his famished stomach, should leave things in doubt, if we had to keep him for a few days. He might die not of the wound, but of inanition, if I did not succeed in giving him suitable food, fairly plentiful and dispensed at fairly frequent intervals. In that case I ran a risk of ascribing to the poison what well might be the result of starvation. I must therefore begin by finding out if it was possible for me to keep the mole alive in captivity. The animal was put into a large receptacle from which it could not get out and fed on a varied diet of insects —Beetles, Grasshoppers, especially Cicadae—which it crunched up with excellent appetite. Twenty-four hours of this régime convinced me that the mole was making the best of the bill of fare and taking kindly to his captivity.

"I make the tarantula bite him at the tip of the snout. When replaced in his cage, the mole keeps on scratching his nose with his broad paws. The thing seems to burn, to itch. Henceforth less and less of the provision is consumed; on the evening of the following day it is refused altogether. About 36 hours after being bitten the mole dies during the night and certainly not from inanition for there are still half a dozen live Cicadae in the receptacle, as well as a few beetles."

The Tarantula lives in a hole dug into the earth. The hole descends vertically for a few inches, then branches off in a sloping almost horizontal direction. It is lined with silk. This silk lining is useful in several ways; it acts as scaffolding and prevents the shaft collapsing or being blocked by falls of earth; it gives the spider a safe foothold in the perpendicular part; and it makes the place easy to keep clean. For the Tarantula after a meal washes herself carefully and sweeps out the debris from her tunnel. The top of her hole is surmounted by a parapet usually about an inch high which is made of what material comes to hand. It is frequently made of small pebbles bound and tied in place with silk. The Tarantula usually stations herself at the elbow leading to the horizontal shaft. It is dark there, and if you look down you will see four eyes gleaming like diamonds in the blackness below. She has eight eyes, but four are smaller and do not gleam in the dark.

Now Fabre wished to capture some tarantulas. There are two instructions given by experts for so doing. One is to get a knife and thrust it down quickly into the earth and block the hole near the elbow and then dig out the Tarantula. The other is to get a long spiked piece of grass and insert it into the hole. The Tarantula, annoyed at this intrusion, seizes it and is drawn out. Fabre tried both methods. The knife method was hopeless from the beginning; the ground was hard and stony and no knife would penetrate. The spiked grass method was easy but had the drawback that no spider ever came out at the end of it. So he tried a method of his own, which we will call the "Bumble-Bee Method."

I will describe it. First, as Mrs. Beeton says about another animal, catch your bumble-bee. Having caught it, put it in a bottle. Insert this bottle over the hole of a Tarantula and the trick is done. For the bumble-bee buzzes in anger and alarm, and then seeing a hole in the earth goes down it. Meanwhile the Tarantula has heard the buzzing and, scenting a meal, has become interested and is already half-way up the shaft.

The operator waits. The bee has disappeared. What now? To his ears comes the sound of a subterranean commotion. Then silence. This is his cue. He puts his forceps down the hole and slowly draws up the dead body of his bee to which is attached the Tarantula holding on like grim death. The bait having been lifted above the surface the hole is blocked and the Tarantula is his. And if, as often happens, the Tarantula gets alarmed and lets go the bee when you are drawing it to the surface and dives for safety it does not matter. All you have to do is to leave the dead body of the bee on the parapet. The Tarantula will soon come back. She will not lightly discard so rich a prize which she has killed herself and feels is hers. At least, so Fabre says, and he adds that his method is fool-proof.

Fabre caught many tarantulas by this method and used them for many experiments and was very pleased with the whole thing. Then he began to have a guilty feeling. His bumble-bee was always killed, which was a thing he had reckoned on, but *how* was it killed? His conscience pricked him because he had never seen it *being* killed.

When a hunting wasp, of the species that preys on the Tarantula, is made by some experimenter to go down the hole nothing of great importance ensues. The Tarantula is not killed and neither is the wasp. Usually after an underground scuffle the Tarantula comes out into the open and stations itself close to its hole and there waits for the wasp and when the wasp emerges knocks it spinning with a heavy clout. After which it goes back into its hole muttering to itself. So, under artificial conditions it is practically impossible to see the way a hunting wasp overcomes a Tarantula. It is the same with many insects: they will not show us their tricks when we want them to. They are like children who are word perfect in their recitations but on the day of the party wriggle themselves about and refuse to perform.

It was so with the Tarantula: she refused to show Fabre how she killed a bumble-bee. He placed the two in a bottle. Both concentrated on one thing only—the getting out of it. So he put them in a test tube where there was room only for one at the bottom. Even then the bee never drew her weapon and the spider refused to bite. The bee lay on her back at the bottom of the tube and tried to ward off the spider with her legs and the spider hoisted itself up as far as possible by pressing with its legs against the glass sides, thus keeping away from the bee. The bee of course did not keep still. Ever and anon it would buzz distractedly and bob up and down in the tube. Therefore it frequently found itself on top instead of underneath, in which case the spider adopted the same tactics and lying on its back fended off the bee with its long legs. There was no fighting and no killing.

Fabre of course tried again and again but with no happier

results. So he discarded the bumble-bee and went back to his friend the Carpenter Bee. He had already studied the results of a bite on this bee by using force on the spider and he now wished to see how the spider acted in natural, or almost natural, conditions. The difference between this bee and a bumble-bee is that the former does not go down odd holes, so if it *is* going to be killed it will be killed up above in the open where the act can be seen. Fabre put his Carpenter Bee in a bottle and, taking it with him, went round looking for Tarantula holes. He found them in abundance, and popped his bottle over the first.

The bee buzzed about and the spider came up from below and stood at her threshold watching the bee. And she continued to watch it until even this observer's patience wore thin. At last however the spider turned round and went back into her hole. She had decided she did not like the look of the bee. So Fabre moved on to another burrow and inverted his bottle over that one. The bee buzzed admirably and the spider came up and after a short inspection went back. And so on from burrow to burrow. And from each burrow a Tarantula appeared, had a long look, and went back.

The morning was hot and getting hotter every moment, but Fabre persevered. From door to door he trudged like a travelling salesman offering a bee to the lady of the house, and in every case the lady shook her head and went indoors. And then he came to the door of a certain lady more interested in his wares. She rushed out and—it was over in a second almost too quick to see. The bee was dead—bitten in the neck.

One would have thought that all was finished now; that Fabre's tiring morning in the heat was over. His perspiring efforts had been crowned with success. He had proved his point about the neck bite. All that remained was to go home and write it up. But not at all. Because one Tarantula bites a bee in the neck it does not follow that they all do. That was what he felt, and obtaining a fresh supply of bees went off on his door to door round once more. He worked that day from eight o'clock in the morning till midday, and for the same period the next day. Eight hours in all, and in those eight hours he saw three Tarantulas kill Carpenter Bees. And they all bit in the same place—the neck.

A short time ago I said that the best thing to do if bitten by a spider is to ignore it. Perhaps I was rash. We have little data on the subject for very few people *are* bitten by spiders. Our bodies are not all made to one pattern like a motor car, and in any case we know surprisingly little about them. To continue with the motor car analogy it is as if we drove highly complicated models but only knew how to steer them and when to put in oil and petrol. Of how they work most of us have no notion. When something goes wrong we take them to a garage in the shape of a doctor, but even he has only a vague idea of how our model works and frequently fails to trace the cause of a break-down. As I said, our bodies are different. Some lack internal agents that others possess. A single tablet of aspirin will cause some people to swell up, peas and beans make others go blue. What is harmless to one man may be very dangerous to another. When in China I used to be very fond of a Japanese sweetmeat made out of a certain seaweed; and so were a large number of people. One day I went on board a Yangtse steamer to see the master, who was a friend of mine. I gave him one of my sweetmeats and he liked it. But it didn't like him. It very nearly killed him. A doctor was called in. I am sure the doctor thought that I had tried to poison him. But the patient did not when he heard what my sweetmeats were made of. He was allergic to iodine and knew it. The slightest trace of iodine in anything he took put him out of action. Some agent lacking in his system of course. What this agent was I do not know, neither did the doctor. So if a spider bites you (and not one in ten thousand ever is bitten by a spider) and really unpleasant symptoms ensue, call in a doctor for you *may* be lacking in some agent that normally deals with spider toxin.

What is this toxin? Scientists do not carry us very far here. They say it is a strongly alkaline fluid containing proteids and an albuminoid. Which conveys little to me.

One cannot make rules about spiders nor lump them together. Nor can one go into their lives species by species— even if these lives were known. We shall study the wolf spider's life by taking again *Lycosa narbonnensis* or the Black-Bellied Tarantula as our model, and again Fabre will be the class master during most of the lesson. We must make the most of him, for after this chapter he has only one more short experiment to show us.

Lycosa, when mature, lives in a burrow above which she has erected a parapet, and from this parapet she surveys the territory over which she holds sway. Should any wayfarer approach she crouches down and gets ready for a quick take-off. Hers is the method of the cheetah, an animal that is a famous sprinter, but no stayer. A gazelle or buck that can keep in front of a cheetah for a hundred yards will get away, but the odds are it will not keep in front, for the cheetah beyond a doubt, holds the world's record for the hundred yards.

So the wayfarer, plodding along, awakens to the fact that something is coming down on him like an express train. One backward look is sufficient; the wayfarer accelerates frantically. But usually it is hopeless; the Tarantula has had a flying start and is on him almost before he has started. The wayfarer is then either eaten on the spot or dragged to the cellar and eaten there.

Lycosa, the Wolf Spider, is not the sadist that Aranea is. If the prey is large she kills it immediately, for she lacks ropes to tie it and has no web to embarrass it. This means of course that she must often lunch in our own manner, crunching her meat. But she does not really eat meat; no spider does. She chews to extract the fluid. Not a nice meal to watch.

In the neighbourhood of the castle of the Wolf Spider tales must circulate. The inhabitants must talk together and shake their heads. Doubtless many a traveller enquiring the way meets with a significant pause and is advised to take a round-about route. If the traveller asks why, he hears vague mut-terings about an ogre and about people disappearing. Anyway he will be well advised to take the route the locals suggest.

But many pass by the castle and the ogress waxes fat. Later on she kills less. For one thing she is bulging with food, and for another a desire for other things than blood stirs in her. With the heat of August she feels the need of a mate. It is no use her waiting where she is. The eager lover she envisages will not come into her bedroom—not if he can help it. Sheep do not *rush* into slaughter-houses. The pros-pective bridegroom is eager, too, for her but he wishes to meet his bride in a place where he has a chance of getting away after the nuptials are over.

So Lycosa leaves her burrow and goes in search of a lover, and in due course, in obedience to that strict disciplinarian, Nature, a small creature appears and stands trembling before her. The bridegroom has arrived.

I shall deal in another chapter with the mating of spiders: what I propose to do now is to study Lycosa as a mother.

We start with this same Lycosa observed by Fabre's children under a bush. The children called their father and he came running. The nuptials were over and the bridegroom had not been quick enough. He had lingered longer than he should in the arms of his bride and she now stood over him eating him. The morbid circle composed of Fabre and his children waited until the obese female had munched and drained her husband dry, then they captured her and put her in a cage which stood on sand in Fabre's study.

In this cage in due course Fabre was able to examine the making of the cocoon of the Wolf Spider. A brief summary will be sufficient for, as I have said, the making of a spider's cocoon is a very complicated process. The cocoons of the web-weavers were stationary affairs, edifices, little houses, placed in certain fixed spots; the cocoon of the Wolf Spider is a large pill that she straps to her person and carries about. It is not so complicated as the cocoons of most of the web-weavers, but since it has to be made detached and portable it presents certain difficulties. It requires space for the making, a cleared patch, so she must leave her burrow to do it. She left her burrow in any case in order to meet the unfortunate whom for a brief period she called husband. Now, as a widow —grass or otherwise according to the alertness and dodging power of her spouse—she probably remains away from home for the ten days or so that must elapse before the laying of her eggs. She takes refuge under stones when necessary and is just as great a menace to passers by—not quite, perhaps; never svelt, her belly is now enormous and must take something off her speed.

Away from her burrow the ogress herself is not of course immune from danger. Other pregnant mothers are abroad. It is the hunting wasp season and amongst the hunting wasps are those who feed their children on nothing but spiders. A smaller, shapelier, deadlier mother may descend on her, overpower her, drug her, and drag her to the cruellest fate that callous Nature ever devised. There are birds, too, and other enemies, but assuming she escapes these dangers she selects a pitch and lays down a carpet. Though made of silk it is a rough affair, more a mat than a carpet. When one lacks a table and has delicate work to do one *does* lay down a mat. The Chinese do it; so do the Indians and many others. It acts as a floor and a protection from dirt and sand. On this floor Lycosa weaves a disc. It is a different affair from the mat, beautifully made from closely woven white silk, and forms a kind of bowl. In the centre of this bowl Lycosa lays a circular heap of eggs which are then covered with a napkin which she weaves over them. The most laborious part of the affair is to come: the silk disc is carefully detached from the mat to which it has been tied and then, legs and jaws working hard, is folded over the bag of eggs, after which the sides are sewn together. The result is a white silk globe nearly as large as the mother, with one side thick and the other side thinner.

The mother is tired. The making of the cocoon has been exhausting work. Moreover, in addition to manufacturing eggs her inside has been drained of what, for a wolf spider, is a great deal of silk. She clasps the globe to her and rests for the remainder of the day.

Mother love is a strange thing. We marvel at it in our own kind, for a new-born child is not *really* enticing. Still less enticing, one would think, would be a mass of jellied eggs. Yet upon that mass, even though enclosed in a case, Lycosa now lavishes an affection greater than that displayed by the most obsessed of human mothers. And what makes it stranger is the character of the mother herself. We have seen the way she treated the father, the part creator of those precious globules. And we have seen her, morose, solitary, dour, dangerous, thinking only of her stomach. That mother love, transcendent, self-denying, prepared always for the supreme sacrifice, should spring from such a source is strange. Human mothers have something that *needs* them, yet in spite of their infatuation one cannot imagine them crooning over a number of billiard balls in a box, which, in effect, is all the wolf spider mother has to cherish. And, or so one supposes, she knows nothing of the future. The human mother thinks her child will turn into something even more beautiful. Lycosa does not even know that her eggs will turn into anything at all. And when they *do* they jettison quite half her affection.

Next day Lycosa will be found to have tied the globe to her with silk tapes and to be moving about with it. She carries it slung beneath her. It is almost as large as herself and at first her movements are greatly hampered. But she gets used to it and by raising her legs as she goes can clear most obstructions. Later on she learns to run quite quickly with it. In a manner of speaking she is a mother that is never seen without her perambulator, and mother and perambulator often go flying along at more speed than one would think right for such a combination. In these chases, which are generally after game, the cocoon is often knocked off, but it is a matter of seconds for Lycosa to strap it on again.

So attached is she, in the figurative sense, to her globular burden that she will fight to the death to retain it. As Savory says, "The possession of a cocoon changes the mother's entire outlook on life." If it is taken away from her she goes frantic. She searches everywhere. She is incredulous, horrified.

Bonnet once found a wolf spider carrying her cocoon and threw her into the pit of an ant-lion. Aware of her danger the spider tried to run away. Too late; the ant-lion seized the under-slung cocoon between its jaws. The mother struggled and in these struggles the cocoon became detached. Now was the mother's chance to save her life, but instead of running away she turned round in the pit and seized the cocoon which was being drawn under the sand. Her strength of course could not prevail against that of the ant-lion, but she retained her hold and was drawn under the sand together with her beloved bag. And she would have been buried alive and that would have been the end of her, but for Bonnet, who dug her out. He got no thanks, for her first act was to hurl herself into the pit again. Bonnet fished her out a second time and for some time kept her from suicide by warding her away with a twig from the fatal chasm. So obviously the Wolf Spider prefers death to life without her cocoon.

Equally striking is her delight when it is given back to her and she straps the beloved possession to her person once more and goes on her way rejoicing.

Some observers say that if the burden is not restored the mother dies of grief in a few days. This is to be doubted.

Those careful observers, the Peckhams, say that Lycosa, having been deprived of her capsule will still eagerly seize it if it is restored to her after 16 or 17 hours. Sometimes she will respond after 24 hours. But after two days she never has any further interest in it.

Dearly as she loves her pill it *is* just a pill and loud has been the laughter of naturalists at the fact that after it has been taken away she cannot recognise it from others similar. But before we vertebrates laugh too loudly let us make quite sure that we are in a position to do so. Any bird will brood over misshapen stones substituted for her eggs. Hedge-sparrows do not throw out the cuckoo's egg, so different from their own. Fowls will sit on potatoes or nothing at all for four weeks or more. A cat, agonised by the loss of her young will suckle baby rats. A sheep dog in similar circumstances will suckle young foxes. A cow whose calf has been taken away will make known its bereavement to all the neighbourhood, yet its lugubrious bellows will cease if the calf's skin stuffed with straw is placed by its side. The story of Romulus and Remus was considered credible by the ancient Romans, and substitution of babies has been made without even human mothers realising it.

Therefore I am not going to comment too scathingly on Lycosa in the experiments that Fabre is about to conduct.

He took a Lycosa's cocoon away from her. He did it with his famous pair of forceps which she attacked with such fury that he could hear her fangs grating on the steel. Immediately he gave her a cocoon taken from another Lycosa. She took it, strapped it to her, and walked contentedly away.

Well, even Fabre did not jeer *very* much at this. He merely said contemptuously, "Her own or another's: it is all one to the spider."

He next tried the same experiment but substituted a cocoon of a different shape, made by another species of spider. This too was taken with as much relief as the other.

"Let us," goes on Fabre, "penetrate yet further into the wallet-bearer's stupidity."

So he made a ball of cork of the same size as Lycosa's cocoon. He made it carefully and polished it with a file. It was accepted.

"The silly creature . . . embraces the cork ball, fondles it . . . fastens it to her spinnerets and drags it after her."

Worse is to come. Fabre made several of these cork balls —four or five—and arranged them with the real cocoon amongst them. The bereaved Lycosa simply rushed up and took the first.

"This obtuseness," concludes Fabre, "baffles me. We will leave her alone; we know all that we want to know about her poverty of intellect."

Fabre thought he had sounded bottom in the abyss of Lycosa's stupidity. But he had not, although he never knew it. Locket records that he saw a *Lycosa palustris* running about with a small snail-shell tied to her. And this was not an experiment. The creature must have lost her cocoon somehow and after hours of frantic search decided that a snail-shell was better than nothing.

But when dealing with spiders, experiments are not of as much value as those made upon many other animals. Spiders are individualists (a horrid but useful word). The experiments have now gone further. Savory tells us that a species in Africa, *Palystes natalius*, invariably selects her own cocoon from that of another spider even of her own species. And yet this same discriminating spider after having bungled in the making of her cocoon and produced a very misshapen object, selected a properly shaped one made by another in preference to her own. So scent has no bearing on the subject. Sight may have; for another of this species selected another's cocoon after her own had been stained with aniline dye.

Other genera also, of the family Theridiidae, will have no dealings at all with *any* substitutes.

By the middle of September in the case of our particular

Lycosa, the pill bursts and two hundred young come pouring out. When the last has emerged the mother unstraps her bag and throws it away. But if she thinks she is now a free female she is very much mistaken. These two hundred know where they are going; they are going with mother. You almost need a lens to see them, but they are perfect spiders in every respect and shaped like their parents. They have their wits about them too and do not delay. The bursting of the pill has scattered them around a bit but they pull themselves together and all come running up to the mountainous form that is their parent. They find her long legs and stream up them and soon are perched on her back like so many passengers on a bus. Their bodies are packed in rows and their legs intermingled together. Fortunately no conductor is present or there would be wholesale ejections and long ago the "No room on top" would have sounded. Once aboard and seated they are very quiet and good.

It is a long journey on which these diminutive passengers have embarked. It will last about six months, and they have brought no provisions. It is a hazardous journey too; the driver is careless and sometimes makes insufficient allowance for obstructions so that the passengers are swept from their seats. On these occasions the bus usually stops and waits and the fares run up and climb back to their places.

The mother has changed. She is still a good mother (to carry two hundred children about for six months speaks for itself) but she does not dote on them now as she doted on them when they were inanimate pellets in a box. Her attitude is that of a good-natured but indifferent riding donkey.

These spider babies pass the whole of the six or seven months without food; at least so far as observers keeping them under scrutiny in cages can ascertain. How they do it is a mystery. It is not as if they were comatose and expending no energy. They expend quite a lot one way and another. Even when seated on top they often have to cling together to retain their positions on the swaying vehicle, especially when the vehicle

sees some prey and accelerates violently. And when they fall
off they expend still more energy, for the mother does not always stop for them. Yet this energy is never replaced by food.
The mother likes to "sun" her babies whenever she can,
turning herself from time to time so that all get the rays
and Fabre suggests that they get their energy direct from the
sun. Scientists however say this is nonsense; only vegetables
can do that.

The mother still likes her food. Babies or no babies, she
runs down what game her burdened state allows. And when
she is eating it the young sit above viewing the orgy with
complete indifference. They are no more interested than
human passengers are interested when their coach takes in
petrol.

Fabre, of course, has not failed to experiment with these
riders. He brushed a complete party off in such a way that
they fell amongst the legs of another Lycosa mother who was
already carrying more than her full complement of excursionists. The mother of the first party he whisked away.
Party No. 1 immediately climbed on to the top of the new
vehicle, without protest either from the driver or the legitimate
fares.

He then repeated the experiment, but instead of brushing
the youngsters into the vicinity of another Lycosa, he selected
an Aranea, a type that does not cater for passenger traffic at
all. The urchins with one accord ran up Aranea's legs and
Aranea shook her legs in horror and disgust. Several juveniles
were knocked spinning but some reached the top, and most
of those that had been ejected ran back and again attempted
the ascent. Again many were flung away, but again many
reached the target and took their seats sedately with the
others.

Their complacency was short-lived: Aranea rolled over on
her back, killing some and maiming others. And she had to
roll several times before she could get rid of them all.

The young, unless brushed off, sit where they are, but in

dangerous situations they alight of their own accord. One such dangerous situation is when two wolf mothers come face to face. In such an event there will be no friendly discussion about the care of children: there will simply be a fight. The children themselves realise this and lose no time in dismounting and making themselves scarce. Peering from cover, they then watch a fight that is no kid-gloved affair.

Eventually one panting matron stands over the other. Fabre has recorded such a fight and shown us the victorious one holding down her opponent, gripping her with her legs and pressing down on her belly. Amongst female spiders no quarter is given or expected. The prone one spits viciously and the other waits her time to avoid those snapping jaws and bite into the brain.

Fabre also relates how, after the *coup de grâce* had been given and the conqueress was eating her opponent, all the children came forth from hiding and climbed on to her back. And there they sat until mother—for she was "mother" now to all of them—had finished her meal.

It follows therefore that a matron, if a good fighter, *may* go out with her own children in the morning and come back in the evening carrying three lots packed several tiers deep.

Three is the limit. Fabre experimented and managed to get three loads on to one mother's back but could not manage a fourth. The mother herself raised no objection, but the load became top-heavy and swayed when the mother moved so that those perched on the summit fell off.

In winter all live in the burrow and the mother eats little, if anything. But in spring she is up and about again and taking her toll of passers-by. The little ones are still on her back and they are exactly the same size as when they left the cocoon—one could hardly expect growth on a diet of air.

Some people, of the class who only give a spider one vague look, have asked me why—if wolf spiders are so common— *they* have never seen a wolf spider running about the garden carrying young on her back? The answer is that they have.

To them a wolf spider even with a three-tier deep lot of passengers would seem merely a spider with a large greyish-coloured back.

In late spring new urges stir in the bosoms of the passengers. The long, long trip is over so far as this particular vehicle is concerned. They alight in batches and are soon seen running away as if they had an urgent appointment somewhere else. They have, for their journey is not over.

The mother shows no emotion at their departure. And they on their part show as much concern as we show when we alight at a junction and go from one train to another. They are well advised. For all her apparent indifference the mother's patience is wearing a bit thin. In a few months she will marry again and have more children and before that time she wants some liberty. She wants to start another reign of terror in the countryside. So if any children stay too long they disappear. Passengers are no longer allowed on top, but there is plenty of room inside.

The little spiders hurry on. They run up short grasses and down again and try others. Already some have reached the tops of railings or tall herbage. It is as if each one carried a banner with a strange device—Excelsior.

And shortly they go higher still. One by one, like prophets snatched to heaven, they are ascending into the blue without apparent agency.

This ballooning, this rising upwards of young spiders, is not confined to wolf spiders: it is the preliminary launching of most species of all our groups and we shall have more to say about it later. Those that escape the many dangers will descend. It may be only a few yards from the starting place or it may be many miles.

There is always something sad in the breaking up of family life and this case seems sadder than most. For six months none of them have quarrelled. Can such harmony continue? No, it cannot; hence the trip by air to widely separated parts. The brother that sat next to a sister on the mother's back and must have got to know her very well, had better not get near to her again.

Descending to land, each casts off its harness. The discarded silken trail floats away and the young spider looks around. It is feeling a completely new sensation—hunger. There are forms around smaller even than itself and one of these it catches and eats—much, no doubt, to the surprise of a stomach that has not yet functioned. It is the most accommodating of all stomachs, being able to cope with much or nothing at all. Had we in these days of indigestion and gastric ulcers the stomachs of—but we have not the stomachs of spiders so let us forget it.

At certain times of the season and in certain places small wolf spiders may be seen running about on the ground in such numbers that they appear to be hunting in packs like their namesakes. But they are not, and constitute as much danger to each other as to their normal prey.

Lycosa narbonnensis, the Tarantula, as we have said, carries her children for six or seven months, which is not far short of the time a human mother carries hers. Not all the Lycosa young are carried so long. Some, indeed, can only book their seats for a fortnight. This is the case with most of the British species, who breed twice a year. But apart from the duration of the journey the way of the mother with her young is the same with all the Wolf Spiders.

CHAPTER 3

THE JUMPING SPIDERS

THE Wolf Spider, as we have just seen, is like a wolf in that it hunts by sight and depends on fleetness of foot, but is even more like the cheetah in that it hunts alone and depends on its first quick rush to get its prey. The Jumping Spider shows us yet another method of hunting—stalking. It practises, in fact, the tactics of the Red Indian or—and this is an even better comparison—those of the domestic cat. The cat, of course, lives a Jekyll and Hyde existence. The dear creature that purrs and rubs itself against your leg is a very different animal when it is outside and has sighted some bird.

We know, its methods. It crouches motionless, and then by imperceptible degrees squirms forward close to earth. Having got as close to the bird as it dares, it springs, and stakes its chances on that spring. The method of the jumping spider is the same, except that most of what the cat knows about stalking the spider has already forgotten. This is fortunate, for did the cat's performance approach that of the jumping spider in technique there would be no birds left in our gardens.

The jumping spider's job is infinitely more difficult than the cat's. If a bird settles on the branch of a high tree the cat never for one moment entertains the thought of going after it. It does not like being laughed at by birds. But supposing the cat were as clever and as well equipped as the jumping spider—what would it do? It would move towards the base of the trunk of the tree taking advantage of every bit of cover. Arriving at the base it would get ready its coils of rope (like an Alpine climber it must have these: the tree is high and a fall would be a calamity). It would now climb up the trunk, fixing its rope every few feet and taking such clever cover from side branches, leaves, and bits of bark, as to prevent the bird ever spotting it.

Then it would arrive at the side branch, at the extremity of which sat the bird. Still trailing the rope, and fixing it firmly at frequent intervals it would move along this branch towards the bird, always of course taking advantage of any cover, however slight. The bird might fly away, but if it did it would not be because it had seen the cat. Then at a certain distance the cat would spring—and this cat would be a marvellous judge of distances and a great clinger to slender footholds and it would land unerringly upon the bird. At least it would land upon the bird nine times out of ten. In the tenth case it would miss and fall off the bough into the abyss below. But only a little way, for its rope would have been fixed a few feet behind and it would merely hang for a second and climb back to the bough.

Enough of this: it is obvious, I think that the cleverest cat operating under these conditions would merely cause the bird to fly off at the fit and proper moment with a derisive chirp.

The jumping spider operates on walls, palings, plants, and even on polished surfaces.

I have had a soft spot for jumping spiders ever since a night in Hongkong. There were only three mosquitoes, but three were sufficient. Whenever I was going off to sleep one or more of them would come pinging round my face, and alight. Finally I turned the light on. One made off to the cornice on the wall and clung there for a rest. A minute later I saw a small dark object moving carefully towards it. The object crouched, made a little run, then stopped and crouched again. So it continued, sometimes crouching, sometimes making little runs, sometimes crawling so stealthily and slowly that movement was hardly perceptible: and all the time drawing nearer. I watched breathless. I allowed the other two mosquitoes to bite without let or hindrance. Not for anything would I have made a sound or movement to interrupt the drama that was taking place. Closer and closer. Barely half an inch to go! Then it came! With a movement so quick I never saw it, the spider leapt on its prey. After that it sucked its blood (and probably some of mine as well).

This left two mosquitoes, but being by now gorged and heavy they did not endure for long. They had grown careless and I soon got them.

I have a soft spot for jumping spiders in any case. They are nice, rather trusting little things and very fond of a game. Our commonest jumping spider in Britain is the Zebra Spider, conspicuous and unmistakable in black with broad white transverse markings. It loves greenhouses and if you see one and wish to please it, play hide and seek with it. It will peer at you from cover and keep coming out to show you where it is. Two days ago three of us were on a veranda when a zebra spider appeared on the railing. I put my hand towards it. It waited till the hand was close and then jumped on to a finger. My friends did the same, and very soon the spider, enjoying this game, kept running up, looking for fingers to jump on.

To operate on polished cornices (and to walk round the sides of glass jars) indicates that there is something about jumping spiders not possessed by other spiders. All of us, in the morning, have seen from time to time a spider trapped in an empty bath. How it got there is immaterial—it either fell in or went there after water. What is very obvious is that the trapped one cannot get out. In short, the ordinary spider cannot walk up a smooth perpendicular surface. The reason a jumping spider can do so is because nature has given the jumping spider special feet. It alone possesses a pad of adhesive hairs, called a "scopula," between the claws.

You can recognise a jumping spider by this alone, but it is troublesome and needs a lens. Moreover you do not need to bother about its feet for recognition purposes. One look is sufficient.

The wolf spider has good eyesight, but the jumping spider has better. It has the finest sight of all the spiders. This of course is to be expected, for stalking needs better eyes than merely chasing something that is running away. We ourselves, when stalking, generally employ field-glasses or telescopes, but the jumping spider has to rely on its unaided vision. In this it is assisted by a rather peculiar arrangement of its main eyes. The normal spider has a rounded head with eight eyes (eight being the usual allowance) arranged in varying patterns on top, but the jumping spider has four of its eyes placed in a row as far in front as possible. These four eyes are large, particularly the two centre ones (the other four are placed behind and are small, insignificant, and little used), and to get these large eyes in a row, the front of the spider must be square-shaped. It is by this square-shaped front that you can recognise a jumping spider.

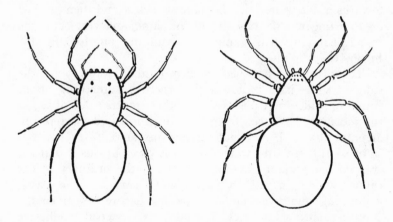

FIG. 15

A jumping spider (*left*) showing square front compared with an average spider of the other groups

Apart from good eyesight jumping spiders are endowed with a visual discernment that is unusual amongst insects, and indeed amongst the majority of higher animals. For the jumping spider will stalk a dead insect. When the wind prevents use of the sense of smell, most of the higher animals are very quick indeed at detecting an enemy by sight, but there must be *some* movement. This was particularly brought home to me when I was stalking game with a camera in Portuguese East Africa. With a camera one must get closer than with a gun, and I adopted the usual crawling tactics, going through the grass from cover to cover on my stomach, or peering from behind trees. But however carefully I moved, the animals could see the slight motion of the grass tops, or see my head when it came above the surface or peered from the tree, and the only photographs I ever got by this method were those of distant hindquarters obscured in a cloud of dust.

So I adopted different tactics which, to my surprise, proved successful. I stood boldly in the open viewing the object through the lens of the reflex camera and thus hiding my eyes, which are often a give-away. Nine times out of ten my unconcealed erect figure caused no lasting alarm. I was subjected often to strict and prolonged scrutiny but, remaining motionless, was taken for a tree trunk or something equally harmless, and in due course the animal would resume its grazing, or whatever its previous occupation had been. Having them fully in sight through the lens the whole time I was able to move only when they were not looking. Progress was laborious and very slow but I used to get surprisingly close, sometimes almost on top of the shyest of creatures. There were anxious moments. Heads would jerk up suddenly, muscles would be tensed ready for flight. One could read their thoughts, "Surely that trunk was not *there* a minute ago!" or "Surely that trunk *moved!*" But complete stillness did the trick. They were waiting for some *movement*, however slight, to confirm their fears, and, getting none, relaxed. Even the click of the camera did not always send them off, though it meant subjection to further and stricter scrutiny.

These tactics would not have deceived the jumping spider. This spider therefore is one of the few animals whose eyes can discriminate without the assistance of motion. Most spiders hate ants. A jumping spider, seeing a moving ant, will take no further notice of it. But a dead ant does not look like an ant; it lacks the peculiar gait and fuss by which an ant is recognised, and a jumping spider will carefully stalk and jump on a dead ant—to go away in disgust of course when it finds out what it is.

For so powerful a jumper, one would expect elongated *hind* legs after the fashion of the grasshopper, kangaroo, or flea, but the jumping spider has the *front* legs longer. This puzzled observers who could not find out how it *did* jump and finally decided that it used either all its feet or only its front ones. Bristowe however showed that it jumped with its short hind legs and that if one hind leg (say the right) was amputated the spider alighted facing to the right owing to the kick-off with the left leg, and that the long forelegs were used to hold down the prey.

The jumping spiders belong to the family Salticidae and although there are about 30 species in Britain only one or two of these are at all common, and the commonest as we have said is the pretty "Zebra Spider" (*Salticus scenicus*). To see jumping spiders at their best one must go to the tropics. There the species are numbered by the thousand and many are supremely beautiful, often in a daring way, going in for ornamentation of a most intricate and lavish description. In colouring the jumping spiders outshine all the others. "More like jewels than spiders" is how Wallace describes them.

It is strange that we have no records of performing spiders. Performing fleas are, or were, common enough, and the spider has more intelligence than the flea. The great trouble with the flea, I believe, is the prodigious height of its jump. To cure this, prospective performers are placed in boxes covered with glass so that repeated headaches may tone down the exuberance of the take-off. This would not be necessary with the spider for, although a strong jumper (being able to clear what would correspond to a standing jump of 40 feet by a man) it is not in the same class as the flea. Moreover it would show no desire for any close acquaintance with the audience.

Mr. and Mrs. Peckham, merely as an occasional pastime easily trained their captive jumping spiders to jump on to their hands for food, and then to jump from finger to finger, gradually increasing the distance until a leap of eight inches was attained. So the thing could be done.

CHAPTER 4

THE CRAB SPIDERS

CRAB spiders are so called because most of them look like crabs and have a crab-like motion, being able to go sideways and even backwards.

It is in this group that we meet the actors and actresses of the spider world. The star performer perhaps is *Phrynarachne decipiens*, found in the East by H. O. Forbes. Her turn, as with many of her calling, is definitely vulgar: she imitates a dropping of excreta. Bird droppings are usually white at the edges, and white mixed with black particles in the centre, and they are frequently found splashed on a leaf.

It is on a leaf that Phrynarachne does her act, and in white silk weaves an irregular rounded blotch. She is even conscientious enough to fashion at the bottom a blob in imitation of the more liquid portion of the bird's discharge that collects at the base. She then squats in the centre of this work of art and completes the deception. For the actress herself is irregularly marked with black and white and her appearance in the centre supplies what was lacking before—the darker and more solid portion of the excreta. Forbes himself could never tell the difference until he made the spider (when it *was* a spider) move.

What is the object of this trick? Phrynarachne is of course enabled to sit unconcealed in the open and snap up anything that comes, for no insect is going to be frightened of the dropping of a bird. But it goes further than that. Butterflies are beautiful, but their ways are not always as nice as their appearance. Both in China and Africa, particularly Africa, I have found exquisite butterflies feeding on animal carcases that stank to heaven. Indeed, at certain times and places I have seen such carcases a blaze of colour from the concourse of butterflies collected about them. Therefore it is not surprising that a certain butterfly in the East makes a habit of visiting the droppings of birds for what it can get from them. Dr. Forbes caught one of these feasting, as he thought, on a bird-dropping on a leaf, only to find that it was not feasting at all but being eaten itself by Phrynarachne.

How this mimicry originates is a problem. A spider cannot study natural history and then decide which object to imitate. The more feasible solution is that *because* it looked like this or like that, it prospered and survived. But even this theory presents difficulties. However we will go into the question later when dealing with spider ants.

It cannot be repeated too often that what we know about spiders is very little, and this goes particularly for crab spiders. All sorts of remarkable performances may be being put on in all parts of the world that lack a human audience. We know a large number of species, certainly, but how half of them live and what they do is a mystery. They are like a human crowd on a railway station. We recognise the guards, the porters, the postmen, the city workers and the rest but we are ignorant about their home lives. We may know, or get to know, a little about some of them; that is all.

The *modus operandi* of the bulk of crab spiders is to lie low having first selected surroundings with whose colour scheme they blend. Many work on the ground amongst fallen leaves and many lie up in flowers selecting petals of their own colouring. Thus hides our *Thomisus onustus* whose special prey is the bee. This might seem rash. Certainly Onustus has a very poisonous bite but her weapon compared with the sting of the bee is like an air-gun compared with an elephant rifle. And Onustus is not the only one; other creatures, including several crab spiders, have made a dead set at the bee. And they are not as rash as might appear. The elephant rifle is a useful analogy and we will use it again. The bee is like a man carrying such a rifle but being a very poor shot. Large standing objects he can hit, but not small moving ones. Moreover this man is not a hunter; he is a botanist. In country full of dangerous animals, all he does is to examine flowers paying no heed to anything else. Therefore it is easy for enemies to creep up to the preoccupied creature and stab him or shoot him where they wish. It is advisable for them to select a vital spot, that is all.

So Onustus lies hidden in a flower and the bee comes and gets to work extracting the riches at the centre. Onustus sidles up, and suddenly leaps on the bee, biting her in the white thread that is her neck. Probably the bee shoots out her sting in her usual random manner, and then all is over. The spider sucks the blood at leisure, throws the drained corpse from the flower, and waits where she is for another visitor. She will stay on the flower probably until it dies and then all she will have to do is to go next door to another.

A sedentary life, but a well-fed one. Incidentally I think that a lot of the commiseration we give to those forced to pass an inactive existence is wasted. A life like that of a cabbage seems dreadful. And it *is* dreadful to some, but not to all. I knew a man of twenty-five who, having been bed-ridden since a boy, was recently cured by some new scientific device. I said how wonderful it must feel to find himself able to walk after all those years in bed. He was not enthusiastic; he told me that at first when learning to walk, propped up by two assistants, he felt a glow of excitement at the thought that he would soon be able to move about himself. But after he *could* walk and fend for himself he took a different view. He wanted to get back to bed and stay there. He wanted to be waited on again and have his meals brought him and not be expected to do the washing-up. He had become, he admitted, incurably lazy. And I know a woman who has been in bed for thirty years, noted and admired for her fortitude under these hard conditions. But when, recently, she was informed that she could be cured she grew alarmed and opposed the idea. I do not somehow think it was the thought of being able to walk that alarmed her but the thought of having to work.

So let us waste no pity on the crab spider whose life consists of immobility interspersed with succulent meals.

It may not be a very high form of art just to find spots alike to oneself in colouring, but some spiders go further. There is a crab spider (*Misumena vatia*) fairly common in Britain as well as America who changes her colour to suit the flower. On white flowers she changes into white, on yellow into yellow, pink into pink, and on pale green leaves into pale green. Few actresses have such a wardrobe. Gabritschevsky investigated the phenomenon with care, starting with the little spiders when they came out of the cocoon and keeping them in glass flasks. Not until they were mature could any of them change their colours. When mature, white spiders transferred to yellow paper became yellow in periods varying from twenty-four hours to twenty days. Replaced on white paper they reverted to white in from five to six days. A pink specimen that Savory put on a yellow flower turned yellow in three or four days. The colour, it was found, was due to a pigment that accumulated in the outside cells, and the white was a negative transparency that showed a sort of crystalline substance in the under cells.

A Brazilian spider, *Epicadus heterogaster*, has made a really good effort to imitate a flower. It has an unspiderlike shape and white prominences tinged with pink that resemble petals.

Shape as well as colour, combined with deliberate acting, plays its part with others of the crabs. The British species, *Tibellus oblongus*, for instance, helped by its shape, gives a remarkable performance. Unlike most spiders its body is exceedingly narrow, of a pale straw colour, with three longitudinal brown streaks which help to break up the pattern and deceive the eye. If disturbed it runs up a grass stem. Nothing is more conspicuous; its long legs wave madly as it goes and its body almost flashes. Then it stops and the miracle happens: the spider disappears. One looks where it stopped, then down and up the stem—there is nothing. And yet it is there, but nine times out of ten only by shaking the stem and putting the spider into motion once more will it become visible.

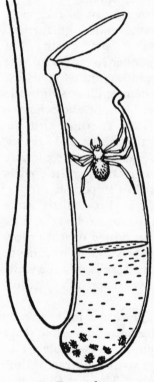

Unconsciously the eye travels on for a fraction of a second after the creature has stopped so that one looks for it a little too high. But what has it done with its long legs? It has stretched them straight out along the stem before and behind so that there is no bulge or protruberance to show their presence.

Philodromus fallax imitates a grain of sand. It inhabits sand-hills and when disturbed goes along like a rolling grain, then stops and draws its legs under it and immediately becomes invisible. Savory says that the only difference between this spider and a grain of sand is that when the grain stops one can still see it, but not so the spider.

In Malaya, and elsewhere, there is a plant that bears calabash-shaped "flowers." It is called the Pitcher Plant and its pitchers are nearly half-full of a digestive fluid and have a hinged top. It is an insect-catching plant and the fluid emits a sweet smell. Attracted by this smell insects enter and get caught.

FIG. 16
The tenant of the pitcher plant

After Bristowe (*from* The Comity of Spiders—*The Ray Society*)

In the remote past a crab spider must have been thus captured but instead of losing its head and getting into the digestive fluid it stayed where it was, weaving a few threads for a foot hold. In due course it came to realise that far from being in a nasty predicament it was on to a good thing. For, attracted by the plant, insects came along in numbers and the spider was in a position to get them before the plant did. In short, the plant had invented a trap merely to feed a spider.

This presumably was the beginning. The spider (its name is *Misumenops nepenthicola*) has now completely adapted itself to life within the pitcher and lives in no other habitat. On the whole, plant and spider get on well together. True the spider lives on game rightly belonging to the plant but it is not indifferent to the needs of the plant, and such insects as it does not require, owing to its surfeit or their taste, it kicks into the digestive fluid as a present. And its sucked corpses —for what they are worth, which is not much—are given to the plant also.

At first the spider must have avoided the caustic pool at the base with great care. Then it realised that it could turn even this to its own advantage. It possessed already, or has developed (probably the latter), a hard outer covering of chitin which is impervious for short periods to the action of the fluid. So now, when disturbed or threatened, it attaches itself to a thread and submerges itself, often for minutes at a time. The danger spots, the air openings, are protected by hairs which form a film of air. Emerging from its mustard-like bath it immediately wipes its mouth against the sides of the upper portion of the pitcher to remove the stinging taste of the liquid.

Bristowe gives an account of this spider. He found one spider in every five pitchers examined. Other species have since been found, also pitcher dwellers; the idea would appear to be catching on.

Sluggards though the crabs are and preferring to wait till their meals come to them, they can move quickly enough when required. Moreover they are prepared to take on larger prey than any of the hunting spiders, including the wolves. We have seen them tackle the honey-bee—no mean antagonist—and they have also been observed to overcome that powerful heavyweight the bumble-bee. Bristowe gives two instances from abroad that might be mentioned. In British Somaliland Dr. R. S. Taylor saw a spider (*Heteropoda venatoria*) attack a large grasshopper. The grasshopper sprang ten inches with the spider on its back. The spider held on like a cowboy whilst the grasshopper jumped again and again the same distance. The spider's poison could not have been as effective as some, or else it could not get its fangs into the leathery hide. It was only after some little time that the grasshopper sank down.

More impressive was the feat of *Platythomisus insignis*, a crab spider that Mr. Hancock caught in Uganda eating a Praying Mantis. The spider must have been mad, or lucky, or both, for the Praying Mantis is one of the most dangerous of all insects and feasts with relish on live hornets. Moreover the Mantis measured three inches in body length and the spider three-quarters of an inch. A pity Mr. Hancock did not see what went before. What a fight it must have been—unless the Mantis was dead or dying when the spider got to it.

I am prepared, however, to believe anything about the gallantry or rashness of spiders after a little affair I witnessed in one of my glass jars in my study. I had a small captive there, a male *Aranea cucurbitina*, which as a member of the orb web weaving family has really no right in this chapter. I got him in my greenhouse—not his normal habitat—and although I searched high and low for days I could find no trace of a female. He was not much larger in body than a pin's head, but seeing him under a lens one gasped at his beauty. The small thorax was a light tan that looked like highly polished leather, the abdomen was light green that shone as if illuminated. His legs were the same bright green with bands of glowing brown. These two colours contrasted remarkably well, and each showed off the other. His wife is a lighter shade altogether and probably the more conspicuous of the two, but her legs are nondescript and cannot bear comparison with his.

Studying him and writing down his colouring reminded me that I had not given him anything to eat for several days. There were no small flies about (there never are when you want them, though the reverse is the case on other occasions) but in a cage was a large crane-fly that I had presented to a portly segestria the day before. I was surprised to find this crane-fly still alive and untouched, for the segestria liked her food. The segestria stood there looking very life-like but the mystery was explained when I examined her and found her dead. She must have died the night before; why I do not know, and it does not matter. I took the crane-fly and put it in the jar with Cucurbitina, though it was a ridiculous dish for so small a creature. My green beauty had been in his jar about a month and had spun some strands of silk here and there in a casual fashion. The crane-fly was caught and, after a little objection, seemed content to hang suspended.

Meanwhile Cucurbitina had registered interest and from one of two twigs I had arranged in the jar was peering at the new comer. Then on one of his invisible strands he went towards it, halting when he was an inch distant. Since he seemed disinclined to go farther I got on with my work. Half an hour later I switched the light on to the jar and looked again. There was no change; a motionless spider, a motionless crane-fly, two motionless pieces of twig, all in the same position. This is where insects are so irritating—their patience is so much greater than ours. They indulge in tableaux that last hours, often days, and when the act comes you are not there. I decided the spider had summed up the crane-fly and decided, as well it might, that it was too big.

I worked for another hour and a half and decided to go to bed and before turning the light off had another look at the jar. There was no change, but this happened to be the identical moment the spider decided to attack, and as I watched, he ran on to the extremity of the crane-fly's wing. Now the spider was a mere microbe compared with the crane-fly. In point of size they were like a man and a Lancaster aircraft. The crane-fly had previously seemed to have given up hope. It had hung motionless, but the moment the spider touched it it awoke into very active life. It threshed its huge wings so that they became invisible; its legs waved madly; its body plunged and reared. It appeared to realise the sinister intentions of its tiny assailant and I feared greatly for my spider. It would be battered against the sides of the jar. I was sorry I had put in the crane-fly. Then, for a moment the crane-fly paused and the position could be reviewed. The green and brown one had escaped death and, what was more remarkable, still clung to the end of the wing. It took advantage of the short pause to run farther along the wing towards the fuselage, and then the crane-fly started off once more. Nothing could be seen; the fly was a mist of motion. Again I feared for the spider.

The mist cleared and crane-fly and spider became apparent. The spider ran farther up towards the body. Again the threshing and plunging—then peace. The spider was on the crane-fly's breast and had administered the anaesthetic bite. He did not stay there long but (apparently not giddy from his ride) ran over the crane-fly's head and along one of its long forelegs. This leg he rapidly bound with silk to its opposite member right to the base, going round and round the two. Then he ran back to the body and inserted his fangs into the crane-fly's mouth. The crane-fly's abdomen moved rapidly during this process but the rest seemed paralysed. The spider now ran up a wing and bound this wing carefully to another leg. Back to the fly's mouth where he seemed to suck for some time. Then to the rear where he bound two hind legs together. Back to the breast; then again to the mouth. Every time the spider attacked the mouth or breast, the crane-fly's abdomen would twitch and curl about. The process was evidently painful.

It was two o'clock now and I went to bed. In the morning the crane-fly was hanging dead with wings and legs roped up but no threads round the body. The spider hung from another thread replete and happy. I have gone into this matter in some detail because the methods of this immature male spider are new to me. I think that journey on the crane-fly's wing had shaken the spider. I think it was scared the creature might start again, hence its inability to get down to its meal, and its frequent rushes to bind up more of those once powerful threshing limbs. Its attacks on the mouth I cannot explain.

"Dirty" and "Repulsive," followed closely by "Beastly" and "Ugly" are the adjectives I have heard most commonly applied to spiders. "Beautiful," never. Yet many spiders, particularly in hotter countries, have a richness of colouring that transcends that of butterflies. Unfortunately the colours cannot be preserved after death. Death seems to turn off a light inside. The most beautiful spider in Britain is a crab, *Micrommata virescens*. The female (she is quite large) is of a glowing green that really looks as if illuminated. The male outshines even his wife. He is of the same lovely green as she, but his back is bright yellow, marked with vivid streaks of scarlet. A handsome couple.

One or two experts have stated that it is not necessary for crab spiders to sit on flowers whose colour they resemble, and, furthermore, that they do not do so. Obviously it is difficult to determine the percentage of crab spiders that *do* tone in colour with the flowers they inhabit, but efforts have been made. Rabaud (the leader of the dissenters) gave figures showing that only 21.5 per cent selected flowers of the same colour as themselves. Pearce, however, a neutral investigator in America, gave, in 1911, an 85 per cent colour agreement, and Bristowe in England, after a count of 50 adult "crabs" found that 80 per cent selected flowers of their own colouring.

On the evidence, therefore, I think we may say that "crabs" *do* arrange matters so that they tone with their surroundings. The second question is, is it necessary?

Berland stated it was not. He was of the opinion that insects would visit a flower whether there were a crab spider of a different colour on it or whether there were not. The rather awkward fact that *Misumena vatia* (and some others) goes to the trouble of changing her colour to suit the flower made no difference to his opinion.

Bristowe went into this matter. He got 16 dandelion heads and arranged them in rows in a square on his lawn. In the centre of every alternate flower he placed a small black pebble, the size of a normal crab spider, and in the centre of the others he placed a pebble coloured yellow. The visitors that came were then noted. Here is his result.

Visitors	To flowers with yellow pebble	To flowers with black pebble
HONEY BEES	10	1
OTHER BEES	2	1
SYRPHID FLIES	42	4
MUSCID FLIES	2	1
TOTAL	56	7

This experiment seems conclusive. Moreover many of the visitors drew back time and again from a flower with a black pebble but always settled without hesitation on a flower with a yellow pebble, while the only honey bee to visit a flower with a black pebble did so by crawling up the stem and getting to the head that way and never seeing the black pebble at all.

It seems to me, however, that these experiments touch only one side of the matter. The desire to get food is strong in all of us, but the desire to avoid becoming food for others is stronger. Spiders are as much hunted as hunting; they are the favourite dish of a host of creatures. The crab spider's method demands that it lies in wait more or less in the open.

Whether camouflage is or is not necessary to enable it to get its prey it is certainly necessary to enable it to preserve its own skin.

The crab spider mother is noted as being the most devoted of all spider mothers—which is saying much. Possibly it is saying too much for I think that Agelena and Lycosa deserve quite as many marks, even though their devotion is not so spectacular. Let us briefly touch on the birth of the crab spider.

The pregnant crab spider mother makes her cocoon. In all probability she, unlike most of the mother spiders of the other groups, is not a widow. Crab spider males understand things. They understand female spiders, for instance, and take steps when performing the functions demanded of all husbands, to safeguard themselves. The cocoon is generally fairly high up in some plant and is thick and strong. It is so thick and strong that when finally sealed up with the eggs inside, the young will have no chance of getting out unless dug out, as it were, by the mother, who mounts guard on top of the cocoon. This cocoon over which she crouches is now her sole interest in life. Insects that venture near are regarded not as food but as possible enemies of her eggs and chased away. She also fearlessly fights pieces of straw and human fingers. She fights anything that comes. She fights, however, on an empty stomach, for she eats nothing even if it is presented to her. One or two very small flies, so small that they cannot possibly be regarded as enemies, *may* occasionally be taken but in the main she starves.

Like the wolf spider she seems unable to recognise the property over which she lavishes such devotion. Transferred to another crab spider cocoon she will nurse it with all the jealous care she gave her own. She will not, however, be put off with an artificial one. Fabre made one with leaves and pieces of silk and the spider left it immediately.

T.S.   H

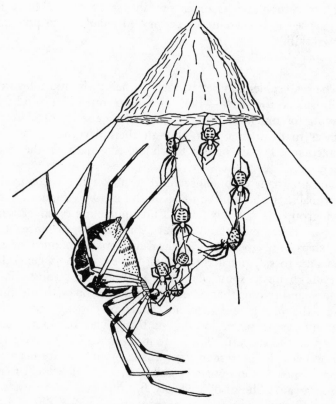

FIG. 17
Theridion sisyphium feeding her young from her mouth
After Bristowe (*from* Spiders—*King Penguin Books*)

In about six weeks the mother hears the movements of the spiders inside and cuts a hole in the silk. The young emerge and the mother usually celebrates the event by dying. And if she does not die immediately, she does not last long.

Fabre, in a paper of his, got very sentimental over the death of the crab spider mother. And with every reason. Such devotion is magnificent—as also was the devotion of the dying Agelena and others. But, in the spider play, these dying maternal farewells are apt to get a bit monotonous, and we turned—or I did—with relief to Lycosa the wolf spider who, though equally devoted, saw no reason for dying because she had brought children into the world. Moreover dying, though a good theatrical gesture, is of no assistance to the young themselves. Bees, ants, wasps, and others, instead of dying, *feed* their infants. Are spiders so far behind? In a way, I must confess they are—though it does not seem to trouble the infants. *But*, as I keep on trying to hammer home, no two spiders, or at any rate no two species of spiders, are alike. Hence we find at least one common spider mother, *Theridion sisyphium*, a very pretty creature dressed in red, white, and brown, who feeds her children from her mouth when they are young, and later shares with them the insects she kills. She is very fond of them throughout, and before they are born weaves them a cocoon of beautiful green silk.

Sedentary though they are in after life, none of the spiders are keener aeronauts than the crabs. The little specks hasten from the eggs in a troupe, and in a troupe climb to the nearest elevated spot where they wait for flying weather. They are restless and eager to be off and wander about within a small area trailing bits of silk until they look as if they were enclosed in a gauzy nest. They do not wait long. They are not so insistent on absolutely ideal weather as the others; anything in which they can take off will do. One bold spirit breaks out and floats away. The rest follow and almost immediately hundreds are floating upwards.

CHAPTER 5

THE TRAP-DOOR SPIDERS

ONE has to admit that spiders have thought out some remarkable schemes. The honey bee has evoked enthusiasm ever since mankind began to write, and doubtless before. The sluggard is advised to go to the ant and study her methods. No one recommends sluggards to go to the spider. Yet if they did they would pick up several things well worth knowing. I yield to no one in my admiration of the honey bee. She has done marvellous things: indeed she has accomplished miracles. The ant also has not wasted her time. She has not been confronted with the chemical and other problems of the honey bee and has not yet evolved a definite colonising plan, but she has gone far and founded communities quite as advanced as those of the honey bees—if not more so.

But these social insects do pull together. For the most unimportant job of work about a hundred of them combine to do it. This has led to great things, but it has also led, I think, to a cul-de-sac. It is difficult to say. If our span of life were a few million instead of a few score years we would be able to judge better whether the various insects are going forwards or backwards. We ourselves have yet to learn what effect "getting together" will have on *our* progress. Until recently all our important advances have been made by private individuals working alone. Scientists cannot do this now. "Research" is a matter of large teams. One highly qualified member of such a team who had previously tasted the joys of individual effort told me recently that he now spent his whole time filing papers.

Perhaps the spirit of the bee and ant research teams is similarly throttled. Or perhaps they have now no research teams at all and consider that they have reached perfection. Such a state of affairs can never occur with spiders. Like Stephenson, Pasteur, Edison and Marconi, they think things out alone.

Violent exception will be taken to the word "think," but objectors can substitute any word they like. It does not matter. The fact remains that spiders have hit upon many remarkable schemes and invented a number of unique gadgets. They have even acted as tutors to mankind, for it is said that the original diving bell was suggested to its inventor by the home of the water spider, an animal we shall meet in a later chapter.

All forms of life have really only three problems to contend with: to get food, to evade enemies, and to bring up young. If a large number of intelligent creatures combine to solve these problems we may expect something clever, and with the bees and the ants we get it. And if a number of intelligent creatures approach these problems, not together but each on its own, they will solve the problems of course (they would not continue to exist if they did not), but they will hit upon many different solutions. We do not for instance find bees making homes under water, but spiders have evolved schemes as remarkable for their divergence as for their ingenuity. So we see some using that great invention the web, some mimicking flowers or the droppings of birds, some with no scheme at all to speak of, some sailing rafts, some defying nature and living under water, and so on. And there is yet another whose scheme is fully as ingenious, and as different —the Trap-Door Spider.

It is only comparatively recently that it was known that there *were* such creatures. It was, Moggridge tells us, in 1757, that they were first mentioned and seven years later the Abbé Sauvages (the church is particularly to the fore in spider investigations) described the nests of certain spiders near

Montpellier which he likened to little rabbit burrows lined
with silk and closed by tightly fitting movable doors.

But before going into any more history I think we will
put the cart before the horse and describe this latest invention
of the spider. It is no use looking for it in Britain; we *have*
one so-called trap-door spider but it does not make a trap-door.
The British species is interesting nevertheless and we will deal
with it in due course.

The Riviera is roughly the nearest place to us where trap-
door spiders operate, and here they have many villas. J. T.
Moggridge put in a lot of investigation and his book *Harvest
Ants and Trap-Door Spiders* is still a classic. The spider makes
a hole into the earth lined with hard material composed of
silk, earth, and saliva, and the digging is done, strangely
enough, mostly with the fangs, those fine surgical instruments.
Roughly speaking the average depth for a full grown spider is
about a foot and its diameter depends on the girth of its maker.
The inside is lined with fine silk.

To think that spiders, those geniuses of the "insect" world,
after making a home that was almost enemy proof, would
sit down and consider it good enough is to show ignorance of
spiders. Nothing can get in when the door is shut but the
spider has to come and go. Lovers must be given entry, if not
exit. At these times the door is open and it is then that
enemies may slip in. So certain species decided to elaborate
the straight simple tube and introduce corridors and *inner*
doors as well as outer doors. We will study them, beginning
with the trap-doors themselves, of which there are only two
types.

The first type of door is what is called the "cork" door.
It is so called not because of its consistency which, unlike
that of cork, is heavy but because of its shape: it fits into
the opening of the hole, which is bevelled to receive it, as
a cork fits into the top of a test-tube. It works up and down

on a broad hinge. But a rough sketch makes things clearer than words (Fig 18).

The door fits so tightly owing to a careful and accurate adjustment of the sloping sides of the door and the bevelled mouth into which it goes that it is hard to open if the spider is not in. If the spider *is* in it is even harder, for the spider runs up and hangs on to the door from the inside, resisting with all her might, just as any other householder might try to thwart the entry of undesirables. In a way this door, owing to its weight and the tightness of its fitting may be

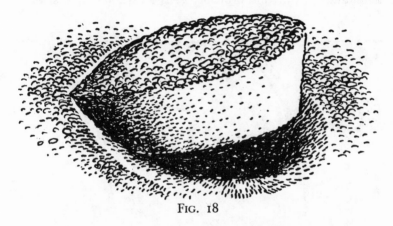

FIG. 18

said to be locked, and few, other than human beings with penknives, are able to open it. Indeed the opening of it must at times present some difficulty to the spider herself and, especially if she is in a hurry, cause her some annoyance. Luckily she is strong and we know no cases of doors jamming so tightly that she cannot open them. Experimenters have found that a full grown trap-door spider can push open her door even when three ounces of lead have been placed on top of it and three ounces for a spider corresponds to several tons for us.

The cork door is made of a large number of layers of silk

and earth, as many as thirty alternate layers having been found, and the top is perfectly camouflaged. This is why trap-door spiders are so hard to find. A place may be full of their villas, but there will be no trace of them, for the top is made to resemble the surrounding terrain. Bits of moss, lichen, cut grass, small sticks, or sand, according to the locality, will be artistically worked into the upper surface of the door.

It might be thought that the spider just works into the top of the door the stuff that is handiest and nearest, so that the top automatically becomes indistinguishable from its surroundings. And this probably *is* the case, but not always.

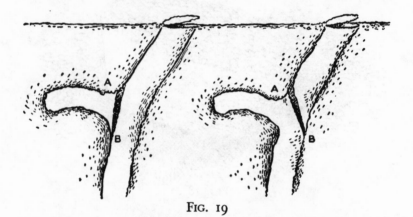

FIG. 19

A certain observer having discovered a trap-door situated in mossy earth, and of course camouflaged with moss, took a spade, or some similar instrument, and swept it over the door, cutting away the moss and leaving a patch of bare earth a foot or so square. A day later he found that the spider had collected moss as before and decorated her door with it, but now the circular patch of moss in a bare expanse of earth—far from camouflaging it—merely called attention to her abode. Still, it *was* rather hard for the spider to know what to do, for the bare patch of earth called attention to it also.

The owner of a dwelling with a "cork" trap-door seems to consider, and with justice, this type of door sufficient. She just sinks a simple tube underneath and does not bother herself about additional corridors or inner doors at all. She knows she has a good thick heavy door, not at all jerry-built, and she relies on it.

There is only one other type of trap-door, though it guards many different types of dwellings, and that is the "Wafer" door. It is well hinged and it is far from being a wafer though it may appear so in comparison with the massive postern of

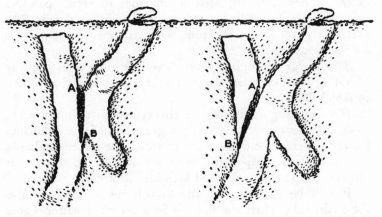

FIG. 20

the cork type. It is the fitting that is different. It has an outside circular flange which overhangs the aperture of the tube. It is rather like the lids of those old time German drinking mugs which if you left open between drinks entailed the "standing" of a round to the company. And if the spider leaves *hers* open she often has to pay a bigger forfeit than that. Often the wafer door is made slightly concave so that it may fit better into the opening of the tube. It also is camouflaged.

The first of these hinged wafer door tubes is a simple tube

like the cork door tube and there is no need to make any sketch.

The second is also a straight tube, but it has another door half-way down. Again there is no need to make a sketch. The reader's imagination ought to carry him that far. This second door is significant. Either the wafer door is proving a failure or the spider is getting nervous. Anyway, if things go wrong she can now dash down the tube and slam the second door.

The next design is what might perhaps be described as the simple branched tube and now our spider architects are growing clever. They have tumbled to the idea of secret passages with smooth close-fitting valves as well as inside doors. The sketch (Fig 19) shows the tube with its inner door, A-B, in its two positions.

This design, though it gives the spider more than one way of hiding from enemies, does not offer the scope of that shown in sketch (Fig. 20).

Hoodwinking an intruder in this type of dwelling must be more of a pleasure than a peril; a game full of quiet chuckles for the spider. The many ways in which the spider can baulk a pursuer will be apparent from a study of the sketch. It can even trap an intruder and keep him locked up.

It will be noticed that the branch tube—which is also the main tube when the door is in a certain position—goes almost to the surface of the ground. It is a cul-de-sac; there is no opening, and the end of the tube is covered with silk to stop earth falling through. But if the spider is trapped it can always bite its way out and escape, a thing impossible in the other dwelling (Fig. 19).

Many and varied must be the adventures of these trap-door spiders when some enemy, such as a hunting wasp, finds the front door ajar. Could they speak we should hear some thrilling tales of swift chases in dark corridors, of slamming of doors, of breathless suspense while running footsteps came nearer and gasps of relief when they turned away in the wrong direction. Unfortunately, however, there is no way at all of knowing what goes on in the subterranean tunnels of the trap-door spiders.

So much for the various houses. We return to the cork door spider. The door is hard and composed largely of earth but the inner lining is of pure silk. This is what enables the spider to hold the door tight when some intruder tries to force it. It grips this silk with its fangs and legs, stiffens its body against either side of the tube and resists with all its might. In Africa I tried to force one open and could not. I had to destroy the whole top. And only then did the spider relinquish its hold and scuttle to the bottom. In gripping the door, holes are made in the silk and it was once thought that these were deliberately made as permanent sockets for the fangs and legs. But this would not be necessary and in an emergency the spider would hardly have time to find them.

A certain trap-door spider, by name *Cteniza ariana*, comes out of its house at night and weaves a web close by. In the morning the web is folded up and put away and the spider goes home, shuts the door, and retires until evening. Most of the trap-door spiders are nocturnal, which accounts for their being so very difficult to find, for until the door is opened there is no sign that there is a house at all. However, a M. Erber found some nests in the island of Tinos and decided to do some night watching and see what happened. He had marked down three doors and in the evening stationed himself close to them and waited.

Shortly after nine o'clock the three doors opened and the spiders came out. They fastened their trap-doors by threads to neighbouring objects thus keeping them open in case a hasty retreat was called for, and then proceeded to make their webs close by. The webs ran among the vegetation and were about six inches long by half an inch wide. The spiders then returned to their holes.

In a little while M. Erber saw two night-flying moths caught in two of the webs. Out from their doors came the two owners and manufacturers of these webs and fell upon the plunging moths. They bit them, sucked them a little, and then carried them home. Later the third spider came out but M. Erber dexterously caught her and popped her into a bottle of spirit that he had ready.

Nothing more happened, and at midnight M. Erber went home well content with what he had seen and with his specimen in the bottle. In the morning he returned. There were other trap-doors around but naturally, by moonlight, he had only been able to concentrate on three close together. The morning visit showed all doors closed and all webs removed—except one. Pathetically, one door stood open, tied by thread to a piece of grass, and one unremoved web lay close by, mute evidence of a midnight tragedy and scientific interference.

In the morning the webs are folded up and taken away. They are not used again, for M. Erber's observations showed that a new web is made each night. What happens to the old, folded-up one? Trap-door spiders do not possess drawers or cupboards. It is known now that they are *worked into the door*, for the cork door can never be too thick for the spider.

America is particularly popular with trap-door spiders and many rare nests have been found there. A long time ago, in some remote spot on that continent, a Mr. Treadwell found one that was either very rare or hitherto unknown—I am not quite sure which and it does not matter for this is merely a story to illustrate the trials and disappointments that beset naturalists. We have a chapter later on about the enemies of spiders but a much longer chapter could be written about the enemies of naturalists. Heading the list, I think, is the common domestic maid, though " common" nowadays is the wrong word. I myself have suffered at her hands by having most of my notes burnt up; and others have suffered too.

Mr. Treadwell, when he found the nest, dug it up and by

a piece of astounding luck managed to dig it up complete with occupant.

He put the nest in an ordinary tin box with a lid and set out with it to London. It was a long way. He was 350 miles south of San Francisco and had to make the journey there overland. The spider survived, and also survived the trip from San Francisco to London. There Mr. Treadwell went to an hotel in the Strand and that evening had his dinner, leaving the tin in his room.

Whilst he was away a chambermaid entered and no doubt turned the sheets down and made all ready. She also had a good look into the trunks and cases of this visitor from abroad, and the tin box did not escape her attention. She took the lid off and looked closely into the interior. A spider rushed out, and with a screech she flung the tin away. It crashed against the wall and fell, and the dry contents disintegrated into dust and earth.

So ended the long journey of this rare trap-door spider and its nest. But for the maid it would now no doubt be occupying an honoured position in the British Museum.

As we have said, most trap-door spiders are nocturnal and this fact contributes greatly to their security. The tightly fitting doors exclude everything that hunts by day, parasitic flies, wasps, ants, and the rest, so that the spider can take the day off in security either sleeping or consuming in a leisurely manner any prey caught the night before. At night their methods differ. Some go out hunting leaving their doors tied open; others stay where they are, peeping from behind a lid only very slightly raised, like assassins crouching behind doors in dark streets.

Let us go after Moggridge who has marked down certain nests and has decided, like M. Erber, on a night's vigil. He has waited for a full moon but even so takes a lamp. In this he is wise. I too have waited up all night and in the brightest of African moons. At first it would seem that nothing could escape detection but as time goes on one finds oneself seeing things that are not there and failing to see things that are. Moggridge has discovered already that these spiders, in moonlight, are not disturbed by the *steady* light of a lamp but on the slightest flicker bang and bolt their doors. Any footfall has the same effect, so the observer must watch his step and his light.

Moggridge took his post and directed the light on the doors he had already marked. They were tightly closed but in due course first one, then another, was slowly raised. But only slightly. Actually, so many murderesses were applying one eye to a cautious chink. Beneath each door Moggridge could see the tips of feet *just* holding it open.

Time went on and this seemed to be all that was to happen. Moggridge, however, did not propose to spend the whole night watching a few feet sticking out from barely opened doors. He lacked the patience of the spider herself and decided to expedite matters. This decision was influenced by the sight of a beetle feeding on a spray of some plant close by. His task was difficult for he must disturb neither the beetle nor the spider. With great care he cut the spray and slowly moved it towards the door. When it touched the edge the door flew open and the spider seized the beetle, drew it inside, and slammed the door. There was a pause, then the door opened again and, like a drunk hurled from some bar, out came the beetle, forcibly expelled, but alive and unhurt.

Evidently this beetle was one of the wrong sort, an inedible kind. Time went on and then into the light walked a woodlouse. The observer's task was even more difficult than before, but with a straw he guided the steps of the unwitting creature in the right direction. Again the door flew open and the woodlouse was taken inside. It was less fortunate and doubtless more edible than the beetle, for the door did not open again.

The villas are occupied by females; very rarely is a male seen inside. But lovers must call, for at certain seasons the female is found with a bevy of children around her—to whom, by the way, she is most devoted. What happens when the male enters? Presumably the door closes behind him and he finds himself locked in with a female very much larger than himself. And what happens after he has satisfied her desires and done his part in Nature's scheme? Does she politely open the door for him and show him out? Or not? It is impossible to say: the trap-door spider after sucking the blood of her victim does not leave the body in the cellar but takes it out and deposits it at a distance from her home. We can never, or very rarely, tell what she has killed.

At the proper time the young say good-bye and swarm out, and each makes a little tube for itself—a kind of doll's house—complete with miniature trap-door.

Trap-door spiders belong to a sub-order (Mygalomorphae) which is distinguished by having downward pointing fangs like a walrus. When these two fangs strike they strike pick-axe-fashion. All other spiders have fangs that operate sideways like pointed tongs bent inwards, or callipers. This sub-order also possesses four lungs instead of the normal two, but that hardly concerns us here. Not all by any means make trap-doors or even tubes and its members embrace the largest of the spiders including the "banana" and "bird-eating" spiders, invariably called "tarantulas." In a bottle of spirit in the Natural History British Museum there is a specimen from British Guiana whose abdomen alone is as large as a tangerine. Count Langsdorff tells us that he saw Indian children leading about a huge Brazilian spider by a string tied to its waist much as we might lead a Pekinese.

These monsters occasionally come over to this country in crates of bananas. Their usual reception is a howl of horror, the precipitate retreat of women, and the advance of brave men with sticks and boots that hunt out the wretched creature and squash it flat. One such immigrant, however, met more enlightened folk when it arrived and was caught alive and

sent to the Natural History Museum. Mr. Browning, in charge
of the Arachnida department, told me about it and I saw its
body. Its passing, I gather, caused almost tears from those
who knew it. I am sure it had a name. Let us call it Horace.
Horace, then, arrived at the Museum and was suitably housed
and was fed on such creatures as cockroaches, grasshoppers
and the like. With that philosophic acceptance of all circumstances good or bad common to spiders Horace soon became
at home. Like a Peke he preferred food given to him by hand
and would come running and take whatever his attendant had
to offer. He was probably six years old when he arrived,
and he lived in the Museum, the idol of all who knew him,
for another fourteen years. Mr. Browning told me that those
deputed to look after and feed him grew "very attached" to him.

It is fairly certain that this spider was 20 years old when it
died. The war killed it. All parts of the Natural History
Museum are well heated normally but shortage of fuel in the
war at one time cut off the entire heat supply. The temperature inside fell below freezing point, and Horace, that tropical
visitor, died. Actually Horace was a female, but I don't think
it matters much. But for the war Horace probably had at
least five more years expectation of life.

These monster spiders have large fat bodies and short but
very thick legs and the whole of them, body and legs, is
covered with a sort of plush like a Teddy-Bear. But one has
no desire to cuddle them when one sees them dashing here or
there in one's room. Most people when they see one . . .
But I will be honest and frank. I too have sinned.

Many years ago police outstations in Rhodesia were rather
crude and I, a just ex-recruit aged 20, found myself drafted to
one. There were about six troopers in this *Kya* and lighting
was by candle. There were hornets and rats above but those
we did not mind; we considered they had as much right there
as we had. The one thing we dreaded was a "tarantula."
The bite from one of these was *death*. Candles were never *all*
doused at night for fear a tarantula might make an appearance.

When one did, the alarm was sounded. Troopers leapt from their beds, seized slippers, boots, revolver holsters, anything, and went in pursuit. An invasion by Cetewayo's Zulus could have caused no more consternation. And then the hairy monster would be seen running here, running there, with six lusty troopers stumbling after it. Then someone would get it with slipper, boot, or what-not and over its molten writhing form would be congratulated and patted on the back and all the troopers would get to bed again pleasantly conscious of a grave danger narrowly averted.

We believed the danger from a "tarantula" was acute because senior troopers had told us so. Senior troopers believed the danger was acute because still senior troopers had told them so. Officers believed it up to the Colonel himself. Everyone believed it. I remember, with morbid anticipation seeking for eye-witnesses of the suffering and death of some trooper or other form of life bitten by a "tarantula." Even at the immature age of 20 I found it strange that no account was forthcoming.

What *is* the effect of a bite from these outsize creatures? Their fangs are huge, like the spurs of cockerels, with holes at the end from which poison is spurted. If even a small spider can cause death to a bird, what of these? One would think they could lay low an elephant.

The first trouble for those rash enough to experiment on themselves is the difficulty of getting spiders to bite at all. One can ill-treat and tease them for hours on end but the peevish creatures will *not* bite. One of the greatest of all authorities on spiders, the American, McCook, admitted that he knew nothing about spider bites because after endless patience lasting over years he had only induced one spider to bite him.

But others, more fortunate, *have* made these great spiders bite. Also the poison has been artificially obtained and injected or placed on cuts on the human body. In the first place the wound, even though it made the blood flow, was no worse and had no more lasting effect than one caused by a thorn, in the second, the effect, to all intents and purposes, was nil. So the size of the spider is no criterion of the effect of its bite. What dangerous bites there are (and they are very few) come from the smaller spiders like the little pot-bellied Black Widow.

When collectors catch a spider they either fling it away in disgust because it is well known, or "preserve" it. They preserve it as a rule by dropping it into neat spirit. In such potent fluid death, of course, is instantaneous. Or so it was thought. I have put small spiders into spirit myself and death is very quick. One little struggle, and then the end. But these spiders were *small*. What of the monsters with bodies the size of a bull-frog? They too are often placed alive into neat spirit. Moggridge always did it with the large trap-door spiders he wished to preserve. He put them direct into pure spirits of wine and they spread their legs backwards and forwards in this bath as if swimming, often for an hour, and often for considerably longer. But Moggridge was convinced that death occurred immediately they entered the fluid and that the swimming for an hour or more afterwards was merely muscular action after death.

This is rather a dreadful tale, but it must be told. I gather it shook Moggridge not a little. I do not wish to harrow you. I merely put down the gist of what Moggridge related lest any collectors have not read it and still think that death by such unnecessary treatment is instantaneous. He discovered a large trap-door spider with her young and managed to secure them all. He decided that the whole lot were worthy of "preservation" and, keeping the young aside for the time being, placed the mother alive into spirits of wine. She swam about as usual in this fluid, death presumably occurring the moment she was put in. Ten minutes later Moggridge flung in all her young. To his horror she recognised them and even in her agony gathered them to her, folding them under her with her legs as a hen folds her chicks; and after that she stayed motionless until death released her.

It says much for the mother love of spiders that it can operate even when the subject is being broiled in a caustic bath—or something very like it. And there is no need for this cruelty. Chloroform or ether is easy enough to procure and can be put on cotton wool in a box with the subject before it is pickled. This is the only humane way. And it is the only scientific way also, for large spiders pickled alive are useless for dissection. After such treatment, as an expert at the British Museum told me, their insides are "all of a mush."

But it will be a long time before any R.S.P.C.A. bothers about spiders. Taking mankind as a whole imagination is the rarest quality he possesses, and it is only imagination that puts an end to cruelty. And to use imagination in this way is to be that scientific pariah, an anthropomorphist.

If the door of a trap-door spider is taken away it immediately gets to work bending down such vegetation as is available to cover the hole. Later it makes a new door. This door is wet and plastic at first and takes several days to harden.

The British trap-door spider, *Atypus affinis*, builds a tube like the others but has not learned to make a door—either that, or she does not *wish* to make one. If a man, working from inside, made a house but omitted to fit a door he would, when the house was completed, be forced to live in it all his life. And this is what Atypus does for the eight to ten years that are her normal span. The male does not live so long, for reasons which will be made clear later.

Atypus is a fairly small spider, half an inch in body length, with the conspicuous jutting out fangs of the trap-door spiders. She builds a tube about a foot deep in the earth and this tube protrudes for three inches or so above ground. The outside part of the tube either sticks right out, being secured in that position by attachments to the vegetation, or lies along the ground. Do not, however, get the impression that by sticking out thus far the house of Atypus is conspicuous. It is so *in*conspicuous that until fairly recently it was not known that we had a trap-door spider amongst us at all. Camouflage of course is the reason, the protruding part of the tube being carefully covered with bits of the surrounding soil and/or vegetation.

A Mr. Joshua Brown first discovered these tubes near Hastings in 1856, and was extremely puzzled by them. So were a number of others. *There* was the sealed tube with the spider inside, but the spider never came out and apparently had no contact with the outside world whatsoever. This perhaps is no bad thing, but even hermits must live. Nests were dug out and taken home and studied. The problem remained. The spider *was* sealed up and seemed to live on what air filtered through its tube. Or on worms; which was a strange diet for a spider!

There was another problem too. Very cunning was the camouflage on the outside portion of the tube—but *why* bring any part of the tube out into the open at all? If the spider wished to be inconspicuous, as she obviously did, why not make the *whole* of her tube underground? There seemed no sense in it.

Mr. Joshua Brown did not solve this problem. He went to a lot of trouble but never discovered the simple but startling truth. Spiders are always deceiving us. The things they do often seem to be so stupid. And then in the end one finds that they are not stupid at all.

It was Enoch, after years of investigation, who found out what happened. The spider waited until some insect touched its outside tube, then, like a flash, she struck *through* the silk covering from within. The amazed insect was immediately dragged inside and taken to the cellar and killed. The killing done, the spider hastened back to the rent up above and carefully repaired it. Only then did she consider herself justified in sitting down to her meal.

Just to wait until some insect alights on, brushes by, or walks over a piece of outside tube might seem a very uncertain way of making a living. But it is not. A single insect a day is enough for any spider, and a good deal more than they often get in captivity, at least, I am afraid, with me. Now if one leaves a twig lying on the ground or stuck up in the earth it is a dead certainty that during a whole day and a night *something* will go by or on or over it. In fact during the warmer months (and spiders hardly eat at all in winter), if one kept watch, one would probably find that a large number of creatures touched it every hour. Patience of course is required on the spider's part combined with the ability to take action in a split second. But the spider has not to be at the ready *all* the time. Having secured one insect she leaves her hunting ground and goes downstairs to eat and sleep until hungry again. Indeed, when not hungry she gets annoyed when insects go on to her outside tube, and gives it a shake to shoo them off. For this recluse likes peace and quietness.

So there she lives for eight years, knowing nothing of the turmoil and troubles of the outside world.

What of the male Atypus? He too is a recluse and lives in a similar but smaller tube. He does not, however, stay there all his life: it would be much better for him if he did. But when summer is drawing to a close, what cinema captions used to call the Laughing Love-God beckons him and he tears a hole in his tube and issues forth. He will never return.

He searches for and finds (with much more ease than Mr. Joshua Brown) the tube of a female. On this he knocks loudly and rudely with his fists, as we are perfectly well entitled to call the ends of his palps. It seems a dangerous thing to do. One expects to see him seized like a fly and drawn inside. But no: he must have a special knock which the lady understands. He knocks again even more loudly, but nothing happens. And then the rash creature tears a hole in the tube and enters.

The female is there and scrutinises the puny form that has broken in. Rather ominously she then goes to the rent he has made and seals it up. This of course *may* be just finickiness or a dislike of draughts. On the other hand she may be making certain that this male, having chosen to enter, does not get out again until she has finished with him.

Various things may happen to the male now. If she likes his looks, and his conduct is good, and she does not become hungry, a happy married life of several months may stretch before them. If she gets tired of him or if he annoys her in any way at all the marriage will not last so long. She may even begin to dislike him after the first night. She may dislike him the moment he enters. It really makes no difference: from the moment she sealed up the hole he had made he was doomed.

She becomes pregnant; but it is not until the next summer that the eggs are laid, and in the autumn—a year after their mother conceived them—they hatch, about a hundred of them. For the next six months the scene is an edifying one: a contented brood and a doting mother who cares for her children in every possible way. The fact that she is a widow with no husband to help her bear the burden intensifies one's admiration.

In the spring the widow faces the fact that she cannot keep her little ones with her much longer. It is not fair to them. They are getting big and the time has come for them to go out into the world in order that they may retire from it in their own sealed cylinders. She bites a hole in the outer tube and through this her young pour gleefully. They too seek the high places, and spreading their balloons, waft away from the home in which they lived so long and which they will never see again.

But if the mother bites a hole and looking out finds it pouring with rain or blowing a gale, or very cold, naturally the young cannot leave. We know how necessary good flying weather is to these aeronauts. So they stay at home and wait and the mother looks after them as before. But only for a time. If bad weather continues the mother goes to the hole and seals it up—that fatal gesture. We do not know exactly what happens now; whether there is any sorting out or any tears or sighs. All we know is that the mother eats every one of them.

At first it was thought that *Atypus affinis* existed only near Hastings. Then Enoch found them at Woking and on Hampstead Heath. They are now known to exist all along the south coast from Kent to Cornwall, and in Cambridgeshire, Essex, Wales, and Ireland as well.

CHAPTER 6

THE AERONAUTS

To be successful it is necessary for species not only to be fruitful and multiply, but to spread themselves over the land. Those who keep to one place, however fruitful they may be, will eventually find themselves amongst the failures. For one thing, they will use up their food supply, so that their fertility, instead of being an asset, will be a drawback. For another they are in a pregnable position; they have all their eggs, as it were, in one basket. Enemies, drought, floods, may kill them off.

Necessity is the mother of invention and we see many inventions. Ants make temporary wings for their colonisers. Wasps and bumble bees send out fertile, cold-resisting females. Vertebrates, such as lemmings, migrate in large numbers for long distances. Others, like man, penetrate afield in small families in search of food. Only the honey bees (with the exception of man in his more recent stages) have put migration on to a considered and intelligent basis and travel to definite places selected beforehand.

Even more varied are the methods of the plants. We look upon plants as innocent and comparatively well-behaved, but accelerated motion films tell a different tale. Do not be deceived by the sweet face of a flower. As often as not it is a merciless assassin. These accelerated motion pictures show an ideal scene at first as the plants begin to grow—then war. We see forms locked together in deadly strife and tendrils stretching out like arms to grasp and choke the life from others. If plants had voices what screams would rend the air as the

weaker were garotted, strangled, smothered, and trampled on!
So the plants *must* colonise or half of them would die out.
Their task is more difficult. Many resort to bribery and use
the motive power of the fauna. Tomatoes, gooseberries, figs,
currants, for instance, are eaten and the seeds voided, possibly
miles away, in excreta. Stone and pip fruit is often carried by
men, monkeys, squirrels, and the rest. Some of our most
prized varieties of apples, plums, and pears were found origin-
ally growing in hedges springing, no doubt, from some stone
or pip spat out by a labourer or a tramp. Some make seeds with
barbs that cling to the coats of animals. Some, of the pod
variety mostly, employ an explosive that in the heat of the sun
bursts the vessel and shoots out the seeds therein.

Incidentally, some of these pods burst with considerable
noise. There is a certain pod belonging to a slim creeper in
Africa, whose name I have forgotten. It was first forced
upon my attention during a shooting trip in Portuguese East
Africa and was responsible for my shooting a good tusker.
I do not like shooting elephants and I would never shoot one
now, but at that time it did not worry me—much. I was
alone with natives and we followed the spoor of a herd for
six hours. The spoor then led into a dark forest where undoubtedly the elephants were resting during the heat of the
day. And here the ground was covered with twigs and dead
branches to such an extent that one could not avoid occasionally
treading on one and making a loud crack. But from time to
time from various quarters of the wood came cracks very
much louder than any we made. They echoed like pistol shots
for it was the season of the bursting of the pods whose name
I have forgotten. Eventually we came upon the herd, silent
monsters difficult to make out in the dim light until one was
almost on them. And then I trod on a branch, the noisiest
branch I think that I have ever trodden on. The elephants took
no notice. It was elephant-hunting made easy for beginners
—but very difficult for elephants. I take no credit for having
got my tusker.

There are many pods and seed vessels in our own gardens that burst also, though not so loudly as this African species.

The last method of the plants that need be mentioned is the parachute method made so well known to us by dandelions. Parachute is the wrong word. A parachute may drift but does not rise like the dandelion seed. The dandelion method of dispersal is the one used by the spiders.

Nearly all spiders emigrate by air when young.* But the weather must be right. There *are*, of course, those who are fool-hardy and take a chance in bad flying conditions, like many of the crabs, and there are those who are over-cautious, but on the whole the rule stands good: the weather *must* be right. So in spring and autumn the whole countryside may be filled by a vast and increasing concourse of baby spiders waiting for suitable flying weather. Many of them, particularly the jumpers, move restlessly about within a small area leaving strands of silk wherever they go. These strands often form a foothold for the aeronaut when he spins the final strand that is to bear him aloft. Others shelter in batches in little silk tents that protect them from the wind and rain. When the right day comes, which is strangely enough an utterly still day without a breath of wind, up go the balloonists in their millions, borne on their buoyant silk. When they alight the silk is cut and drifts away and comes to earth.

Next morning lawns, meadows, stubble fields, and every other place will be covered with filmy lengths of silk, particularly visible if there is a dew. This gossamer, as it is called, greatly puzzled our forebears. Chaucer placed it amongst the unsolved riddles of the universe. Spenser attributed it to dew and called it "scorchèd deaw." Thomson in his "Seasons" referred to it as "Dew Evaporate."

* The exceptions, as Bristowe has shown, include the more primitive types such as Oonopidae, Dysderidae, Scytodidae, and most of the Mygalomorphae. That is why oceanic islands do not usually possess these types. When they *are* found there they were carried by the agency of man and not of air currents.

How still the breeze! save what the filmy threads
Of dew evaporate brushes from the plain.

Gilbert White in his *Natural History of Selborne* describes how
on September 21, 1741, a "prodigious" shower of flakes of
silky web fell all day over an area of many square miles. His
dogs were blinded by them and had to keep scratching to clear
themselves.

If you are interested in the origin of words the name
"gossamer" is probably derived from the French "Gaze à
Marie," and this gauze of Mary, legend tells us, came from the
threads that fell from the shroud of the Virgin Mary on her
Assumption.

Later on, when gossamer was known to be a spider product
it was supposed to come from one species of spider, and this
spider was called the gossamer spider.

Really heavy showers of gossamer are most uncommon in
this country. I have seen them several times in Africa and
shall never forget one morning in Portuguese East Africa.
I was in a tent and when I looked out in the early morning
I thought a low lying mist covered the country. I dressed and
went out and found that my hob-nailed boots were breaking
into a delicate silken film a few inches deep leaving footprints
as if I had walked through snow. And soon I saw marks where
antelopes and other beasts had passed. It was an eerie experience: tearing through the fine silk garment the earth had
donned seemed like sacrilege.

The spider's thread can function only when air is moving.
In *completely* still air it is useless. Then why, it may be asked,
does a spider wait for a day of complete calm? For it nearly
always *does*. It is because on such days there is a steady *upward*
current from the warmed ground. You and I do not perceive
it, but dandelion seeds or soap bubbles will, if you care to
try with them. This current bears the spider gently aloft and
gives him his initial altitude. It is significant that the day of
the "prodigious shower" was recorded by Gilbert White as

being "cloudless, calm, serene, and worthy of the south of France itself."

Although the reason why terrestrial bodies can rise in air that is apparently still is clear to us now, this was not always the case and observers were greatly puzzled by the "impossible" phenonemon. They searched round for an explanation. Thus J. B. Waters in 1868 claimed that the ascension of spiders in such conditions was due to the sudden expulsion of silk in frequent jets—like a rocket! Others attributed it to air-sacs in the spider's body, and others to a rapid vibration of the legs which thus acted like wings.

This is what Gilbert White says:

"Every day in fine autumnal weather do I see these spiders shooting out their web. They will go off from the finger if you will take them into your hand; last summer one alighted on my book as I was reading in the parlour, and running to the top of the page, and shooting out a web, took its departure from thence. But what I most wondered at was that it went off with considerable velocity, in a place where no air was stirring; and I am sure I did not assist it with my breath; so that these little crawlers seem to have, while mounting, some locomotive power, without the use of wings, and move faster than the air in the air itself."

What is to happen to the spider on that calm day in that gently ascending current no one can say, least of all the spider. He may come down to earth a few yards or a few miles away. Or he may rise and get into high altitude currents that will take him long distances. Darwin tells us that whilst on his famous voyage on the *Beagle* the ship was covered with thousands upon thousands of these minute voyagers when 60 miles from land. The American, McCook, describes a similar occurrence on a ship *200 miles* from any land. What is particularly strange in the latter case is that after a short rest the spider host all set sail again. There is little doubt that these creatures, getting into trade winds, are often carried from one continent to another. T. Foster in his *Pocket Encyclopaedia of*

Natural Phenomena of 1827, writes, "In crossing the channel from Calais to Dover I have observed that the captains of the vessels have sometimes foreboded fine settled weather from the settling on the masts and rigging of a certain sort of web which we take to be the woof of some spider, though we may have observed it to alight on the ships when some way out to sea."

It is obvious that ascending currents of warm air may take the young spiders to great heights. Naturally it is impossible to find out how high they do go, but we have the following observations to serve as a guide. In 1670 Lister climbed to the summit of York Minster and saw spider aeronauts above him. Lincecum in 1874 saw spiders sailing at 2000 feet over Texas. Bristowe in 1928 actually approached the Air Ministry for assistance to collect spider airmen at high altitudes. The Ministry refused to help but informed him that aeroplanes frequently ran into masses of gossamer. In 1931, in America, R. C. Coad collected spiders at 14,000 feet, and jumping spiders (residents, of course, not aeronauts) were found on Mount Everest at a height of 22,000 feet, thus being in the proud position of the highest permanent inhabitants of the world.

Fabre experimented in order to ascertain what strength of current is necessary to bear aloft the young spider. The experiment took place in his study and he had by him a bunch of newly hatched spiders in a box. (*Is* there a name for a collection of spiders. We have a "covey" of partridges, a "gaggle" of geese, a "wisp" of snipe, a "pride" of lions, a "swarm" of bees, and all the rest, but nothing apparently for spiders. So let us call them a "purse" of spiders.*) It was a calm day. The door and one of the study windows were open. Fabre himself could feel no movement of air whatsoever, yet the little spiders when the box was opened were soon sailing up and disappearing through the open window. An

---

* Since writing the above I find that there *is* a name for a collection of spiders. Bristowe coined the phrase "A smother of spiders" and this is quoted by Ivor Brown in one of his books on words.

unperceived draught of course existed between the door and the window.

Fabre closed both door and window and migration ceased. But not for long. Soon the small mites were sailing straight up to the ceiling. A shaft of sun was shining on the carpet, slightly heating it; heating it enough at any rate to cause a faint ascension of air imperceptible to our senses but sufficient to lift the spiders.

Fabre now blocked up every aperture and shut out the shaft of sunlight. He then placed a small chafing-dish on the table whose heat his hand could not feel except when close to it. Motionless before, the gang, when the chafing-dish was lit, began to rise and were soon clinging to the ceiling. Fabre opened the window. The faint current from the chafing-dish (as proved by liberated dandelion plumes) curved round and went out at the window top. The spiders followed it and were wafted into the open.

"Let us wish them," says Fabre, "a prosperous journey."

Before the spider becomes mature it has to cast its skin many times. Even before it takes its air trip it has to moult. But this first moult often occurs inside the cocoon. In any case moulting at that tender age is a matter of no consequence —like pulling off a set of rompers. But when the spider is approaching maturity moulting is a different matter. The first feeling is obviously one of discomfort and, like some of us when we feel our clothes getting too tight, it goes on a diet. The diet is strict; in fact it eats nothing at all for several days. This does no good; a new suit is necessary; but before donning a new suit one must remove the old one. The spider hangs itself upside down and squirms and wriggles. This manoeuvre causes its suit to split, and it gets rid of most of it fairly easily. But the difficult part is to come. The old skin remains on the abdomen and on the legs. The abdomen part is nothing, it soon shrivels off; the legs are a different proposition. They are as if enclosed in riding boots. Not the riding boots you generally get, that are made with due allowance for detachment, but riding boots almost sewn on to the calves, knees, and thighs. In China an alleged boot-maker made me such a pair to measure and I shall never forget them. They went on without *too* much difficulty but could never be pursuaded to come off within ten minutes, even with two boys pulling at them. The spider has no boys and it has eight riding boots instead of two. Savory timed a spider getting *one* of its boots off. It jerked, pulled, heaved, at regular intervals and it took 600 pulls and 40 minutes to get the one boot off.

It is obvious that the first (and last) migration of the spider is, like that of the dandelion seed, haphazard. Dandelions establish themselves anywhere and everywhere. But strangely enough spiders do not. That is to say, certain species are found only in certain parts. We have noticed *Tegenaria larva* living in Southport. And there is Zygiella, the maker of the orb web that is like a cake with two slices cut out. Zygiella has in Britain two very common species, Atrica and X-notata, and although the young in both cases fly away with the rest of the crowd and leave it to chance where they come to earth Atrica is only found in bushes in the open and X-notata outside houses, spinning its web generally in window frames. So fixed are these two in their choice of locality that, although they are hard to distinguish, one always knows which species one is dealing with; for if it is in the open it is Atrica, and if on a window frame or a paling, X-notata.

One could cite innumerable other instances; spiders found only in certain areas, in certain types of vegetation, spiders rare here, common there, etc. And in many cases no explanation is forthcoming. The distribution of animals can generally be attributed to the food supply; the snipe keeps to marshes because its prey lives there and is accessible to its beak; the heron, living on fish, need not be sought in the Gobi desert. And so on. But the spider eats most things that come its way; it dines with equal relish on a grasshopper or a daddy-long-legs, a fly or a mosquito. And it can weave its web anywhere. So the special distribution of many, in view of their haphazard methods of colonisation, is rather a mystery.

CHAPTER 7

THE HERMIT OF SÉRIGNAN

IN writing on Natural History one inevitably owes most of one's knowledge to the work of others, and one rarely gives these others adequate acknowledgment. This sounds very wrong, but to do so would make a book so cumbersome and tedious that very few would read it. For instance, if one said that an insect did a certain thing, one *would* probably say that the discovery was due to Jones. But if one was determined to be really fair one could not stop there; one would have to go on and say that Jones had been much assisted by the previous observations of Smith and that Smith had got on to the idea by a discovery made by Brown, and that Brown had been influenced by a treatise written by Black.

Therefore every naturalist works, not for honour and glory, but from a wish to advance knowledge. The utmost a naturalist can do—in his own chosen field—is to provide a stepping-off place for another. By entering the field of literature however, naturalists *can*, if they write well enough, make a name for themselves that will live. Such an one was Gilbert White of Selborne, and another, probably, was Fabre. Whether or not Fabre's books will live, he was certainly the greatest observer the world has so far known, and he put down his observations clearly and concisely. And he has another claim on our attention; he was unique in that he never used the work of others but started always from the beginning.

This method, however, needs not only patience and hard work but long life.

Fortunately long life, a very long life, was granted to

Fabre, and it is his life—as distinct from his studies and discoveries—that have always intrigued me. Going through his works one finds little bits of this life here and there, tucked away amongst observations on spiders, wasps, and other creatures. I find digging out these bits and pieces and putting them in order fascinating, and I propose to present them now —not in the form of a lengthy "Life" (that has been done already by the Abbé Fabre and others) but as a series of little pictures—a kind of Magic Lantern Show.

This is going to interrupt, for the space of one chapter, our studies of spiders. But perhaps that is no bad thing. It will act as a break; and I have always wanted to do it. I feel, too, that since Fabre does not appear again in this book I ought to do it now.

Fabre, towards the end of his career, won great fame. Statues were erected to him and princes and governors went to see him. But do not be led astray by this and think of taking up natural history as a career. There is no money in it—and very few statues. Moreover, a real naturalist never does take up natural history; it is natural history that takes up him.

As a matter of fact all of us are naturalists—in the beginning. In my garden is a small pool and to this pool in the mating season come frogs in their hundreds. Where they come from or how they know of the pool is a mystery. Then they depart, leaving the water almost solid with a gelatinous mass that looks like dirty tapioca pudding. Not long afterwards comes another invasion to the pool—the invasion of the naturalists. All carry jam jars looped at the neck with string and their ages vary from four to about eight. Where *they* come from and how *they* know it is the season of spawning is also a mystery. They too depart in due course, well stocked with tadpole specimens, and return the next spring.

My daughter, aged nearly five, coming into my study noticed my spiders in their glass receptacles. Never before had she realised that I, too, was of the elect; the sort that keeps things in jars. And spiders seemed a good and new idea.

Out came *her* jars, no longer tenanted by tadpoles, and soon five of them were occupied by *Tegenaria domesticas* of varying sizes, together with sundry flies. In hardly any time she became obsessed by spiders and drew them in her drawing book. They had about thirty legs at first, but later, and by herself, she found out that spiders have eight and thereafter drew them with more or less that number. But in a few more years what will have happened? Alas, she will care nothing for the legs of a spider nor any other part of it.

One more example: a girl of three or four and her mother came to my house for the day last summer. The spawn had vanished from the pool but there were plenty of things that swam and wriggled. The girl, bored by the conversation, wandered into the kitchen and was later found to be missing altogether. I went out hastily: the pool is not deep but it is deep enough for a child of four. (The tadpole naturalists had been safe by reason of their numbers: when one naturalist fell in the other naturalists would pull him out.) She was safe; kneeling by the pond, a large cooking spoon in hand, engaged in getting something from the water. I paused—for I too have known these tense moments. Apparently all went well for, with a small expanse of tongue showing between lips, the spoonful was decanted into a glass jar to the accompaniment of an audible sigh of relief.

I called her then. She did not hear me. She was examining the jar and suddenly a loud wail came. Whatever it was she had been after she had not got it. The jar was devoid of life and I led her weeping back to the house, where more weeping took place over the matter of a ruined best frock.

But these naturalists do not remain naturalists, and this same girl when she grows up will probably take no interest in things that swim in ponds and still less in those that wriggle. Nor will she count a best frock well ruined in the cause of science.

Luckily there are exceptions, and it is to these exceptions that we owe the knowledge we possess. Fabre was one. But

enough has been said by way of introduction. We will turn
off the light and show the slides.

The year is 1829 and the first slide shows Jean Henri Fabre
at the age of six. His parents, poverty-stricken and quite
illiterate French peasants, have found themselves unable to
feed him and have sent him to the farm of his paternal grandparents. One wonders how the grandparents fed him either,
for the "farm" was a ridge of granite covered with heath and
gorse. By setting fire to the heath and gorse, small patches
of oats and potatoes could be grown that apparently derived
their nourishment almost entirely from the ashes. There was
stock; some sheep and geese and poultry, but these must have
led a hazardous existence for the place was over-run with
wolves.

As for Jean himself: a ragged little urchin, but as decent
as it was possible to make him. His grandmother had provided
him with a handkerchief tied to his waist with string but he
admits that he preferred to use the back of his sleeve.

Even at this age he possessed the inquisitive nature of the
biologist as one of his experiments will show. How, he asked
himself, did one perceive light? He shut his eyes and opened
his mouth—darkness. Not therefore with the mouth. He
shut his mouth and opened his eyes—light. With the eyes
therefore. He ran to his grandparents with news of his
discovery and was hurt by their laughter. Nevertheless it *was*
unusual for a child of six to fail to take light for granted.

The next slide shows him at seven at the village school.
There is only one class, composed of boys of all ages. There
is a fire on which boils continually a large pan of pig food
from which the boys with knives or pencils surreptitiously
spear potatoes and other edibles when the master is not looking.
The smell of the pan attracts others, notably a sow with piglets

and a hen with chickens. They push in through the door continually, assisted by the boys who, on the excuse of "leaving the room" go out and return, carefully not quite shutting it.

One gathers they learnt little. Adequate instruction is difficult to provide for ages so mixed. Moreover the schoolmaster, besides being schoolmaster, was the manager of the large farm of an absent landowner, was the village barber, bell-ringer, clock-mender, and leader of the choir. It was only by chance that Fabre even learnt the alphabet. His father gave him one of those books where the letters are decorated with animals. So animals, he avers, taught him to read. They were to teach him a great deal more later.

He is ten when he appears next, a day boy in the Lycée of Rôdez and a serving boy in the chapel—a position which entitled him to free instruction. There were four of these servers and they would take up their posts near the altar in cassocks, white surplices, and red skull-caps. Fabre was the youngest and was, he says, always "all of a tremble" and never knew when to ring the bell or move the missal from one side of the altar to the other, or when to perform his genuflections. On the other hand it is pleasant to learn that he was "well thought of" and "cut a good figure" in composition and translation. That he was a born scholar is evident for we soon find him confessing a love of Latin. He attributes this to Virgil with his intriguing accounts of the bee, the cicada, the turtle dove, the crow, and the nanny goat. The animals apparently taught him Latin too.

The next picture is a long time coming. I knock impatiently with my pointer. A tall, lanky youth appears. Fabre is 18 years old and a teacher in the primary college of Carpentras. Many of his pupils are older than he is and their "one ambition is to play tricks on their youthful master."

That short sentence holds quite a lot if you think it out: a lot of joy and a lot of sorrow according to the angle from which you view it.

But he had compensations. He sat at a desk in front of the class and from time to time peered within. Masters' desks hold many secrets from bags of sweets to cribs and Wild West romances, but *this* master's secret hoard breaks new ground. It contained beetles' wing casings, wasps' stings, snap-dragons' seed vessels, and things like that.

A master in those days had one advantage over his present day prototype. He could teach what he wished, and when. There was no set curriculum. This suited Fabre's avid desire for knowledge. To him at this stage, and for a long time afterwards, teaching was only a camouflage for learning. So he decided to teach his class chemistry, a subject of which he knew nothing. True, on one occasion, and one only, he had attended a chemistry lesson—and that ought to have been sufficient. The master had tried to make oxygen. There are several ways of doing this, but the best way *not* to do it (especially if the manganese dioxide is not pure) is the method employed by this master. He boiled manganese dioxide in strong sulphuric acid over a fierce charcoal fire. The boys of the class blew with all their might on the charcoal so as to get up a good fierce glow. The retort exploded and boiling sulphuric acid shot all around. Screaming boys dashed away in agony and the master's clothes were a mass of smouldering holes. The unobtrusive Fabre, being at the rear behind another boy, escaped. Yet it was this same method he used for *his* class in the first chemistry lesson he gave them. Admittedly he made them stand well back and he did the blowing himself, and what is more there was no explosion. After this his weekly chemistry lessons became a big success.

A subject of which he knew even less than chemistry was (not surprisingly) practical surveying. So of course he felt compelled to give his class lessons in practical surveying. This meant a whole half day in the country and the class were all for it. Fabre bought most of the apparatus out of his own pocket, and the boys quarrelled for the privilege of carrying it. This quarrelling is significant. They wanted to *help* their master now. There is no more talk of " tricks."

The locality selected for these lessons was a place well out of the way; a sweet-smelling plain full of pebbles and flowering thyme. Things went well, and both boys and master picked up the subject admirably. Then things went wrong. There were inexplicable delays. Boys sent to plant the stakes or pick up the arrows lingered by the way, went off at tangents, lay down, or disappeared altogether. The diagonals and measurements of angles went hopelessly astray. It was some time before the harassed master found out what was wrong. What was wrong was a big black solitary bee. This bee made clay nests on the pebbles and filled them with honey from the thyme. The boys preferred abstracting this honey with bits of sticks to practical surveying.

It is hard to blame them. Certainly their master did not. Indeed, instead of handing out impositions he joined the hunters and "acquired," he says, the taste himself. Personally I feel that a taste for pure thyme honey can hardly have been one that needed much acquiring.

This incident, besides giving Fabre a taste for thyme honey, led him to make enquiries as to the identity of the big black velvet bee that had so disorganised his class. He saw a book on insects for sale and though it took a month's salary bought it. After buying it he devoured it; every page thrilled him to the core. In the lives of great men one seeks always for turning points and it would be nice to be able to say that this book —and the interrupted surveying that had made him buy it— turned the footsteps of the "Great Observer" towards entomology. Perhaps it did, but I am quite sure that nothing on earth could, in the long run, have kept Fabre from insects.

Some years go by and Fabre decides to rise above the level

of the primary school; to get degrees and a post in the secondary school. This meant taking up mathematics, physics, and chemistry. He taught himself, as usual. Alone he pored over conic sections, differential and integral calculus, and the rest. Physics and chemistry presented more difficulty. He had no laboratory and could not afford to buy one. In the end he made one, more or less out of jam jars; a Heath Robinson affair—what he himself called an "impossible" laboratory.

Another thing remained to do—the hardest of all. If thy right hand offend thee, cut it off. Natural history was offending Fabre, occupying his thoughts, becoming a part of himself. He must cut it off. Into the bottom of his trunk went all his natural history books and when he met a new grass or an unknown beetle he looked the other way. And in so doing he states he "did violence" to himself.

Even without natural history one would have thought that his regular teaching and his new studies would have kept him sufficiently busy, but when a certain young man came to him with a proposition he listened. This young man was preparing for an engineering examination and he asked Fabre to coach him in algebra. It was as if a man with normal sight asked a blind man to lead him, for Fabre knew nothing of algebra. He did not even know why they talked of x and y. The lessons, said the young man, must start the day after the next.

We know how Fabre liked to learn himself under the pretence of teaching others. It was a bait he invariably found all but impossible to resist. And *complete* ignorance only made the bait the more alluring. But in this case it was a dangerous game to play and he knew it. The young man must never guess the truth; must always think the coacher knew the subject from A to Z (including x and y.). A path beset with pitfalls. Fabre hesitated, and was lost. He agreed to teach the young man algebra, beginning the day after the next.

When the youth had gone Fabre came to his senses. Not only had he merely one day in which to master enough algebra for the first lesson, but *he had no book*. The local bookshop, he knew, would have nothing on a subject like that, and if he wrote and ordered one it would be a week before it arrived. He was on the point of dashing after the young man to call the whole thing off.

How often, later on, when long observation and infinite patience had failed to elucidate the behaviour of some insect, did he say, "Shall I abandon the project? Not a bit of it!" He said it now. The science master might have a book on algebra.

Now the science master was by way of being a big noise and as such lived in a house in town and not at the college. But he had a small room in the college where he kept his books and other things. Fabre decided to burgle this room.

One would have thought it simpler to ask the science master for the book direct, but Fabre feared his questions and his scorn when he learnt what Fabre proposed to do. He would tell everyone and the whole college would rock with laughter. Furthermore the science master did not like him. None of the masters did if it comes to that. Fabre's own explanation was that if he had asked for the book he was sure his "amiable colleague" would have received him "superciliously" and refused his request.

The next day was a half holiday. It was almost a certainty that the science master would not put in an appearance. Fabre went to his room and found that his own key—after persuasion —could force the lock. In a cupboard he found a bulky tome, six inches thick, on algebra. He took it and tried to make towards the door. But the strain and suspense had told. His legs gave way and he collapsed on to the carpet. Shaking in every limb he found that he no longer had the power of movement. Luckily no one came along as he lay there and in the end he recovered sufficiently to get up and stagger back to his own room with the stolen book.

There remained but one evening to master the subject. Turning the pages over before commencing he noticed, somewhere about the middle of the book a chapter on *Newton's Binomial Theorem.* The title intrigued him, for he could not think what a "binomial theorem" could be. He began to read it, got interested, took up his pen, and became lost in permutations and combinations. It was to him a fascinating, irresistible game, but the result was that when the pupil came the next morning Fabre still knew nothing about algebra. But he *did* know quite a lot about Newton's Binomial Theorem and started on that, which was putting the cart before the horse. His enthusiasm infected the pupil who conceived a vast respect for the erudition of his tutor.

Before the next visit Fabre had turned over other pages. He found algebra "less digestible" and "heavier fare" than the binomial theorem but managed to keep a short length ahead of the pupil and bluff along. And then, in one of his preliminary readings, he got stuck. We know what a man he was for the essentials. It was not sufficient for a thing to *be*, he must know the reason. And he could not understand why minus multiplied by minus made plus. Neither can I. On the morrow he faced his pupil determined to brazen it out. He made his explanations, taken direct from the book, and asked, "Do you understand?"

"No,"said the pupil.

" Let us then," said the tutor patiently, "try another method."

He stumbled on, anxiously watching the other's eyes. At any gleam of intelligence in those eyes he knew that he was working in the right direction and hoped that light might come to him also. He felt his way, the pupil's face being his guide. And suddenly light came. It came to both of them at the same time, but the pupil never knew this.

"My pupil triumphs," says Fabre. "So do I, but my inner consciousness says, ' you understand because you succeed in making another understand.' "

Fabre is thirty when next we meet him, and a professor in the Lycée of Avignon. He has got his degrees and is no longer an irresponsible young master. He lectures on physics and chemistry at set hours. This means that he has more spare time, and spare time to Fabre is like gold. How to use it to the best advantage? He decides on higher mathematics.

And all this time the natural history books had been lying at the bottom of the trunk, and beetles had passed him by and seen only his averted face. He appeared to have put the devil fairly and squarely behind him. And he had, but the devil had never ceased to nudge and whisper. He whispered now, in fact he shouted, and his plausible argument was that the professor could easily study the two subjects together.

Tempted thus, Fabre fell and decided to divide his spare time between mathematics and natural history. The books came out of the trunk and the devil chuckled. Getting out those books was like letting the imp from the bottle.

For some time Fabre kept strictly to his contract and divided his spare time honestly between the two subjects. He did very well in mathematics; but he did better in natural history—so much so that a distinguished naturalist urged him to abandon mathematics altogether. Fabre climbed to the top of a high mountain to think it out.

He need not have bothered to climb that mountain. Once it came to a direct fight mathematics had no chance.

"Bug-hunters" are often classed as mad. This is mostly unjust, but there was some excuse in the case of Fabre. At any rate, as time went on he certainly became peculiar. It was enough for an insect to appear to make him drop anything he was doing or saying and dash off after it. Women going to work in the vineyards in the early morning would see his tall form crouched down and his eyes staring at some spot on the ground. Returning in the evening they would see him still there and would look at each other and cross themselves and murmur a word that means a harmless as opposed to a dangerous lunatic and hurry quickly by.

In the next picture we see a renowned but still timid scientist. He must have been renowned for it was quite common for famous men to come and see him. Louis Pasteur was one. He had just been commissioned to investigate a disease that threatened to exterminate silkworms. As a matter of fact when Pasteur took on the job he would not have recognised a silkworm if he had seen one, but, like Fabre, the unknown attracted him. He came to Fabre to ask to be shown a silkworm cocoon. Fabre brought one. Pasteur took it and shook it. Something rattled inside and Pasteur stared

"Something rattled," he said.

"Of course," said Fabre, "the chrysalis."

"What's that?" asked Pasteur.

And this man, who did not know anything about chrysalises, had undertaken to investigate a disease that had confounded all the experts! There is something to be said for ignorance. Plodding slowly over ground that experts have taken in their stride one possibly notices things that have escaped them. Anyway Pasteur saved the silkworms.

He called again on Fabre. This time it was his cellar he wished to see. Pasteur was busy with those famous experiments on germs and yeasts that have given his name to half our milk bottles. But now Fabre could not help him. He could not afford a bottle of wine from the grocer, let alone a cellar. With his usual shrinking from questions or ridicule he made vague excuses. Perhaps he pretended he had lost the key.

Later came a summons to appear before the Emperor, Napoleon III, to receive the ribbon of the Legion of Honour. Terrified at such publicity he had almost to be dragged to Paris by force.

When the time came the Emperor moved from one to another of the assembled savants and showed "a fair amount of information" about their various activities. When it came to Fabre's turn he answered as best he could a question about his last essay, *The Hypermetamorphosis of the Meliodae*, but forgot

to address the Emperor as "Sire" and called him "Monsieur."
His description of this august personage is terse: "An ordinary
man, round and plump with a large moustache and a pair
of half-closed, drowsy eyes."

He did not enjoy it. He was pressed hard to stay and visit
the museums and collections, but refused. "I had had enough
of Paris. Never had I felt such tortures. To get away, to
get away, was my one idea."

The next picture brings tragedy—and all through a class-
room of young girls. Fabre, as we know, was disliked by his
colleagues. At ease with young people he was tongue-tied
with men, and his timid manners did not endear him to them.
But the dislike went further. He wrote about science in a way
that ordinary people could understand. This was considered
to cheapen the profession. He was a born teacher too, and
pupils almost fought to attend his classes. Naturally the
other masters did not like it, and were ready to take action
at the first opportunity.

It happened that at this time a scheme for the secondary
education of girls was put on foot. Fabre volunteered his free
services. The scheme went through, so on certain days he
gave these girls lectures on physical and natural science. He
explained why a man breathes, what causes the lightning,
how a plant flowers and seeds—subjects like that. It seems
innocent enough now, but it rocked Avigon. Girls ought
not to be taught such things.

A lot Fabre cared. He went on teaching them, and the
days of *his* lectures were red-letter days to the girls. Elderly
ladies, the clergy, and of course Fabre's "amiable" colleagues
were shocked—or pretended to be. The ladies were also angry
and when ladies become angry things happen, generally nasty
things.

Fabre was married and had a large family. He occupied
a house owned by two old ladies. Very religious were

these ladies but lacking in the virtue that Saint Paul prizes so highly. Fabre, simple soul, had no agreement in writing and one day bailiffs appeared, armed with stamped legal documents. He and his must go within the month or be thrown out on to the street together with their furniture. Moreover, his vilifiers had been working hard for he could obtain no other house. He had to resign his professorship and go to distant Orange. From here he secured an isolated house in Sérignan and moved into it with his family.

He was 74 years of age. All seemed over. Actually, all was beginning; the Hermit of Sérignan was coming into his inheritance.

The house at Sérignan (and this, by the way, is our last picture) had a large garden which soon became the apple of the hermit's eye. He worked on it from morn till late at night. But let no one think of closely-shaven sward, neatly-edged paths, herbaceous borders, or manured roses. Thistles did best, but couch-grass flourished and most of the more pernicious kinds of weeds were kept in check only by competition from equally noxious flora.

This is what he says of his garden:

"The Eden of bliss. Eden . . . this accursed ground which no one would have at a gift is an earthly paradise for the bees and the wasps. Never in my insect-hunting memories have I seen so large a population at a single spot. Here come hunters of every kind of game; builders of clay, weavers of cotton goods, collectors of pieces cut from a leaf, architects in pasteboard, plasterers mixing mortar, carpenters boring wood, miners digging underground galleries, workers in gold-beater's skin, and many more.

"In front of the house is a large pond. Here from half a mile and more around come the frogs and toads in the lovers' season. In May, as soon as it is dark, the pond becomes a deafening orchestra; it is impossible to talk at table, impossible to sleep."

It was here that Fabre, living in almost complete seclusion, made the bulk of the studies and experiments that have made him famous. He shunned his fellows to such an extent that on his entomological expeditions into the country he never passed through the village, though this meant making a detour of several miles. Such men excite suspicion—particularly in the breasts of policemen and game-keepers. And a botanising case *does* look rather like a ferret box. So, unknown to Fabre, the village game-keeper began to follow him on his excursions and to note with growing interest his stealthy movements and his long hours spent poring over what might possibly have been rabbit holes. It culminated in a hand on Fabre's shoulder and the peremptory summons, "You come along with me."

He got off: there was no direct evidence against him, but the game-keeper never believed his story that he went into those preserves merely to watch flies.

Fabre's family, his wife and eight children, were enthusiastic collaborators, but they dispersed or died and the hermit's last years—the years of fame and honour—were very lonely ones. He died in 1915, after 18 years hard work at Sérignan.

Knowledge increases. As I said at the beginning of this chapter, naturalists and scientists become superseded. Later discoveries have left Fabre behind in some respects, but during his life he gave natural science a tremendous shove forward.

And now we must return to the spiders.

CHAPTER 8

ENEMIES

"WILL you walk into my parlour . . ."

Popular conception classes the spider purely as an ogre, a lurking menace that deals horrible death to the unwary. And so it is, but this is only half the picture. The other half shows a wee, timorous, cowering beastie, a creature so persecuted and preyed on that it is a wonder it survives. For a long time "Animal" tales have been popular. "Uncle Remus," Ernest Thompson Seton, and Mortimer Batten amongst a galaxy of writers and observers have enthralled us. As a boy I used to shed tears over the hard lives and often dreadful fate of the heroes and heroines of these stories. When reading of Molly Cotton-Tail, had it been in my power, I would have exterminated every enemy of the rabbit. And likewise when the hero became a bear, coyote, wolf, or fox, their enemies would have gone too.

I rarely faltered in my allegiance to the hero of the moment but I was troubled once. I had read about Molly Cotton-Tail and had not had time to readjust myself to the story of a fox, the hero of the next animal tale. He was hunted a lot and had a family of cubs. In between being hunted he had to feed these cubs and when he was stalking a rabbit my heart was in my mouth lest he should miss it. Then I realised that he was stalking Molly Cotton-Tail and for the first time I was up against the facts of life and was puzzled, and I have been puzzled ever since. The hunter and the hunted, with the hunter often becoming the hunted—with which shall we sympathise? We ought really to sympathise with neither: we ought to look down on this earthly scene of slaughter

with the Mona-Lisa-like smile of nature herself, but it is hard
to do it when one sees a robin caught by a cat or a pregnant
antelope ripped open by wild dogs. With spiders however
this academical aloofness is easier to maintain. The cruelty
of the spider herself has nothing to do with it. The fox is
cruel and has a love of slaughter for the mere sake of slaughter
greater than that of the spider, as has the leopard and the wild
dog who in a farm gnash and maul every living thing within
their reach for the mere fun of it. But we are akin, in a remote
way, to foxes and leopards. We can understand their ways,
indeed we can even imitate and improve on them, but the
spider is an "insect," a member of another world whose
doings are no concern of ours but on whose wickedness we
can look with complacency and, at times, interest. So when,
as in this chapter, the spider becomes the persecuted heroine
few are likely to get wrought up.

. . . "Said the spider to the fly." But not to *all* flies. Flies
belong to the order Diptera, which means two wings and
there are a lot of insects that have only two wings. Nor,
incidentally, does the lack of another pair incommode them,
as anyone who has tried to catch a house fly knows. Out of
the vast order of Diptera are flies who actually prey on small
spiders or parasitise their eggs. Other species have been found
eating spiders and have been classed as their enemies on this
account. But an important link is missing in the chain of
evidence against these latter. They have not been *seen* killing
the spider. A jackal will feast on a dead lion but that does
not mean that it is an enemy of the lion.

In general, however, flies are the favourite food of spiders
and so must be classed as friends rather than enemies.

In drawing up a list of enemies in order of merit it is hard
to know where to begin, but probably the wasps come first.
Not the social wasps—these may take an odd spider or so just
as a spider takes an odd wasp or so—but the solitary wasps.
These latter want meat for their young, and their *modus
operandi* is briefly as follows.

T.S.   L

The female solitary, or hunting, wasp makes a chamber in the ground, or a mud cell, or a tunnel in some plant stem according to her species, and provisions this chamber with meat. She lays one egg, seals the chamber up, and leaves the forthcoming child to its own devices. The egg hatches, the grub consumes the meat, then spins its cocoon. The meat is in the form of corpses—grasshoppers, beetles, spiders, and the rest. The meat has to be kept fresh until the time of consumption, so the corpses, unfortunately for themselves, are alive. They are alive but scientifically paralysed by a clever injection of dope into the nerve ganglia. To perform such an intricate surgical operation the wasp mothers have to be specialists possessing an intimate knowledge of the nervous system of the subject. Therefore the species of wasp that gives treatment to caterpillars gives treatment to no other prey. Similarly with the beetle, grasshopper, bee, cricket and spider hunters—all confine themselves to one subject.

Naturally, only the spider-hunters come into this chapter and these include the genera Pompilus, Calicurgus, Pelopaeus, Agenia, Ceropalis, Aporus, and Trypoxylon, with a multitude of species. So it will be appreciated that such a host is well able to reduce the spider population considerably and to make the spider's life at certain times a most uncomfortable one.

A little investigation will give some idea of the slaughter inflicted. The number of spiders stored per cell varies, but it may be as many as 30, and one wasp will make ten or more cells. The commonest place for a cell is underground, but the Peckhams found 400 in a single haystack. Putting the average contents as low as ten, this gives 6000 spiders stored in one haystack. How many paralysed spiders, then, would there be in a few acres of average ground?—millions, I should think.

Opinion varies: as enemies of spiders, some class the wasp first and others the Ichneumon fly—which is not a fly at all. Savory thinks that the solitary wasps account for more spider casualties than all the other causes put together. No one knows. One makes what investigation one can, and then guesses.

The spider's eggs at any rate are safe from the hunting wasp but not from the Ichneumon, who attacks both the living spider and her eggs according to her species. Here, too, the enemy is a mother and a vegetarian also. Females *are* more dangerous than males but to be really terrible they have to be mothers. The mother Ichneumon that preys on adult spiders is faced with the same difficulty as the mother hunting wasp—the meat for her child must be fresh. Up to a point she solves this problem in the same way as the wasp, by giving her infant live meat; meat, as it were, on the hoof. But her task is easier. The hunting wasp egg or baby is dislodged and killed even by a shudder from the live corpse on which it lies, hence the need of expert paralysing. The Ichneumon mother simply lays her egg on a hale and hearty spider. And after receiving this precious burden the spider runs off and attends to its affairs in its normal way, apparently unaware of the infant jockey that now rides it.

But although her child is a born jockey and gives his mother no cause for anxiety after she has provided him with a mount it does not follow that the mother's task is simple. It is the getting him into the saddle that is—or should be— the difficulty; a panic-stricken animal is not easy to mount. But the spider, although terrified of this mother, offers no resistance to her.

Ichneumon chooses her victims mostly from among the web-weavers and when the spider sees her coming it dashes away and drops from the web on a long line. Here it remains, hoping that the mother will not find it. A forlorn hope. The mother follows sedately down the line and scrutinises the trembling form. She even pats it and strokes it with her antennae. She then mounts it, arches her abdomen, and with her ovipositor lays an egg just beneath the skin on its back. This done she descends, cleans and combs herself, and walks. away. It is as easy as that.

The strangely docile spider stays motionless for a few more minutes, then comes to life and resumes its business as if nothing had happened. Quite why the spider, after its first panic-stricken drop from the web, offers no resistance has been the subject of much speculation. Personally I should think it is too petrified with fear to move, but some have suggested mesmerism and others, including Bristowe, think that the Ichneumon actually stings and paralyses the spider. Certainly, at times, the Ichneumon feels about with the tip of her abdomen but probably she is only searching for the right place to put her egg. And if it were a paralysing sting that quietened the spider what about the preliminary period when the mother often almost fondles the beast before she mounts it? No sting can have been inflicted then but the spider rarely moves. And finally what sort of a sting is this that induces paralysis from which the subject recovers completely in a few minutes? We know the effect of the sting of the hunting wasp and the bite of the spider. From the one no recovery is possible; from the other recovery is but the prelude to death. It is poison, not a sleeping draught, that insects inject.

Moreover the Ichneumon does not *want* to incapacitate the spider. On the contrary she wants the spider to live a normal, active life for as long as possible after being saddled with her baby. And this the spider does, but towards the end it is not a happy life.

The egg hatches out and a tiny cream-coloured grub emerges. There is a kind of saddle in a depression in the centre of the spider's back and to this the grub attaches itself. It is the one place where the spider cannot get at it.

The spider does not seem to mind, though the grub is actually feeding on her juices. She spins and renews her webs; she catches flies, mates, and sometimes even lays eggs. But all the time the grub is growing: not fast—unlike most grubs it is a small feeder and a slow grower. But it *does* grow and in time the spider begins to show signs that all is not well.

She makes sudden rushes round her web for no apparent reason; she ignores flies that get caught, and if she renews her web at all she does so in an amateurish and uneven way as if she were too troubled about something else to give the work the necessary attention.

When it is ready to pupate the grub kills the spider. *How* it kills her is another problem, but the real problem is how it manages to avoid killing her before. For time here is of the essence: if the spider dies too soon the grub will not have reached the stage of pupation, and will die without a host to feed on. If on the contrary the spider lives on, the grub will be unable to leave the saddle without receiving dire and well-merited vengeance immediately it dismounts.

Moreover, apart from the danger of retaliation, the grub now *needs* a dead spider. It has exercised restraint for a long time and is a bit thin. To pupate successfully a grub should be fat and well nourished. So the grub kills the spider and eats as much of it as it can hold. It then retires to a quiet spot, generally on the outskirts of the web, and there weaves its cocoon.

It is a neat cocoon, in shape very like those leaf coverings in which some cigars used to be wrapped. Everything about the Ichneumon is neat, precise, well-ordered.

While some Ichneumon species attack the living spider others (a large number) attack the cocoons and lay their eggs inside. The grubs hatch and feast on the spider eggs. The hard outer covering of the majority of spider cocoons is made to protect the contents from just such enemies as this, and most insects *are* thwarted. But the Ichneumon mother, that efficient creature, somehow manages to penetrate almost any cocoon however thick and hard. No wonder the Ichneumon race is on the increase.

Ichneumon lays quite a lot of eggs in one cocoon (the number varying) but for some reason or other few of these reach maturity. Often it is only one, and very rarely more than five. This suggests cannibalism amongst the young, though it has never been observed. Bristowe once saw an Ichneumon laying her eggs in a spider cocoon. He caught her and placed her, together with the cocoon, in a glass-topped box. The Ichneumon circled around in the usual way of captured insects but whenever in her ambit she stumbled onto the cocoon she immediately laid more eggs in it—about a dozen each time. In all, he tells us, quite 60 eggs were laid in the one cocoon. And of all these only four came to maturity. Under natural conditions of course this Ichneumon would have found a fresh cocoon for each batch of eggs and laid about a dozen in each.

Here again careful timing is important, for if the spider eggs hatch before the Ichneumon eggs the Ichneumon eggs or young will be devoured.

It is impossible to assess the amount of damage done to spider eggs by Ichneumons. They do not fill in forms for us. But from observations made in certain places and amongst certain susceptible species it is quite 50 per cent.

Ants eat spider eggs (and spiders too if small and if they can catch them) but in their case the protective envelope of the cocoons is usually sufficient to keep them out. Ants also eat many paralysed spiders that have been stored away by hunting wasps and by so doing reduce the wasp population. Thus, indirectly and very slightly, they may be of benefit to spiders.

Obviously, insects being what they are, there must be a large number of species that kill spiders, but these two, the Ichneumon and the Hunting Wasp, are far and away the most important and are the only two that have concentrated on spiders to the exclusion of other game. Therefore we will leave the insect class and review a few of the more important of other types of enemies.

Two hard working and self-satisfied members of the opposition are toads and frogs. Spiders run about everywhere on the ground (to an extent that is little imagined by most of us) and if the frog and the toad just sit, spiders will come. The stomach of the toad is gross; obviously it can hold a lot. It is also expanding. Even so anyone who has watched a toad picking up bees outside a hive wonders where they all go—or rather how they find accommodation, for there is no question as to where they go. And as his stomach becomes more and more distended a look, not, strangely enough, of distress but of smiling beatitude grows on the toad's face. Presumably there *is* a limit to his capacity but I have never been there to witness it.

The frog too is a good trencherman but cannot compete with the toad. Also his field is more restricted and he likes to keep near the edges of his pond instead of wandering around.

Painstaking investigators have gone to incredible trouble sorting out the contents of the stomachs of thousands of toads and frogs. Unfortunately a stomach is not a specimen cabinet. Its function is to destroy, not to preserve. In about six hours to twelve the contents vanish; in half this time they are unrecognisable. Only things just swallowed can be identified and listed. And if, for instance, a lot of spiders are found in a toad's stomach it does not mean that the toad particularly selects spiders as food, it means that a lot of spiders were in the toad's vicinity an hour or two before it was killed.

Statistics concerning anything rarely give us the true picture and I should think statistics based on the stomachs of toads are less reliable even than other statistics. Nevertheless if a sufficiently large number are examined *some* idea can be obtained. Cott is one who has been to great pains in this matter and on his figures the number of spiders consumed in one year is 277 for one frog and 1190 for one toad. This sounds a lot, especially for the toad, but if you work out the daily consumption it is surprisingly little, even if you remember that the toad works only in the summer months.

If a bird is not singing it is generally eating, or at any rate looking for something to eat. Swallows, Flycatchers, and others take insects on the wing. But thrushes, blackbirds, and starlings and others that run about the lawn—what are they eating? They are not confining themselves to worms and snails; they are taking creatures that run in the grass, such as spiders. How to find out what they *are* taking? According to circumstances they take insects either for their own consumption or that of their nestlings. The ordinary man would leave it at that and merely deduce that they must catch quite a lot of spiders. Possibly in this deduction he has gone as far as the experts, and with much less labour, but this is an age of statistics and enthusiasts have again gone to fantastic lengths to determine the number of spiders taken by birds both young and adult. For instance Kleuver on the Continent extracted 17,933 invertebrates from the insides of starling nestlings and found that 677 of these were spiders, while Florence in Britain has a record of the contents of 2897 stomachs. That is a lot but it fades to insignificance beside the feat of McAtre in America who examined 80,000 stomachs of birds (9966 spiders were found). Let us pause, let us indeed take off our hats, while we try to think of the work involved in dissecting 80,000 birds and separating, classifying, and counting out each tiny creature inside, most of them half dissolved and barely recognisable. For the stomach of the bird acts even more quickly than that of the toad and consumes its contents in four hours.

Such painstaking investigation is of great value to agriculturalists, and it is of interest too to know to what extent the various species of birds feed on spiders. The examinations of stomach contents have been pursued to the bitter end and tables have been made out which show (striking an average of course) the number of spiders eaten by one bird of each species for every month of the year. And quite possibly these figures give us a fairly accurate idea. But we cannot determine the "value" of the bird as an *enemy* by such simple means. Complications arise. For instance if, for the sake of argument, a bird eats ten spiders each day it does not follow that this bird reduces the spider population by ten per diem, for that same bird may have eaten also a number of hunting wasps and ichneumons as well and thus instead of reducing spiders by ten saved hundreds to come to maturity.

Contrariwise, a bird by eating the spider's natural prey and impoverishing its hunting grounds or by eating its allies who prey on its foes may cause much more loss than ten per day.

Going still further, the bird is comparatively large and naturally selects a substantial spider in preference to a small one, just as we, if a pheasant and a quail get up together blaze at the pheasant. Spider preys upon spider (Bristowe indeed classes the spider as the greatest enemy of the spider) so naturally big spiders eat a lot of little ones. Therefore by eating big spiders birds may save the lives of a host of small spiders just as the capture of cannibal trout will lead to better stocked rivers and lakes.

But the big spiders may be pregnant mothers. . . . It all gets very involved indeed and anyone who can work out tables to allow for all these things will be a very clever man.

In view of the above I will not copy down the tables that the dissectors have worked out. Briefly, from their figures, starlings are far and away the biggest consumers of spiders; nestlings consume more spiders than adults; and the stomachs of birds generally show that a much smaller percentage of spiders is consumed than might be expected, in spite of the lusciousness of this dish.

Fish take insects (if they did not half the joy of life would be extinguished in the breasts of thousands of men and quite a number of women) but the only serious insect taker is the trout. Fishermen often open the stomachs of trout to see what they are "taking." I myself, on the few occasions I fish, often open the stomach of one of my catch, provided the catch amounts to that number, though I have never found the practice to yield much profit. No record is made of the contents of stomachs opened by casual fishermen, but fishery officials and other investigators have provided us with abundant data taken over many years. Some species of spiders live near water and often hide *in* water, and several of these, no doubt fall victims to trout; but it is only after floods that statistics show any appreciable quantity of spiders in trouts' stomachs. These were evidently washed-away spiders, the majority of which would have perished in any case. So I think the trout should be classed more as an undertaker than an enemy.

Mammals, as enemies, are still more difficult to assess. Men have already been mentioned and the impression given that they, and particularly their women-folk, are the foes of house spiders. So they are, but on the other hand men *make* the houses that shelter spiders. They also make the stables, sheds, cellars, garages, and outhouses where spiders flourish secure from elements and normal enemies.

Horses, cattle and sheep are said to pick up a lot of spiders amongst their herbage. This may be so, though having tried frequently to pick up spiders amongst herbage myself I rather doubt it.

Monkeys and baboons however destroy large numbers. Baboons especially can be seen in the veld spending most of their time turning over stones and eating what harbours there, both spiders and scorpions—taking the precaution in the case of the latter of plucking off the sting first.

Smaller mammals take their toll. The insatiable shrew who dies if kept without food even for a short period adores spiders and must account for a lot of them, especially at night when both are most active. Mice and rats probably eat many also, but nothing can be proved. Statistics are impossible —it is little use examining the stomach contents of creatures that *chew* their food.

CHAPTER 9

DEFENCE

OUR investigations into the damage done to spiders by their enemies was not, on the whole, very satisfactory. A better idea is gained by the statement of certain authorities that only two per cent of the spiders born into the world survive to maturity. . This *does* give a picture of the slaughter inflicted. But any attempt to get sympathy for spiders on this account is impossible. I went into the matter once with someone and he said, "Well, who cares? The brutes are always killing other creatures and eating *them*." And this from a man who had his joint on Sundays and (being a city worker) meat at restaurants all the other days of the week! Just because he did not have to kill his meat for himself he sneered at spiders. Is then the lion more despicable than the jackal?

The fact must be faced that so long as certain animals have to eat flesh in order to live slaughter will be an everyday thing and ferocity will never be extinguished. Not that *all* those innocent of shedding blood for a living are as amiable as they might be. There are a lot of people who would sooner meet a lion than an irritated buffalo or rhinoceros, and human vegetarians are not *always* docile. In fact, the good-nature of no herbivorous creature can be taken for granted, not even that of a rabbit. For there is a certain species of rabbit the bucks of which can kill or seriously hurt a small dog or a cat. Most people are very surprised to learn this, and still more surprised are the dogs and cats. They are probably annoyed too, for defiance from the meek and mild is much more irritating than aggression from a bully. The Frenchman who wrote of a certain antelope, "This animal is exceedingly wicked. When attacked it retaliates," had the same idea.

The spider retaliates also. One might not think it when one sees it cowering under the cold scrutiny of the Ichneumon mother or dashing here and there like a distracted sheep on the approach of a hunting wasp. But these two insects have concentrated on spiders for untold ages and have developed a technique. The spider on its part has developed an inferiority complex and the two go together, the one no use without the other. It is as if they had been cast for roles in a play; murderer and victim. There seems no real reason why the victim *should* be the victim but this is the part it is expected to play, and it plays it. Confronted with the ichneumon or the hunting wasp the spider is like a rat confronted by a weasel. The weasel is very small and the rat could kill it. But the rat never even thinks of trying; it just crouches squealing while the weasel runs round it in narrowing circles. There is a sort of mesmerism here, too, probably. When the weasel finally draws in and sinks its little teeth into the rat's neck, the rat still makes no movement; still merely squeals until the squeals are choked. And the teeth of a rat are wicked things that can bite through metal.

When off the stage, however, the spider sees no reason why it should play the part of victim; it prefers that of murderer. The familiar surroundings of the open air theatre being exchanged for those of a jam jar or a glass-topped box the spider no longer shows fear of the hunting wasp, its hereditary killer. Indeed the spider knocks and buffets the wasp about and often finishes up by putting it to death. Similarly if you stick an Ichneumon into a web so that it is held fast the spider treats it like the rest of its prey and occasionally sucks its blood. The only reason it does not always suck its blood in these circumstances is because it does not care for the flavour.

In its natural surroundings, unlike the others, the Segestria spider puts up a bold defence when threatened with its hereditary hunting wasp enemy, *Pompilus apicalis*. Indeed, it puts the wasp to flight time and time again and generally remains unharmed on that account. It is only when Pompilus, by a trick, tumbles it to the ground that the spider loses its poise, and without poise no spider can survive—not at any rate when confronted with a hunting wasp.

But almost any animal will show fight when cornered. Retaliation hardly comes under the heading "Defence." In a way I suppose it does, but it is a last ditch sort of defence. We expect something better than that from a spider and one very adequate defence has been studied already but from a different angle. The web is an effective means of getting food: it is also an effective protection for its maker. Did it catch never a head of game it would still be well worth the making for protection purposes only. It is a barbed wire surround, and the telegraph bell not only sounds the dinner gong, it sounds the "Alert" as well. The sticky web, as well as being the best snare, is the best protection, and I doubt if the owner need fear any insect except Ichneumon. And if only the owner would take up her position in the middle of the web and stay there when that lady draws near I do not think even Inchneumon would dare to tackle her.

But no. Stage directions insist that she drops on the end of a long, non-sticky line where the murderess can follow her.

The crab spider's effective methods we have studied already. Its coloured pose brings it game without its having to go to get it and camouflages it from enemies as well.

The others, the hunters, are perhaps not so clever. They do not need to be, but several have a trick or two up their sleeves. In the main, however, these types, having good eyes and quick feet, can see an enemy coming and if necessary dodge him, twisting and turning like a rabbit. That in itself is defence, and good defence, as rabbits and hares prove by still inhabiting our earth in great numbers. But the larger hunting spiders, like tarantulas, do not wish to spend their time dodging and twisting. They have their castles and like to stay near them, and being well armed see no reason why they should *not* stay near them. They will fight in defence of their stronghold, but they do not particularly want to do so. Their aim and object in life, as with most of us, is to keep their bellies full.

The best way to avoid having to fight is to be strong and formidable. There is, I fear, in this imperfect world no other way. But it is no use being formidable if no one knows it; at least it does not save one from having to engage in fights which take up time and possibly damage one. So to avoid misunderstanding and an engagement which would bring no profit to either party, the tarantulas (or most of them) wear black marks on their bellies, or like the dangerous Black Widow of America black and orange, or red, to advertise their aggressiveness. And when some foe approaches they rear up, thus adopting a threatening attitude and at the same time displaying the warning colours.

The scheme, of course, as I have mentioned before, is an old one in the insect world and has been much abused by dishonest members who, innocuous themselves, have adopted the colours of creatures dangerous to a degree and thereby secured a life of tranquil ease to which they are not entitled.

Being unashamedly anthropomorphic I am reminded here of a miner in Rhodesia in the earlier days. He was an ex-pugilist from Northumberland who had been known there as "Dynamite Thompson," or something like that. He could even produce newspaper cuttings about himself—though none of those showed any photographs. The mining camp was a tough one and any argument was settled by a fight, which is as good a way as any of ending an argument provided you do not call in whole nations to help you. From these final arbitrations Thompson, by virtue of his fighting record, was immune until one day an aggravated miner hit him on the nose. A fight of course was a sheer necessity and eager supporters escorted to the clearing outside a Thompson who seemed strangely reluctant to go there. One blow decided the issue. The real "Dynamite Thompson" is now probably the jovial landlord of some Northumberland inn. Where his understudy is I do not know but I imagine he did not have too happy a time after his exposure. Nevertheless his false colours *had*, like those of many insects, brought him immunity over a long period which with a bit of luck might have been even longer.

Another plan, if a creature is edible (as almost all spiders are) is to contrive to look like something that tastes nasty. The subject selected must be common and must run about in numbers so that all know it and have learned to avoid it. None fulfil the necessary conditions better than common ants: they are everywhere and, with a few notable exceptions, birds, reptiles, insects, and mammals avoid them. Ladybirds are nasty in flavour but they are not very common and have other obvious disadvantages. So if a spider can pass itself off as an ant it will enjoy almost complete immunity from its natural enemies.

And many spiders *do* disguise themselves as ants; not just spiders of one species but spiders from several different genera. These look like ants (and the imitation in certain cases is amazingly good), act like ants, and often live amongst ants. How they have managed to acquire the *shape* of ants it is difficult to say. Our useful friend Natural Selection is responsible I suppose but one is still left with the impression that this does not entirely explain the phenomenon, for some spiders have imitated even the unusual protuberances that occur in certain species of ants.

Good as the impersonation is in the case of some spiders, with others it is not so marked, and indeed the eye of faith is required to see any resemblance at all. But *looking* like an ant is really not so important as *acting* like an ant, and these spiders play this part to perfection. An ant has two antennae and six legs and some spiders place their front pair of legs over their foreheads and wiggle them as if they were antennae. They thus—apparently—possess six legs and a pair of antennae themselves. And the spider imitates the gait and jerky movements of the ant—so much so that when in motion ant and spider are indistinguishable but when the spider is dead one wonders how it could ever have seemed even faintly like an ant. This deliberate act of the spider is remarkable enough but something even more startling has come to light fairly recently. In Brazil Bristowe noticed one day a "large-headed ant" walking along. He caught it to identify its species and found to his surprise that it was not an ant at all but a black spider *bearing over its head and shoulders the hollow skeleton of an ant.**

He could hardly believe that a spider could go to such depths of deception, and then, later, Hingston, in British Guiana saw exactly the same thing.

If these spiders were deliberately disguising themselves as ants in this manner we must readjust our impression of spiders and grant them—or some of them—an intelligence almost equal to our own, however loath we are to do so. There were of course only two instances noted but when one considers the paucity of adequate observers, especially abroad, this is quite a lot. And even Bristowe, the expert, was deceived: the spider in these circumstances looks exactly like an ant so that hundreds might run about without being noticed—even by experts.

It will have been noted that what was being carried was a "hollow skeleton." *If* the spider was one of the few (if such exist) who eat ants it *might* have been bearing the corpse in this most unusual manner to eat later, but no spider of any species is interested in a skeleton—*as food.*

The ant-mimics often live amongst ants. Donnisthorpe records having found them *in* ants' nests. Why the ants do not kill them I do not know. Ants are peculiar creatures, pugnacious and aggressive to some creatures including, often, their own species and strangely lenient to others. One can hardly suppose that by waggling its front feet and trying to

*The "skeleton" of an insect is outside, and usually consists of the hard chitinous covering of the head and thorax.

make them look like antennae the spider, though it deceives others, can deceive the ant herself. The ant is too clever for that, and the spider is too clever to run about with ants if the ants are likely to hurt it. Who would win in a fight between the two I could not say—the hardy brittle ant I should think—but the spider would never be able to fight just one ant, for ants unite both in attack and defence. Perhaps these spiders doing their act amuse the ants. An insect with a sense of humour sounds absurd yet I am convinced that flies possess one—and a very distorted one too.

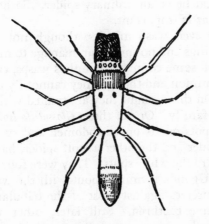

FIG. 21
A British ant-mimicking spider (*Myrmarachne formicarius*)
After Blackwall (*from* Spiders of Great Britain—*The Ray Society*)

The ant-mimic is in the happiest of positions. The inedibility of the subject mimicked protects the spider from nearly all its ordinary foes and the act it puts on protects it also from the greatest enemy of all, the hunting wasp. The latter, since she never eats her prey, is not interested in its flavour, but she loathes ants above all things and gives a wide berth to anything that looks even remotely like one. She spends half her life trying to hide her prey from ants and if ants *do* get to it that is the end; she writes it off and goes and kills something else. So anything that looks like an ant is safe from her, and no ant-mimicking spider has ever been found in her larder.

Possibly (Bristowe says certainly) the greatest of all enemies of spiders are spiders and the mimics are protected from these also. In captivity even fierce species withdraw uneasily if touched by the quivering imitation antennae of the actors, and some run away and erect a defensive silk barrage immediately. But if the actor is ill, or dead, he is seized at once and treated as what he is, an ordinary spider. So here again it is the acting that is important.

There are even wasp mimics, though not many. Most wasps have wings and no spider can manage to make imitation wings. But in some countries wingless wasps, called Mutillid Wasps, are common and though they cannot fly they can sting effectively. On this account they are treated with respect even by their own family. One of these, *Glossotilla liopyga*, has four large white spots on its upper abdomen and two spiders, one a jumping spider and the other a wolf spider, have imitated it closely, down to the white spots. They were found by Dr. Hale Carpenter in Uganda running about with the wasps and thus insuring themselves against most of the tribulations of their less imaginative brethren. Still later, other wasp mimics have been found.

It would seem then that spiders in increasing numbers are taking up acting as a career. Acting has been described as the lowest form of art but what spider cares about that if it carries with it an insurance against personal risks? Spiders are not slow in appreciating a good racket and we may look forward to many more performers. The present amateurs will improve their parts and others will step into their place. Indeed the day may come when almost any insect found may be a spider in disguise.

CHAPTER 10

COURTING

"FAINT heart," sings the Lord Chancellor in Iolanthe, "never won fair lady." In this scene, it will be remembered, two men are encouraging another to pluck up sufficient courage to propose. They go on tunefully,

> While the sun shines make your hay.
> Where the will is there's a way.
> Beard the lion in its lair.
> None but the brave deserve the fair.

The stirring nature of this encouragement seems somewhat uncalled-for in the circumstances. A proposal, if couched in the correct form, entails no danger to life or limb. But if the actors in Iolanthe had been spiders then every word of this well-known song would have been singularly appropriate. For the spider suitor *does* need all the encouragement he can get.

Off the stage, the diffident human wooer, if he seeks advice from a friend, is usually reminded that the girl can't eat him. But this is just what the female spider *can* do to her wooer and furthermore *will* do unless he watches his step very carefully.

The courting male spider has many obstacles to surmount before he can accomplish his desires. But before he goes courting at all he has to perform an act which no other form of life is called upon to do. Structurally, as well as in other ways, spiders are different from other creatures. This particular peculiarity is that the testes of the male are not connected with any organ capable of being inserted into the epigyne of the female: they are connected merely to a hole in his belly. His sperm therefore can only be shed straight on to the ground, unless he chooses to make some receptacle to receive this fluid. He generally takes the latter course and weaves a small mat, called a sperm web, and makes his emission directly into that.

I have compared the palps of spiders to arms, which, to all intents and purposes they are—arms and hands. Those of the female are used for feeling and probably possess a highly developed sense of touch. In the male they fulfil a further function. The tips of them—the hands as it were—are bulbous. It looks as if he were wearing boxing gloves (see Fig. 24, page 208), and, incidentally, it is by the boxing gloves at the ends of his arms that you can always recognise the male. These bulbs, which are of varying shapes according to the species and are of a highly intricate design are used to scoop up and absorb the sperm fluid which he has shed on to his mat.

The mat, which is about half the size of the spider, is either rectangular or triangular—again according to the species— and the male rubs his belly against it and stimulates himself to eject the sperm. Having shed the liquid he charges his palps by repeatedly inserting first one and then the other into the tiny pool, waving the one palp in the air while the other is absorbing more liquid.

These two arms, with their charged attachments, will be the organs to be inserted into the female opening which is situated under her belly near her waist. Amongst spiders therefore fertilisation of the female is by artificial insemination, but both parties derive as much excitement and pleasure from the act as if it were conducted in what we consider the natural way.

This complicated arrangement inflicts a lot of trouble on the male, but on the other hand it enables him to escape the dreadful fate of the male honey bee whom callous nature orders to mate, and sentences to torture and death for obeying her commands.

It may be objected that having started with the subject of courting we have gone on abruptly to that of mating. The reason is that, with spiders, courting and mating take place at the one meeting. With creatures like grasshoppers and crickets you may see dalliance brought to a fine art: shyness, violin playing, gentle touches, soft caresses, continued for days and days (a long time in the life of an insect). Not with spiders. Apart from mother love (and sometimes this is non-existent) the female spider has only two emotions, or rather appetites, her belly and sexual lust. But predominant is her gluttonous love of food.

To spiders almost anything that lives is food, provided it is capable of being overpowered. There *are* creatures whose taste they dislike though such are not common. Unfortunately for themselves, male spiders (except for one species only) are smaller than the females, sometimes ludicrously so. For instance, there is a certain foreign orb web weaver (*Nephila chrysogaster*) whose body measures two inches in length while that of her husband measures only one tenth of an inch, though this, of course, is an extreme case. Now the female spider may hesitate to attack something her own size, but when she sees something smaller and weaker she has no hesitation. Under the excitement of the sexual act the demands of the stomach are in abeyance but when the act is completed the puny creature under her, recently encouraged and favoured, becomes what he is—a spider smaller than herself. In other words prey, and prey, apparently, of a particularly succulent kind.

This is where the male spider must time his actions with precision. It is the cue for his exit, and directions add "hurriedly." Those males who realise this and run away in time survive. There are exceptions: there are long-suffering females who allow their husbands to live with them, and, consequently, husbands who have the temerity to live with their wives—very much, it may be added, under dictation.

But we will return to that. At the moment we have put the cart a long way ahead of the horse. We are discussing an obstacle our male spider has not come to yet. He has others to surmount before he gets to that one. Let us go back.

Having charged his palps with sperm the male has now to find his female. This may entail a very long journey but in the end he finds a female of his species. This is the first obstacle. He must tread with care now for he is in the danger area and his life depends on his technique. First of all he must make the female realise that it is a suitor who calls. This necessitates a change of outlook on the part of the female. She is waiting for callers and welcomes them, but only as a butcher welcomes a lamb or a fat pig. Her mind dwells on trussing-up and bleeding, not on love. We must not judge her too harshly; we must try and put ourselves in her place. Let us imagine a stout lady, a good trencher-woman too, who thinks she hears the dinner gong and sits down to table. But instead of a succulent joint a puny and unknown man presents himself and announces that dinner is off but in its stead he can offer her love. Would such a man *always* meet with a gracious reception? Or would he at times get something very much the reverse?

In fact luck comes largely into this first fence of the male spider. If the female has fed recently his chances are greatly improved. If she is hungry they are not so good. Luck enters too in other ways; if the female has previously received a suitor and is sexually satiated for the time being, or if she happens to be pregnant, she is less inclined to be indulgent to another candidate and forego a good meal on his account.

The way the male intimates his identity to the female is the most interesting part of the subject and varies with the class of spider. The web-weavers, being next door to blind, have to be particularly careful. They twitch the web, or drum on it, in what must be a sort of code. But we shall study the various methods when we sort the spiders.

All being well and the female having decided to indulge in a little dalliance she often becomes quite coquettish and minces forward. It is an attitude that seems rather absurd in some of those fat-bellied ogresses. I saw one such run away from a tiny male and peer anxiously round the edge of obstacles to see if he still pursued her or had taken the wiser course and bolted in the opposite direction. In the main, having decided on love-making, the female enters into it whole-heartedly and does all in her power to excite her partner. Occasionally however females have been observed to go about their ordinary affairs during the act, paying little or no attention to the male clinging to them. Others are so carried away that they swoon or go into a trance and remain for some time devoid of life.

The position taken in the act of mating varies according to the species, the respective size of the parties, and personal idiosyncrasies. Usually the smaller male gets underneath the female so that his head is beneath her belly, the two facing in the same directions. In this position he thrusts his charged palps repeatedly into the female opening, generally one after the other but sometimes both together. Others may mount the female and leaning over her flank to one side insert a palp into her opening underneath. This method has the advantage of enabling a quicker get-away to be made after coition is over. The male of the species *Hypomma bituberculata* has two hard knobs on his head. As he approaches the female he keeps his head down so that the female, when lunging at him to kill him, grips these knobs between her jaws and the jaws enter grooves at the base of the knobs. She maintains her grip and holds him down while the sexual act is performed. Males of other species have jaws so adapted that they are able to hold the dangerous female fangs closed together or, in other cases, wedged open and thus, for the time being, rendered harmless.

At times the act is over immediately; at others it occupies several hours. Once again we are up against the impossibility of generalising about spiders. Those who like their facts cut and dried and insist on order and system must not study spiders. Almost any other animal would be more satisfactory from their point of view.

The act over, one of three things happens: the male retires unobtrusively with all the speed he can compass, or is killed, or, if he is the husband of one of the tolerant species, lives with his wife.

So much for generalisation. Love-making varies between the different classes and we must now examine their methods, class by class.

I. The Web Weavers

With these short-sighted females the males have had to develop a technique to suit the conditions. We have compared the female to the wet fly fisherman who operates almost entirely by the sense of touch. At the first pluck of some unknown fish the fisherman strikes and then takes action according to circumstances: if the tugs and struggles of the unseen fish amount to little and thus denote that something small is at the end, the catch is merely whipped up contemptuously and killed. If obviously big, more cautious methods are required and the fish is "played" until it has little strength or heart to resist further. This is where the fisherman gets his thrill; and probably the spider also. Anyway, the strike on the line, be it slight or heavy, is the signal for both to take the necessary steps to secure something to eat.

Now the male spider to get to the female has to go on her web. By touching her web at all he signifies to her that *prey* has arrived. This, especially if she is hungry, starts her gastric juices working. This makes things dangerous for the male. Not only has he aroused the hunting instinct in the female but he has initiated in her the appetite which of all others he would avoid. It is imperative that he cancels this appetite and substitutes in its place the appetite of sexual lust.

How can he accomplish this? Certainly he must steer clear of her for a time, but he must also take prompt measures. She has already come out and is trying to fix his whereabouts. He *does* take prompt measures; he drums and plucks on and at the web as if his life depended on it—which it does. The web vibrates in no uncertain way and the female pauses. She *knows* now, but it takes some time for the gastric juices to subside.

The actions of both parties after this differ very considerably according to the species and within the species itself. Our friend, *Agelena labyrinthica*, whose life story we gave earlier, behaves in a way which seems to me commendable from every point of view. Indeed should I, like Arachne, offend some goddess and be sentenced to be turned into a spider the one request I would make would be to be allowed to become the husband of Agelena. For not only does she suffer her husband to live with her after marriage, and on the whole treats him kindly, but at the marriage time itself—— But it would be better to get on.

Agelena's boy friend, drumming continually, advances towards his lady who has come out of her tunnel and is waiting, showing every sign of subdued excitement. Her friend's approach is gradual and his drummings on the web might be compared to the guitar-playing of a troubadour. The vibrations surround her and as they continue and the male gets closer she appears to be falling into a trance. (The approach of nearly all male spiders is gradual, for very adequate reasons.)

At last he gets within touching distance and very gently strokes her with his forelegs. These advances grow more intimate and soon he is tickling her. Tickling is a process used by a large proportion of males to excite the female. The effect of this caressing and tickling on Agelena is remarkable: she swoons right off. Like some Victorian young lady she faints and becomes an inanimate corpse. The male is not at all put out by this. He makes no efforts to revive her. Instead he hauls her off by one leg to a quiet place and has his will with her.

Immediately after the act Agelena recovers.

If my first wish were denied and I were not allowed to be turned into a male *Agelena labyrinthica*, then I would put forward a second plea. Do not, I would ask, make me a male *Aranea diadema*. I would not object so much to being greatly smaller than my wife, though I would not choose it. What I *would* dislike would be having a wife who thought husbands were made for two purposes only, the second one, to be eaten. For of all the spiders who go out to woo, the Aranea males suffer the greatest percentage of loss. Lucky is the husband of Diadema who lives to tell of his amorous adventures.

Termeyer once saw a male courting a female Diadema. He captured both and put them in a box. A web was made in the box and courting was resumed. The female liked this male and plainly took a stance offering herself to him. Emboldened by this, the male thrust his palp into her epigyne. But before the act of mating was accomplished, and when his palp was still inserted and could not be withdrawn, she began to tie him up, and as soon as he was bound and helpless she killed and ate him.

The suitor of the commonest of all the Aranea, *Meta segmentata*, is wise but certainly not dashing. He does not drum on the web or advertise his presence at all; he hides at the edge and waits until he sees the object of his desire engaged in killing some prey and then comes up behind her and attempts union. It is a far-sighted plan, for not only is she busy at the time but she also has by her something to kill and eat and is not likely to go to the trouble of killing additional prey just then. Moreover Meta is one of the few "frigid" spideresses and it probably would be impossible to excite her in any case.

In spite of her frigidity she is not an Aranea that is particularly hostile to her mates, and generally one, if not more, will be found living with her, but always keeping at a safe distance on the outskirts of her web. And this mate will always postpone any advances until she is occupied in trussing up or killing game.

Frigidity however is very much the exception and of those who show enthusiasm none go further than the females of the family Theridiidae, whose webs we looked at in an earlier chapter. The males of several species of this family need fear nothing from their females except their inability to satisfy them. Indeed the initial advance and excitation comes from the female and long after the male is exhausted she will try to excite him to further efforts. As Savory says, she is "quite insatiable."

II. Wolf Spiders

The male and female web-weavers recognise each other by their tactile sense, the web acting for the time being as a communication cord between the two. The web therefore constitutes both a danger and a safeguard to the male web-weaver. By going on it at all he invites treatment similar to that received by an insect, but by using it as a signalling apparatus he is able to calm down the female before she can get at him. Indeed, although, as we have said, the male spider who goes courting entails great risk, this risk is not half so great as that of the male who is *not* courting.

We have heard of certain players on pipes and flutes who charm the cobra which, under the influence of their music, allows unheard-of liberties to be taken. The male spider who is not courting at the time he meets a female is in the position of a cobra charmer who, having made contact with his cobra, discovers that he has forgotten his flute—or does not get it ready quickly enough.

The wolf spider has good eyes and signals his approach by

visual methods; semaphoring with his arms and legs. And the female sees these signals and understands them. But the eyesight of wolf spiders, though good, is not so good as that of jumping spiders, and in this very slight deficiency lies an element of danger to the male. He can see things well enough when they are moving, but not when they are motionless. And the female often is motionless, waiting for some game.

He follows the female when he gets near by the scent she leaves on the ground, or so one has to presume. But I get on to tricky ground here. The sense of smell is one very difficult for us to understand, even in our fellow mammals, even in ourselves. In insects it is more difficult, for we have not yet located where their organ of smelling lies. This has caused much argument. It has been observed that the male spider trailing a female "feels" the ground she has covered with his palps and his forelegs. The organs of smell therefore must lie in one or both of these members, though not necessarily confined to them. To emphasise the "touch" nature of the smelling of spiders certain scientists have refused to admit that they "smell" at all and have termed the sense a "chemotactic" sense. The idea of explaining by inventing a long word is common in many fields including psychology. The spider, it is argued, touches the ground as it goes along. But so, quite frequently, does a foxhound or any dog following a bitch. We ourselves, unless the smell is disagreeable, generally touch the object we smell. A girl "buries her nose" in a rose or a man his in a scented handkerchief. So why not call the sense by which a male spider follows a female simply "smell" and have done with it? Why call it something else harder to pronounce and still harder to understand?

We are so ill-endowed with the sense of smell ourselves that we shall never understand it—especially that side of it that in so many forms regulates the selection of a mate—and could get along quite well without it. It warns us occasionally of unsuitable food or insanitary conditions but for the rest, it is a luxury, even though it is also an important factor in our sense of taste. Not so with the dog; if *his* sense of smell were taken away, if, for instance, the nerve that communicates that sense to the brain were severed, he would, we are told, among other disabilities, no longer be able to perform the sexual act. The dog would be as if castrated, the first necessary stimulus being lacking.

As compensation *we* have those over-worked members, the eyes. I had a dog in Africa named Sam that I locked up once when I went by horseback to a mine six miles away. I stayed the night at the bungalow of one of the miners. At two in the morning Sam jumped into my bedroom via the window. He had never been to this mine before, therefore he had done the whole thing by smell. After breaking out of the shed he had connected me with the horse, followed the smell of the horse to the mine, through several native compounds, to the mine office, and then to the miner's bungalow.

This is remarkable if you think it out, but equally remarkable is the fact that a man could have done the same thing with his eyes. He could not have done it in the dark of course, and the man would be neither you nor I but some bushman or skilled native hunter. Nevertheless he, too, could have followed the spoor of the horse, even as Sam did, by infinitesimal signs and marks, most of them invisible to the eyes of the untrained.

The sense of smell has a great advantage over the sense of sight in that it operates at all hours including the hours of darkness. This is an important consideration for most dwellers of the wild, including many spiders, who would gain little advantage from a sense that functioned only during the time they were not abroad.

In the case of the animal, man, who uses the sense of sight more than any of the others, a strange phenomenon is taking place—the sense is deteriorating, and artificial distorting aid is the form of spectacles becoming increasingly necessary for each succeeding generation. Now nature usually rewards the continued use of a member by improving that member and punishes neglect in the opposite way. In other words deterioration comes from under- nor over-use. That is why domestic hens cannot fly and seals cannot walk and why we cannot recognise our friends in the dark by their smell. By right we ought to be able to demand from nature increasingly efficient eyes. And we are not getting them. Why, I do not know, but evolution moves slowly. You cannot force it. Mankind likes to take short cuts, and does. He goes rapidly from one invention to another, but there is no short cut, apparently, to good eyesight. We have made unusual demands on our eyes too suddenly and nature has not as yet been able to adjust things. She *will* give us even better eyes, but only in her own time. And not if we wear spectacles. Spectacles are another "shortcut" of man's that will bring no profit, at any rate to his remote progeny. I am not suggesting that we discard spectacles for the sake of our remote progeny. And certainly, if we do, our remote progeny will give us no thanks for it.

Many experiments have been made to try and locate the position of the olfactory organs in spiders. Parts of legs and palps have been removed, and certain minute organs, called lyreform organs, coated over with varnish or vaseline. Nothing definite has so far come to light but it seems probable that the scent organs are located at the tips of the first two pairs of legs and possibly in various scattered places in the body as well.

The question of scent leads naturally to that of taste, the two being inter-related. With its catholic diet a keen sense of taste is not necessary to the spider, and one has been known to eat part of a fly that had been previously dipped in parrafin. On the other hand a spider was observed in a greenhouse to give one bite to an ant and then rush to a porous plant-pot and grasp the edge between its jaws so that the nasty fluid taken from the ant might be absorbed. Hingston soaked a fly in quinine, a substance possessing neither scent nor irritant action, but plenty of taste as most of us know. A selected spider bit the fly and then ran back to its lair where it frenziedly tried to wipe away the quinine from its mouth with its palps. That they do not rely very greatly on their sense of taste is shown, I think, by the frequency with which they are sick after eating something that they discover they do not like.

To return to the male wolf spider following the female like a bloodhound on the track. The scent probably warns him when he is getting "warm," but not always. If she has been stationary for some time he may come upon her unawares. If she is on the move when he gets close, all is well. He sees her at once and semaphores to her in a special way with his arms or legs or both. She understands and knows what he is and what his intentions are. But if he comes upon her so unexpectedly that he has no time to semaphore, his wooing may terminate abruptly. He has not seen *her* but she has seen *him* plodding his way along and has sized him up as something edible. At the right distance she may spring and inflict her fatal bite.

Afterwards she may realise her mistake and suffer a feeling of faint regret. Licking her lips and shaking her head as she goes away from the corpse she may say, "It's a pity, but he never waved to me. It's his own fault." And she will console herself with the thought that she has fed well and that another suitor will come along shortly.

It is another instance of the danger to the male of being caught not courting.

He is aware of this danger and so will often semaphore when no female is there at all. For instance, if put in a box recently occupied by a female he will strike his attitudes and make the advances that convention demands amongst wolf spiders: at least, so very competent and painstaking observers tell us, but I must confess that my own efforts to get several of our common male wolves to act in this way have been unsuccessful.

Concerning the dangerous position of a male who is found not making advances, a faint, very faint, analogy exists in human affairs. At any rate women take a more lenient view of an offence due to a liking for themselves than to one unconnected with such weakness. There was a sergeant in France in the first world war who, during a period of recovery from wounds, sat every day and all day in an estaminet drinking brandy. Continued brandy drinking is apt to have unpleasant results and with this particular sergeant the bout ended with his raping the proprietress. He knew nothing about her and cared less, but she happened to pass at the wrong moment.

The punishment for such an offence was death and the proprietress brought a charge against him. Now when sober he was an excellent sergeant and, in further extenuation, his brandy drinking had been caused partly by some trouble at home. So the authorities did not wish him to be shot and tried to get the proprietress to withdraw her charge, on the grounds of the sergeant's excellent war record. She refused, and the adjutant went with a French interpreter to plead with her. He explained that the man had been completely drunk and had not had the faintest idea what he was doing. At least, the adjutant told the interpreter to say that, but the interpreter demurred and asked if he might put things his own way. *He* told the proprietress that the sergeant had fallen a victim to her charms; hence his presence day after day at that table. And in the end his passion for her had overcome him. It was very reprehensible but, in a way, due to Madame. And after hesitation the proprietress withdrew the charge.

It would be tedious to go through all the courting postures and methods of signalling of the various species, even if we knew them. The palps or front legs or (less commonly) both

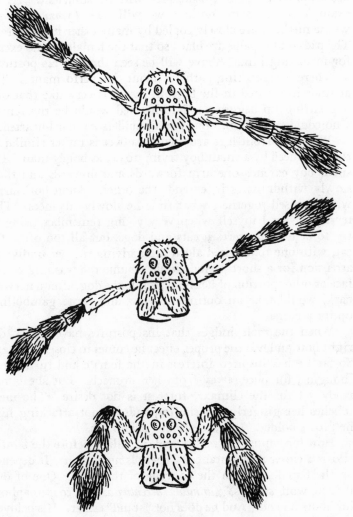

FIG. 22

Courting attitudes of the male wolf spider (*Lycosa amentata*)

Drawn by G. H. Locket

are employed. A few examples will be sufficient. As an example of the arm motions we will take *Lycosa amentata*, whose methods are closely copied by many other male wolves. The pads on his palps are black so that the female has no excuse for mistaking him. Above will be seen three of his postures.

There is something pathetic about this performance. The attitude illustrated in the bottom sketch is very like that of a dog sitting up begging. Hard-hearted would be the female who could resist him. But female spiders *are* hard-hearted.

When the front legs are used the effect is rather similar to that produced by a small boy trying to act as bogey-man. The small boy extends one arm forwards and upwards and then, slowly withdrawing it, extends the other. Anon both arms will be raised together, what time he slowly advances. This terrifying act I myself when very young remember using to try to demoralise certain cats and dogs, but all too often the cat, with one foot raised aloft, after giving me her undivided attention for a short period would resume the washing of her face or other portion of her body, while the dog, after a nervous bark, would take an optimistic view and come gambolling up for a game.

When the male judges that his postures have struck the right note and had the proper effect he comes to closer quarters. So far he has inspired interest in the female and turned her thoughts, for once, away from her stomach. But she is not ready yet for the climax. Interest is not desire. The male touches her gingerly. If she responds by not attacking him he grows bolder. He caresses and tickles her.

How long must the male stand signalling before the female allows a closer acquaintance? There is no answer. It depends on the female, and on the courage of the male. One of our British wolf spiders, *Tarantula accentuata*, has to semaphore for hours on end. And he does not "stand" either. His beloved is as tough a proposition as will be found in female spiderland, which is saying much. Luckily for him, although larger she is fatter than he, and he is usually able to avoid her murderous rushes. For hours he circles round her at a discreet distance, signalling every now and then. And every now and then she goes for him, often so viciously that he streaks off like a hare. But he comes back—they all come back. When she finally submits, her endearments, as might be expected from such a termagant, are more like a wrestling match than love.

The front legs of many male tarantulas have a portion coloured a conspicuous black that shows up vividly. This marking by Nature of those portions of his anatomy that the male presumably desires to be conspicuous is one of our puzzles. We ourselves like to appear our best before our womenfolk but to do so have to destroy a lot of Nature's handiwork. A man whose hair had never been cut and who had not shaved would be hard put to it to find a mate. What he would get, at any rate, would not be out of the top drawer. Nor does Nature provide us with Savile Row suits. Yet with many spiders and birds and others she goes all out to make the male look attractive when he goes a-wooing. She clothes these males herself—and what a costumier she is! Look, for instance, at the peacock or at the male bullfinch. Consider the egret whose lovely courting dress had been so coveted by women that he has been massacred and well-nigh exterminated in the female rush to tear his clothes from him.

It must be admitted that with birds these glorious costumes do not appear to have the result that might be expected. The peacock walks away, then wheels round and confronts the hen with his distended tail—one of the loveliest sights in nature. It takes *our* breath away but appears to have very little effect on *her*. That plain creature, with all that male magnificence before her, pecks about on the ground looking for bits of seed. And so do the consorts of most of the others, whose raiment excels that of Solomon in all his glory and the lily of the field as well. *Our* womenfolk do not behave like that: the glittering uniforms of bye-gone days used to have devastating effects.

Perhaps the very passivity of these female birds makes the male displays necessary. Doubtless out of the corner of a demure eye they are noted and have an accumulative effect resulting in ultimate surrender, though Nature, one would have thought, might have attained the same result simply by making the hen more responsive. But it is not for us to quarrel with Nature. I suspect too that, woman-like, she is herself fond of colourful displays and pretty clothes and likes excuses to make a splash from time to time—though in this respect she has been singularly niggardly with *us*.

Whether the courting dress of male birds is an advantage or not, the tufts and markings of male spiders certainly are, for not only do they help to excite a much more attentive female than any bird, but often preserve the male's life by advertising his identity and intentions in good time. It is a pity we have no statistics on the matter: a record of the pre-nuptial casualties of males with markings and of those without would be instructive. Perhaps Nature has given markings only to those spiders possessing more than usually formidable wives.

We are apt to speak very casually about Nature "giving"; as if she were a nanny who opened drawers and got out various articles of clothing for her charges. How did the male spider *get* those tufts and markings just where he wanted them? It is convenient to talk of Nature as a person or at any rate as a thinking force and refer to her as "she," a kind of wife of God. But Nature as we conceive her has no more existence than the Santa Claus of childhood. "She" did not look on and watch a male spider making passes at a girl friend and decide to look him out a pair of black mittens.

Nevertheless, I am still going to believe in Santa Claus and talk about Mother Nature.

But how *did* the male spider get his black mittens? I do not know, and I do not know how the peacock got his painted tail, and I do not know why *I* was not given a pretty suit when *I* went courting.

And whilst on the subject of problems let us face another. The male spider decides to go courting, and wedding as well. He has to seek a mate and may have to go a long distance to find one—an incredible distance sometimes. Now on that journey he will meet, or at any rate go near, female spiders in plenty. But out of the multitude of females all round him he must often journey on and on until he finds one of his own species, correct down to the last minutest detail. We ourselves know nothing of this problem: black, yellow, red, white, we can mate indiscriminately if we choose.

Take rats. You can take almost anything else if you wish, but I select rats because I have had some dealings with them and because their species are not so confusedly multitudinous as those of spiders. I once collected rats in Portuguese East Africa. I have known people who think there are only two species of rat, the brown (or grey) rat that came from the Orient, and the old English Black Rat which the brown rat is, or was, killing off. Similarly I have met people who think there are only three mice, the dormouse, the field mouse, and the house mouse. There are a lot more than these. And there are also a lot more rats.

In Africa, in addition to the brown and black rat, we had (though not all in one place) the Black-tailed rat, Darling's Rat, Smith's Rat, the Golden Rat, the Damaraland Rat, Verreaux's Rat, Wahlberg's Rat, Brant's Rat, the White-Nosed Rat, and so on for at least 36 species. Now many of these species are running about in the veld together. Some can only be distinguished the one from the other by such slight differences as a small circle round the eyes, more whiskers, or more mammae. The male rat is a lusty creature—that is partly why there are so many rats—and when the female is in season, which is often, he goes after her eagerly. And yet, in nature, the species remain separate. The Verreaux Rat remains the Verreaux Rat, and Brant's Rat Brant's Rat. Mr. Verreaux and Mr. Brant never have occasion to quarrel; there are never rats that are a bit of both. How does this come about? Mating time is not a time of nice discrimination. Does the male, full of urge, count the mammae of the female and finding six instead of the necessary ten, walk away? Does another, staring at a female's eyes, notice the rings and give her the sad news that union between them is impossible? Absurd of course, but the problem remains. We never find rats that are a mixture of species.

As a matter of fact I am wrong. We *do* find rats that are a mixture, but this mixture, when found, is such a *rarus rattus* that it merely helps me in my argument and proves the rule.

On this expedition of mine in Portuguese East Africa when a friend had persuaded me against my will to put a few traps and collect him specimens whenever I had the spare time, I got to a place where there were no rats. At least nothing was caught in the traps, for which I was grateful. On the eve of pitching camp and moving on I went to bed and slept soundly in my tent on the bed of cut grass with blankets laid over. In the morning down came the tent and the blankets were taken up. Underneath were quite twenty brown rats.

Note the fact that these were *brown* rats—those most detestable of rodents. I had never seen *one* before in that type of country. Near farms and kraals, yes, but not in almost virgin veld. Infinitely preferable would have been the rats of Messrs. Smith, Darling, Brant, Wahlberg, or the rest: indeed some of these are not at all unattractive. I can only conclude that one of those migrations had taken place and an army of brown rats passed us during the night. The cosy hay underneath my blanket and the smell of eatables had proved a temptation to twenty footsore and hungry defaulters who fell out and invaded my tent. Thank heaven I was asleep !

Brown rats have large scale migrations fairly frequently.

I have only seen one, when I was about fourteen years old. It was dusk and I was cycling along a country road in Lincolnshire. The road was deserted and passed through quiet countryside. Ahead, about five rats ran across, and then a ragged bunch of rats about two yards deep. I rang my bell and rode through them. They took no notice and made no attempt to avoid my bicycle. On my right the grass was rustling and moving. Farther on, not too close, I dismounted and looked back. I could not see things clearly in the growing dark but a brown river seemed to be flowing across the road. How I should hate to meet that river on foot!

While brown rats often migrate, and in large numbers, they occasionally plan a super-mass invasion. At any rate they did so once. It was in 1727 and at that time, although a few had doubtless imported themselves in sailing ships, brown rats were practically unknown in Europe. The brown rats decided to remedy this state of affairs and in that year, and in such swarms that the previous eruption of the Mongols seemed like a visit from a party of excursionists, swam the river Volga. Almost immediately they conquered and occupied Europe and by 1730 had reached Britain.

A migration is a different thing from a plague. In Britain we do not get plagues of rats. Goodness knows we have enough and at times get serious increases in certain places, but not real plagues. There was a plague of them in a portion of Southern Rhodesia once. I was there at the time, and when on a patrol called at a remote farm and stayed the night. The farmer said, "Wait till the moon gets up later on and I'll show you something." His place was only a shanty and there were few outbuildings, for the stock was simply left on the veld in charge of a herdboy. Not a place to attract rats. When the moon rose he took me out and the whole terrain seemed to be covered with lights. They were tiny lights, not unlike glow-worms, and they came from the eyes of a multitude of rats. And as one's eyes became accustomed one could see that there was nothing much anywhere but rats ; and occasionally faint chirruping squeals could be heard. They had been there, the farmer told me, about four days and had eaten up most of his provisions before he had managed to make his larder rat-proof. But on the whole these rats did not seem to seek human habitations; they seemed content just to cover the country outside and where they got their nutriment from I don't know. Neither do I know what breed they were. I was young then and to me a rat was just a rat.

This is a book on spiders, not rats, so I will not pursue the subject further. Before leaving them however I should like to point out that the rat begins to breed when only half grown, that it breeds at incredibly frequent intervals after that, that it has about 15 young at a litter (all of which are breeding themselves in next to no time), that it can use its paws with almost the same dexterity that we can use our hands, that it has a brain in many respects equal to ours, and in some respects better, that it can pass information to others and to succeeding generations, that it is brave, fierce, wicked, can eat anything, and that the female at breeding times feels she *must* have blood.

Such animals are dangerous and deserve more of mankind's thought and attention than he has given them so far. They have every qualification to become dominant in the world over an evolutionary period.

I return with relief to the estimable spider. The male will probably come upon many females before he meets one of his own species, and to some of these, it is said, he occasionally makes love. Perhaps responsibility for keeping the species separate rests with the female. Of course the size and shape of the palps of the male and the epigyne of the female vary greatly according to the species. Union between many different species would be physically impossible. But this is not an explanation, for matters never in nature get to the stage of the two parties trying but failing to have connection.

Here is an example of how useful anthropomorphism could be if it were applicable. Were the genus Homo divided into thousands and thousands of species all living together and with the species often barely distinguishable—to put it in another way, did a man live in a town with thousands of women almost but not quite like him, and did he, if he wished to mate, have to travel to another town by foot and perhaps from there on to other and other towns before he could meet a woman of his species: did we have these obstacles to contend with when spring stirred our blood, then we should know exactly the nature of the veto imposed on spiders and others when they meet one of the opposite sex not of their species.

All things have an origin and there must be an origin to the complicated and long-drawn-out postures of the male while courting the female. I think the most plausible theory is that they were inspired in the first place by fear. Two of the most powerful forces in nature pulled at the male, but they pulled in opposite directions. Sexual excitement urged him forward, fear, with equal urgency drew him back. So he stood rooted, his indecision betrayed by nervous movements, many of them obviously of a "warding off" nature. Similarly the web-weaver males plucked anxiously at the edge of the web, afraid to venture farther on that dangerous platform, though longing to do so. And in time these motions developed into a sort of ritual.

It is, with us, a fairly common practice for a lover to give his chosen a box of chocolates nicely wrapped up, and there is a spider that does the same thing except that *his* parcel encloses a dead fly. This spider is the wolf, *Pisaura mirabilis.* It is a common species and one of the largest of the British hunters. The gift is wrapped in silk and presented to the lady. Very occasionally he cheats and has been known to hand her a parcel beautifully wrapped but containing either no fly or one from which the juices have already been sucked. A dangerous thing to do. It would be dangerous even for a human wooer. Imagine the feelings of a girl when she opened the box her lover had presented to her and found therein either nothing at all, or chocolates from which the centres had been eaten. It would go hard with the lover.

And the deceit of Pisaura rarely goes unpunished. He has little to gain from such meanness and duplicity, for his present, if intact, would not only have advanced his suit but would have dulled the edge of her hunger. Indeed such a gift is a good investment, carrying with it a sort of life insurance policy.

Neither Lycosa nor Pisaura are females to trifle with. There are many stories about their ferocity. Mrs. Treat in America saw a female Lycosa just inside her burrow. A male stood near in that dreadful state of indecision so common with male courting spiders. He longed to go to her but feared to do so. For hours and hours this diffident suitor just hung around. When a male refuses to woo only one thing remains; the female must do it. So this Lycosa came out of her hole and approached him. The suitor turned and ran. She followed him up and after he had made many more attempts to escape got close enough to caress his trembling form. After that things went well, for when the observer returned in the morning she saw the two of them half in and half out of the burrow and in the act of coition. This act Mrs. Treat cut short by catching them both and putting them in a bottle. The female resented this abrupt termination of her enjoyment. She also resented being put in a bottle, and altogether was in a very nasty mood. Feminine-like she put the blame on to her husband and springing at him grasped him by the throat. He barely resisted and allowed himself to be killed without a struggle. "In fact," said Mrs. Treat, "he acted as if he rather enjoyed being eaten." The observer shook the bottle but the female would not let go her hold. So Mrs. Treat jerked the two of them out of the bottle on to the ground, and the female immediately dragged the remains of her lover to her burrow. Fools, they say, rush in. In two more days there was another lover waiting at her door.

The Peckhams also made studies, and amongst their observations we read, "In each of two species of Lycosa whose mating habits we were endeavouring to discover two males were destroyed by a single female."

One wishes to give so excellent a mother as Lycosa full justice, but the evidence piles up that she is a cruel and savage wife.

III. Crab Spiders

The wooing of crab spiders is rough. It has to be so. With the other groups there is, to a certain extent, a line of retreat for the male. The wolf spider, signalling and gradually approaching can, if things get too dangerous, change his mind and run away. The web-weaver male, too, has generally time to reconsider his matrimonial intentions. But crab spiders (and certain short-sighted hunting spiders which in this sub-section we will lump together with them) by reason of their short sight or the absence of vibrating webs, often blunder on to a female before they see her or she sees them. In these circumstances it is necessary for the male to act quickly and he generally seizes the female immediately by one of her legs—probably in such manner that she cannot reach him with her jaws. She makes off, dragging her lover tumbling along behind her, and soon they are rolling over and over on the ground.

But by now she realises what has happened and knows that it is a male who is clinging to her. In other words the danger period is over. The crab spider's idea of an introduction has been effected—and female spiders are as insistent on an introduction as any Victorian lady. Moreover desire has been aroused, so evidently with this group sexual excitement is induced more quickly than with others. There is little danger now to the male unless this particular female is pregnant or so hungry that that appetite overrules other considerations. If she *is* unwilling the male soon knows it and relinquishing his hold tries to get away. He is thinner and more agile than she and has longer legs so his chances are fair.

One can never lay down rules. At no time is the courting male spider *entirely* out of danger. Once the crab spider has got to the stage of caressing a responsive female he can generally consider himself safe, but not always. The females of many species of the genus Xysticus are particularly dangerous. Talking of one such in America, De Geer tells of a male which was seized by a female in the midst of his preparatory caresses, bound up, and then eaten. A sight, he said, which filled him with "horror and indignation."

To continue with the general lay-out. The battle continues, but it is a mock battle, and soon he is on her back performing the inevitable stroking and tickling which female spiders seem to find so irresistible. He then crawls underneath. After union, of course, he has to get away and no rough measure will help him then.

The problem of getting away after the sexual act would appear to have been studied by several spiders of this group. Bristowe first discovered one method in the species *Xysticus viaticus*, but it has since been observed in others. These have not insured themselves against the lesser danger of the first encounter, the bumping and rolling and (as they fondly imagine) "subduing" of the female, but they have the last part—the getting-away part—very well mapped out.

With them the cave-man-like beginning of courtship is much the same as with the others, but the caressing and tickling after the male has mounted the female is more prolonged. Probably the female wonders why things *are* so protracted, little realising that her deceitful lover while pretending to caress her is roping her down to the ground in such a way that she will have the greatest possible difficulty in freeing herself afterwards.

The pegging-down completed the male has his desires and then departs, in a nonchalant manner strikingly at variance with the panic-stricken dash that most males make from the nuptial couch.

Reprehensible as is the conduct of Xysticus it fades to insignificance besides that of *Drassodes lapidosus* (and others) whose

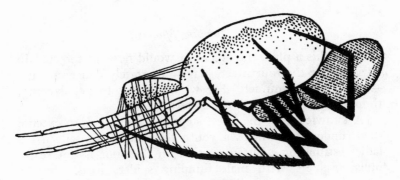

FIG. 23

A male crab spider (*Xysticus lanio*) indulges in intercourse with a female after he has roped her safely to the ground (the male is shaded).

After Bristowe (*from* The Comity of Spiders—*The Ray Society*)

act is reminiscent of that of the worst villains of Victorian melodrama. He *kidnaps* an immature female and keeps her in a prison until, in the course of time, maturity comes to her and she is ripe for his designs. Her prison is a silken tent over which he himself mounts guard, chasing away any creatures or any other spider that comes near. After the prisoner's last moult she is mature, and he assaults her at a time when she has not yet gained the strength to resist him.

Before judging such unprincipled conduct too harshly it must be remembered that the female of this species is not only one of the largest of the British spiders but also, when mature, one of the fiercest.

Hitherto we have given very little attention to the male. That insignificant form has been passed by. The impression may have been gathered that with spiders all the brains go to the females. The crab spiders force us to readjust that impression. Here we meet subtlety in the male and something very close to stupidity in the female who allows herself to be roped down without knowing it.

IV. Jumping Spiders

Were this a play, the orchestra would now, as the curtain is rising for the fourth act, play some stately dance measure —a gavotte or minuet. For we are going to get dancing, though it will not always be stately.

A knowledge of the latest steps and an ability to execute them undoubtedly helps a youth to advance himself in his lady's estimation. But perfection on the floor is not really indispensable. With male jumping spiders it is. In the following pages you will hear of one uncouth and awkward male to whom the dancing mistress was kind but he, or rather she, was an exception.

The courting jumping spider, then, must dance before his mistress, often for hours at a time. He is frequently dressed up for the occasion in frills, plumes, and colours, like a Zulu warrior, and not infrequently his dance is of the negroid type consisting of a posturing and a wriggling of the abdomen combined with slow or jerky steps. Throughout the dance the female looks on and follows every step with critical interest.

As the British jumpers are outclassed by foreigners in beauty so are they outclassed in the art of dancing. Probably *Salticus scenicus*, the ubiquitous Zebra Spider, is top of the British class but his performance is nothing particularly wonderful. He raises his first pair of legs and zig-zags to and fro in front of the female, moving and jerking his abdomen the while in a way very similar to certain Honolulu dances. If the dancing mistress does not attack him he gains confidence and dances with more exuberance, still keeping his arms, or rather forefeet, raised on high and getting nearer and nearer to the mistress who in the end, and if his dance has passed the test, suffers herself to be embraced.

In all cases what the male has to fear is a sudden rush and he generally has at least one eye ready and watching. But he never really knows what impression he is making. She is all attention but that means nothing: she may be thrilled by his efforts, or disgusted. And even if he dances faultlessly she may have taken a personal dislike to him. If she runs away when he gets near he generally takes it as a good sign and dances gaily after her. And it may be a good sign, she may be employing one of the oldest artificies of the sex to lure on the male. On the other hand it may mean that she has turned him down and wishes to see no more of him, in which case he will be ill-advised to go after her. Wooing is perplexing for the male jumping spider.

The movements of some males seem to be a deliberate attempt at hypnotism and sometimes the female does indeed appear to get into a hypnotised state, rooted to the ground and feebly following with her own limbs the various motions of the male. Bristowe describes a typical case. *Euophrys frontalis*, a handsome spider when viewed from in front, raises his black, cream-tipped legs above his head with a jerk, then slowly lowers them to the ground. This goes on and on, the movements being varied occasionally by two rapid jerks. These motions are very like those used by our own hypnotists, at any rate in the earlier days. And as he makes these passes the spider gradually advances upon the rooted female.

The actions of the common *Ballus depressus* may also have an hypnotic effect. His legs are black tipped with yellow and he holds them pointed towards the female. Meanwhile he sways over to the left then to the right like a drunken man moving from side to side in front of her as he does so.

To go through the list of the British dancers would become tedious. It is, after all, only the beginners' class. We will pass on to some of the experts in America.

Before 1899 nothing to speak of was known of the mating habits of jumping spiders. One year, that remarkable couple, Mr. and Mrs. Peckham, decided to study them. Usually they went into the country for their holiday at the end of June

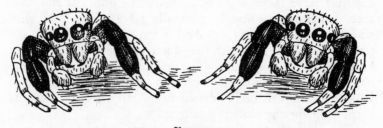

FIG. 24
The drunken sway of the courting *Ballus depressus*
After Bristowe (*from* Spiders—*King Penguin Books*)

but in the year in question they arranged their arrival for May 22nd in order to be present in good time for the opening ceremonies. For dance halls they took with them several boxes.

When they arrived the males of *Saitis pulex* had reached maturity and were waiting in large numbers until the females should have reached that state also. At last the Peckhams found a mature female and put her in a box with a male. "Her glance excited him" and he advanced slowly until about four inches from her, when all his limbs on one side collapsed. To prevent himself losing his balance (or apparently so, for all this was part of his "dance") he sidled rapidly towards the collapsed side for two inches in a semi-circle. Then the other side collapsed and he moved in another semi-circle in the opposite direction. To and fro he circled in this weird manner, getting closer and closer to the female. He got too close too quickly and she made a rush at him. He raised his legs to protect himself and turned and fled.

But she had not finished with him. On the whole she was not displeased with his performance. Her rush had been merely a gesture to teach him his place. She had him come back and dance again and she kept him at it until he had made 111 circles. One would have thought that she herself would have become weary of so prolonged a display. But no, she followed every step with the utmost concentration, and as he went on her mood began to soften. At last, when almost within touching distance, he whirled madly round and round like a dervish. This last effort completely won her heart and she suddenly joined in and whirled with him "in a giddy maze."

This particular spider must have been a good performer for not all the males got on so well. Some were made to dance for many hours, only to be contemptuously turned down in the end.

Nevertheless, the female of this species must be fairly amiable. Hard to please perhaps, but never really brutal or cruel. And one of the females was *most* exceptional. The province of the dancing mistress normally is to criticise and reward incompetence either with withdrawal or with punishment. In one instance however the male that the Peckhams introduced was a "very glum-looking individual." His looks did not belie his nature for he made no attempt to perform but stood sulkily like a boy who has been made to go to dancing-class when his friends have arranged to play games. In spite of this, the mistress tried in every way to make herself agreeable to him. In vain. He just stood there like a log. She turned him this way and turned him that way; she prodded him and pushed him; he would not dance. In the

end and after a lot of this treatment he did make a slight
effort and shuffled clumsily about. Did he realise, I wonder,
how lucky he was to get a mistress like that?

In dealing with our friend *Salticus scenicus*, the Peckhams
put six males and six females into a large box. With most
species this would have been simply asking for trouble—a free
fight all round with heavy casualties. And certainly, at first,
the utmost confusion ensued. The males all started dancing
and the females made a rush for them like that of women in
a store on the first day of a sale. They ran amongst them,
bewildered as to which one to choose. But gradually they
sorted it out and each female secured a male. The male, as
soon as he had been selected, got to work building a nest
and next morning there were six tents, nicely separated, with
a couple inside each. A cosy scene, and an unusually happy
ending.

Collecting jumping spiders so that males were available
for presentation to a female at the proper time meant keeping
a large number of males together waiting for the time when
their act came on. And one is not surprised to hear that
fights took place amongst this herded mob. The Peckhams,
not wishing to lose the specimens they had been at such pains
to collect spent most of their time parting the combatants in
order to prevent their killing each other. But in the end they
had to give it up; it was a day and night job and they had
other things to do. They decided to let them kill each other
and use what remained—if any. And afterwards, though
fighting was going on incessantly, "we could never discover
that one of the valiant males was wounded in the slightest
degree."

But on with the dance. *Hasarius Hoyi* holds his first pair
of legs high in the air and skips from side to side in a sort of
variation of the Highland Fling. The exact opposite is the
tango exhibition of *Marpessa familians*, so slow and dignified
that the Peckhams described it as "almost ludricous." The
"dance" of *Phidippus rufus* consists chiefly of a conceited display

of beautiful white plumes. He advances towards the mistress
with a swaying motion like a mannequin or a Georgian dandy,
not dancing but merely displaying his costume. The one the
Peckhams saw seemed to be making a great effect as he minced
before the female; so much so that when he got close to her
she ran coyly away. He went after her, his pansy gestures
becoming even more extravagent and assured. It is a
mistake to be *too* assured even if one is beautiful. He
thought this female was luring him on. And in a way
she was; for with a sudden pounce she caught him and
killed him.

Unlucky is the male born of *Phidippus morsitans*. The
female is a "savage monster." The Peckhams had only two
males to offer a female specimen of theirs, and neither had
much time to dance for she killed them one after the other
when (in those now famous words) "they had only offered her
the merest civilities."

In those parts *Dendryphantes capitatus* was far and away the
most abundant jumping spider, and the males of this species
were more quarrelsome than any other males. Since they were
so common the Peckhams collected ten males and put them in
a box just to see them fight. "Cruel sport," they said, feeling
rather guilty about it. They need not have worried. It was
the same story as before. After two weeks of incessant
fighting the Peckhams were "unable to find one wounded
warrior."

The males of this species may fight amongst themselves
but they are very abject before a female. They do not dance
at all but run up to her and lie down and grovel and twist
in front of her. She likes this and insists on their keeping up
the performance for several hours before she condescends to
accept their addresses.

Both sexes of *Dendryphantes elegans* "shine with the metallic
splendour of humming-birds." The female (very much larger
than the male) reflects a beautiful rosy hue from a background
of shining green and "her loveliness is accompanied by an

extreme irritability of temper"—a phenomenon not confined to female spiders. She too insists on a very prolonged display from her partner in spite of the fact that his dance is the most fatiguing of them all. He must stand on tip-toe, he must prance, he must wriggle his abdomen; and all the time he must keep whirling round and round. And any mistake, even after he has done it for hours and is exhausted, brings him a savage rush from the instructress. Indeed a lot of these performances seem like deliberate torture inflicted by a sadist even though the male is not obliged to be there if he does not wish it.

Astia vittata dances the tango, gliding, advancing, and retreating in a smooth way. The Peckhams put a number of both sexes into one of their boxes. The females, though keeping strict order amongst the males did not observe it themselves and several fights (resulting always, of course, in death to one of the parties) took place amongst them. One of these females was pregnant and it was noticed that the males gazed ardently at her from a distance but never attempted familiarity with her.

In *Philaeus militaris* we meet another kidnapper of undeveloped female children. He keeps his captive in a tent and erects another tent close by for himself. From time to time he goes off and brings back food but never on any occasion offers her any. Perhaps he feels that a starved prisoner will be less able to resist him when the time comes. In about a week his captive undresses for her final moult and is immediately violated.

The Peckhams kept several pairs in a box and much unruliness prevailed amongst the males. There was one large bully who tried to rule the whole place and who seemed to consider that all the young females belonged to him. Pathetically, these females used to crouch under their own particular kidnapper when the bully came raging round. Later, things quietened down and each male mounted guard over his own captive. Unfortunately the bully's female moulted first and after he had raped her he tried to get at the others and became almost as great a menace as he was before.

From the foregoing it might appear that the Peckhams had rather a good time; a private seat, as it were, at a ballet. But, even they described it as "very tedious." Unlike the female jumping spider they could not watch enthralled the same few steps repeated indefinitely. They said it used to take them a whole week, looking on for four or five hours a day, to get an idea of the habits of a single species.

WATER SPIDERS

IN Britain, and in fact in the whole of the northern hemisphere, there is only one spider who can really be called a water spider, but there are many others who live, like our fishermen, by and on the water. They are all of the wolf class; they are indeed wolves who have taken to water somewhat after the fashion of the otter (though not quite so expertly). This is not surprising : competition on land is severe and food often short. Spiders lead hard lives. We ourselves in time of stress often have to take to the water to keep body and soul together. We do it by proxy through our fishermen but without fish in times of war we should go very hungry. The "fish" of these water-going spiders usually takes the shape of emerging nymphs or spent water-hatched flies, but real fish and tadpoles are often caught. All this is a source of supply for spiders denied their hungry land-dwelling relatives. Furthermore, the water is a refuge, a retreat from their normal enemies.

The only ocean-going fisherman we have in this country is a species bearing the cumbersome name of *Lycosa purbeckensis*. He lives on our beaches and the incoming tide never worries him. He likes it, and will remain under the sea for many hours, catching what comes his way.

By dykes, ponds, and lakes you will meet at least four other water-loving wolf spiders in Britain. And they not only love water but insist on it, and die if taken away from it. The Pirate Spider (*Pirata piratica*) will serve as an example of all four. Like most pirates he is vain and cuts a striking figure in a swaggering dress of glossy yellow and brown and black and white. He hunts both on the banks and on the surface of the water and so, I should imagine, lacks little in the way of food. To these creatures calm water presents no obstacle. They run over the surface film just as easily as they run over dry land. Nor are they dependent on the surface film but will break it and dive underneath in pursuit of sub-aquatic prey or to escape enemies. Anyone who has tried to catch the Pirate Spider knows how difficult he is to outmanœuvre or bring to close quarters.

What impresses one most about spiders is their philosophical acceptance of whatever befalls. It is not as if they were sluggish or unintelligent, yet when caught and put into appalling prisons such as small glass jars they do not fret their souls away trying to escape; nor do they just sit and mope. They go round and round and this way and that at first but soon realise that there is no profit in such conduct and no escape for the time being from the jar. So then they get busy and erect scaffolding on which they can walk and threads which could hold flies if any entered. If none do enter —and unless their gaoler gives them some none will—that is not their fault; they are prepared for them if they come. And in the meantime the job has kept them occupied and their minds away from their sorry plight.

I once caught a female spider and put her in a match box. I had collected a number of other spiders also in match boxes and took the lot home and put them into jars. But for some reason I overlooked this particular box and it lay on a shelf for a month before I noticed it. And I only noticed it then because I was hunting for matches. When I opened the box, there she sat beside a pathetic little web she had made . . . waiting.

The Pirate Spider, adventurous and energetic as he normally is, accepts confinement as philosophically as the most sedentary of web-weavers. I have never kept one myself but Savory tells us he caught one and put it in a jar. The jar was placed in a tilted position and had water at the bottom. The pirate made a silk tube just above the level of the water and more or less lived in the mouth of this tube with his two forelegs resting on the surface of the water. He was kept in this jar for a whole summer.

But the real pirate amongst spiders is *Dolomedes fimbriatus*, the notorious Raft Spider. He is one of the largest of our spiders and a handsome one as well; beautiful in fact, but it is hard to convey in words the markings of a spider. Let us just say that he wears a uniform of chocolate brown with two broad golden stripes down it.

A pirate without a ship, whether a spider or a human being, does not command our attention to the same extent as a pirate with a ship. Dolomedes *does*—at times at any rate—have a ship, though whether he makes it and launches it himself is a matter of doubt. It was once said that Dolomedes sewed leaves together with silk into the form of a raft, and then "put to sea." Now there is nothing unusual in spiders sewing leaves together—they often do it, to make cabins or cover cocoons—but the awkward fact is that no living observer has ever actually *seen* Dolomedes make a raft. More probably the rafts he is found on are mere chance leaves. I must however tell of a "raft" spider I once saw, though whether it was Dolomedes or whether it had constructed the raft itself I cannot say for I was not particularly interested in spiders at that period.

I was travelling by junk along a Chinese river. The country on either side was half reedy, half grassy, with a few trees here and there. Then I heard the throaty squark of snipe and saw one or two shooting up and falling like stones farther away. This was enough for me. I had the junk pulled to the bank and got out and went after them, dressed in shorts, shirt, and a pair of canvas shoes. But the snipe were not really "in" yet. Those I had seen were merely the forerunners of the vast army that was to come in May. In an hour's walk only three got up, two at an impossible distance and one very close, which I missed. Then, unexpectedly, I came to a shallow lake from which with a concerted quacking, splashing, and flapping of wings a number of duck got up and flew away. Twenty yards from the shore was a clump of tall reeds. If I could get there I could hide behind them and be ready for the duck when they came back.

I found the lake was shallow and when I had waded to the reeds the water was only up to my thighs.

The afternoon wore on, and becoming tired of watching the sky for duck that never came my attention wandered to the water around me and I saw over the ripples caused by a gentle breeze what seemed like a large leaf sailing towards me. It passed close by me and idly, more for something to do than from curiosity, I pulled it towards me with the butt end of my shotgun. As I did so an average-sized spider jumped out and ran across the water to the reeds, where it disappeared. I took the "leaf" up in my hand and found that there were about four or five leaves matted together with whitish stuff. Alas, I cannot say what that whitish stuff was. I never examined it closely. It *may* have been spider silk. On the other hand it may not. It may have been just mould.

If anyone wishes to hear the end of this story I got no duck but I *did* get a bad infection of hook-worms through walking in marshy country without greasing my feet.

Having once pushed off, Dolomedes—whether his boat is a single leaf or a raft or whether he has launched it himself or commandeered it or even found himself cast adrift in it— is in a happy position. Up goes the skull and cross bones and the pirate sails merrily along. He keeps a smart look-out and on the appearance of any prize jumps from his boat and captures it, bringing it back and eating it in comfort on board. He is fortunately placed too as regards enemies. His hereditary foes are all seeking spiders on dry land, but if anything likely to be dangerous should put in an appearance he has only to submerge until it has gone. He prefers stagnant water and the southern counties.

Not until about seven years ago was man able to imitate in any way the actions of the Water Spider. And it was a very crude imitation that the Frogmen made when they swam under water to the hull of some ship. Even for this, special apparatus was necessary. The water Spider has no special apparatus. Nature made him to the same pattern as all the other land-living air-breathing spiders and must have been very surprised when she saw him swimming about in water without her permission: and living in it too, and spending his winters at the bottom. If any animal ever defied Nature and got away with it, it is the Water Spider, otherwise known as *Argyroneta aquatica.*

His method is well known: he gives a flop on the surface of the water and in some way imprisons a globule of air about his middle (where the breathing tubes are). Holding this globule of air to him he descends and, swimming with ease and rapidity, catches water animals and small fishes. The globule lasts him a long time, but when the air in it becomes foul he goes to the top and gets another in a matter of seconds.

Man imitated the Water Spider's house about 200 years ago, but here again the Diving Bell was but a crude copy of the spider's water residence. People were impressed by it because it was the first time man had ever been able to stay under water for any length of time without being drowned, but man did not, like the spider, live in it, keep his wife in it, and bring up his children in it—all of them being completely air-breathing.

The Water Spider has a summer cottage and a winter house. The summer cottage is a small and rather flimsy affair not far beneath the surface of the water. It is more of a tent than a house. The winter house is at the bottom, secure from gales and the risk of icing up. It is made of much more solid material and sometimes takes the form of an inverted shell filled (by the spider) with air.

The first step in the making of an underwater house is to weave a web the corners of which are affixed to certain points such as (for the summer house at least) the stems of water weeds. The web is very dense and certain observers state that after making it the spider covers it with a kind of liquid glaze. Whether she does or not the web is waterproof. It is also, in its first stages (being under water) completely invisible even when looked at closely in an aquarium.

Hard work is ahead, but hard work is ahead of anyone who wishes to build a house worth having. Aquatica again makes a trip to the surface and gives a flop, but this time manages to imprison an extra globule of air between her hairy hind legs in addition to the personal globule about her stomach. She swims down and releases this extra globule underneath the web. She does this time after time and gradually the web inflates and becomes a bell-shaped container of air, helped to take on this form by its own elastic material and by the yielding of the weeds to which it is attached.

The Water Spider deals with air as if it were a commodity. She carries it about like a builder carries cement, she measures it out and carves it into portable portions.

As we have said, the other house is near the bottom and made of more solid material.

When mating time draws near the male erects a house close to the house of some female, whom he may have seen but to whom he certainly has not been introduced. He then constructs a corridor leading from his house to hers and makes everything watertight before breaking into her wall and thus uniting the air in the two houses.

We have emphasised how necessary it is for a male to use tact when dealing with a female and how desirable to get her into a responsive frame of mind before making advances. The male Water Spider rudely demolishes a part of her wall and enters her house. It is hard to think of anything less likely to please her, especially when one realises that at this season of the year she is more irritable than usual. She *may* of course have heard him at his work outside and sensed what was going on. And this painstaking preparation may have softened her so that she *may* receive this breaker into ladies' boudoirs with only a faint show of indignation. On the other hand she may not. And if she *has* heard his busy preparations the audacity of the whole thing may merely have filled her with rising fury.

Anyway, the male enters and encounters either a yielding form or something very much the reverse. In the latter case it is to be hoped that he is in training, for a fight lies ahead that will last many rounds.

Let us introduce the contestants before the gong goes. On the one side we have the lady, length of body 11 millimetres, on the other the male, length 16 millimetres.

Quite! You have noticed a strange thing. A male spider larger than the female of his species. And the only one. Alone of all the spiders the male *Argyroneta aquatica* is larger than the female.

And he needs to be. Nevertheless, for once we can sit back and watch the spectacle of a female spider, spitting, cursing, and using every unorthodox fighting device she can think of, being gradually worsted by a male.

It is no kid-gloved affair. The fact that the two houses, and the corridor as well, are often wrecked beyond recognition will give some idea of the nature of the fighting.

Lady spectators, were such present, might wish to separate them; might even wish to take away and kill the big bullying male. But it never pays to interfere in these matrimonial disputes. The next day you will find these two busy repairing one at least of the wrecked houses, the work being interrupted from time to time by amatory caresses.

In due course a cocoon appears securely attached above the water level. The mother loves it and if experimenters break open her house she rushes to it and holds on to it.

The big male hangs around and when not fishing the two indulge in a certain amount of dalliance. This consists usually of an interplay with their feet, but the innate irritability of the female often causes her to change her mood and lash out most wickedly at the husband she was caressing a moment before. He is on his guard at once, springs aside, and gets ready, if she wants it, for another fight. She rarely does. She has had one and that was enough. But strained relations exist for many hours afterwards, though next day they will probably be found "holding feet" as before.

The young hatch and the mother cares for them for several weeks. Then, holding a bit of air, their sole legacy from the old home, they dive beneath the floor of the cottage and become tiny freelance water spiders hunting microscopic prey on their own.

The Water Spider is confined to Europe. Even America, that happy hunting ground for spiders, has nothing like it. Spiders, however, that live on or about water are common all over the world and if you are interested in fishing stories here are one or two from abroad.

One day in America, New Jersey to be precise, Professor E. T. Spring, with a companion, was on a journey to see what he called the "fine place" of a certain Mr. Stevens, then deceased. Going by the side of a stream they were halted by the sight of a commotion taking place in mid water. A spider had caught a fish and was trying to haul the struggling creature to the shore. The length of the fish (as they found out afterwards) was three and a quarter inches and the length of the spider three-quarters of an inch. Eventually the spider got the fish to the shore and commenced to try and haul it up the steep bank. The two observers were evidently in a hurry and felt they could wait no longer, so got a bottle and put both spider and fish into it. The fish swam about weakly near the bottom and the spider stood sentinel on the water above watching every motion of the fish, following it, and turning when it did.

Leaving the bottle there, they proceeded on their way and returned after three hours. The poor spider was dead, drowned in the water. The fish was alive, but weak, and died 24 hours later.

One feels annoyed with the conduct of these observers. "The fine place of the late Mr. Stevens above the hill," as they called it, could surely have waited. It would have been interesting to learn whether the spider *could* have hauled such a fish up the bank. And they themselves admit that they probably damaged the spider in their hurried bottling. The spider weighed 14 grains and the fish 66 grains.

A Mr. Wadey in Australia had a gold-fish pond and over this pond there was an outjutting piece of rock festooned with spider web. One morning in 1935 he saw much splashing there and found one of his gold-fish, two to three inches in length, entangled in the web. Going nearer he saw a large black spider on its back. The fish died. So did the spider, for Mr. Wadey had a kink in his make-up and preferred gold-fish to spiders.

In Philadelphia two sunfish in a bowl were killed by a species of wolf spider which bit one and then ran over the water and bit the second: both fish died in a few hours.

An Australian species, *Dolomedes facetus*, stands motionless for hours with its forefeet resting on the surface of the water and its hindfeet grasping the bank or overhanging vegetation. When some tadpole or fish comes close enough the spider plunges into the water and grasps the creature with all her legs. The fangs sink in and the struggles of the tadpole or fish grow weaker and weaker.

Father Pascalis Bomberg has given accounts of the hearty appetite of a South African species of Dolomedes. One, in a jar, he says, ate five tadpoles in one night. This was nothing for another ate nine out of twelve tadpoles and then "dealt in a similar manner" with a full grown frog. One hesitates to question the veracity of the reverend father but I must confess this made *me* blink.

Considering that a spider can take in no solids how does it eat a fish or a small bird? According to McKeown, it first makes an incision with its fangs and then regurgitates a digestive fluid over the wound. This fluid is potent and dissolves the adjoining flesh, the solution being then taken in by the spider. And so it goes on, the spider crunching away at the flesh and sucking in the fluid part, and ever and anon bringing up its digestive juice to help the liquefaction process.

The maggots of the bluebottle and some other flies are like the spider in that they can eat no solids. They too emit a fluid, which dissolves the meat and turns it into a putrefying liquid as they go along. In a recent book, I mentioned this fact and, impressed by the quick-acting potency of this fluid, idly suggested that, some time perhaps, a use might be found for it. This brought me a letter from a surgeon, part of which I will quote :

" . . . you refer to bluebottle grubs exuding a liquid which you think might have some use. You may like to hear of one use which I believe is now recognised.

"During the first World War I was surgical specialist at a Casualty Clearing Station which was posted first behind the salient and for the rest of the war on the Somme. We were usually five to ten miles back from the line and it often happened that we did not get the casualties for two or more days, and the numbers were so great that some did not get attended for another day. The soil of the salient, and the Somme, was teeming with tetanus and gas gangrene organisms, and if wounds could not be excised and cleaned up soon after infliction the chances were that they rapidly developed gas gangrene, often with fatal results. Perhaps you have come across such conditions, but if not I may tell you that a gangrenous wound is most unpleasant both to nose and eye.

" We found that many wounds on arrival at the C.C.S. were swarming with maggots and we soon noticed that when the maggots were cleared away a red, healthy, granulating surface appeared where they had been and that the men were not so ill as one would have expected. We therefore took to exposing some of the wounds to the flies and got them fly-blown and the results were often good, but the question always arose as to whether one was justified in holding up operation while the flies did their job. The operation consisted of very complete excision of the wound and all infected tissues. Anyway there is no doubt that the maggots did a very good job and I believe the pathologists did some research into the subject later on, but I did not hear much more about it."

All this, of course, was new to me. In Africa the sight of a maggot-infested wound always roused in me a burning fury against Nature who could so add to the sufferings of the injured. But apparently Nature knew a little more than I did.

CHAPTER 12

INTELLIGENCE

THE easiest way to evade the tricky task of assessing the intelligence of spiders, and other lowly forms of life, is to follow the example of many observers and say that they have not got any; that their minds, such as they are, work in a way that is totally different from our own, that they cannot think backwards or forwards; that, in fact, they cannot think at all. This may be so, but such an argument postulates a knowledge of the mind of the spider that we do not possess, and to be dogmatic negatively is just as rash as to be dogmatic positively. No one knows the mind of a spider. No one, if it comes to that, even knows the mind of his fellow. We take it for granted that it works like our own, but we do not know. And frequently it does not work like our own. How often do we hear such exasperated comments as, "I cannot understand what he was thinking about to act like that," or, "I don't think he knows what he's doing half the time." Indeed amongst certain peoples one meets *Homo sapiens* with much less intelligence—or so it seems—than any spider. How would the severe Fabre for instance comment on the intelligence of men if his only subjects for study had been certain Chinese labourers who saw off a branch from a tall tree while perched on it, and suffer grievous injury and much surprise when the branch on which they sit goes hurtling to the ground; or who water their masters' gardens with an umbrella in one hand and a watering can in the other?

So, not knowing the mind of the spider we must judge its intelligence by its actions when circumstances arise that call for thought, or something allied to thought. And the thought must be conscious. We ourselves, though less than any other animal, are ruled by our sub-conscious brain from the time we get up to the time we go to bed. If we always acted consciously we should be the slowest and most blundering creatures ever created. Take tennis as an example: if a man who has never played tennis in his life is as fit physically and muscularly as a Wimbledon champion there seems no reason why he should not stand a chance of beating him at his very first game. Action is the result of telegraphed instruction from the brain to the muscles concerned. So all the non-tennis player has to do is to hit the on-coming ball with the centre of his racquet into some place in the opposite court where the champion will have the most difficulty in getting to it. He therefore gives his brain instructions to move the necessary muscles, but something goes wrong, for he either misses the ball completely or sends it into an adjoining court. Why? Merely because he is trying to do things consciously. What he must do is to persuade his sub-conscious brain to take over from his conscious brain and play his strokes for him without himself having to bother. The sub-conscious brain however needs a long course of instruction as to what is required. This is called practice. In the end it does take over and plays the man's strokes for him, leaving his conscious brain free to attend to the more general policy and wider outlook of the game.

Similarly with walking. When taking a stroll in the country we can notice and think about things around us and leave the act of locomotion entirely to our sub-conscious mind. It does practically everything for us, this mind; it tells us when to wake up, how to find the bathroom, and how to recognise our wives.

So we must be quite sure when judging the intelligence of men and insects that the actions we study are *conscious* ones. At the same time the subjects studied must be pursuing their normal lives. Above all they must not have been subjected to demoralising treatment. We must not snatch them from their homes and fling them into prisons, or destroy their homes or massacre their children. Yet this is the form that many "experiments" on insects take, and if the subjects—in circumstances that would send most men into a lunatic asylum—fail to behave with cool and calculated sagacity they are given a black mark. We will have none of that here.

But the other way—just to watch insects and pick out such actions as indicate either intelligence or stupidity—yields no spectacular results. Nevertheless, that is what we propose to do.

Spiders can learn. That alone shows that they are not controlled entirely by instinct. They soon learn to disregard a tuning-fork placed against their web, though the sound excites them greatly at first; they learn to distinguish between colours; and (after first fleeing in terror) to come and take flies from human fingers.

Where shall we go now to watch a spider that is not acting in an automatic or instinctive way? To its home, I think; to the web in the garden. The making of that web was instinctive, but the spider's treatment of what goes into it is not. Each type of prey requires selective handling. Watch for yourself. The prey arrives; the spider comes out and views it. It views it often from various angles. It is summing the creature up and turning over in its mind what steps to take. It may decide on biting or roping or both. It may decide to cut it loose altogether and get rid of it. If the creature is powerful or dangerous one can see in the spider's hesitation the mental anguish it is undergoing. It seems to be, as it were, gnawing its nails. The spider therefore can *think*, and follow up thought by a plan of action.

As a site for the web some species have a distinct preference for a place just above a footpath where the first passing man or tallish animal will obliterate it. Here we seem to have a good example of stupidity in spiders. But have we? We have been deceived so often by spiders that we have to be careful. Many of the "stupid" things they do have been found recently not to be stupid at all; indeed the boot is on the other foot and the stupidity is ours for not realising the intention. Consider what a spider asks of its web; it asks for food. Some of them manufacture a web that is only meant to catch one insect, and think the trouble worth it. A path through meadows and between hedges is used by men and cattle and these destroy most webs in the way. But what of the night and early morning and the days when no men or cattle pass by? The same path is used by foxes, rabbits, weasels, stoats, cats, hares, dogs, and others. In their progress these animals "flush" large numbers of insects which jump or take to flight before them as they go along. So the spider in its web just above this path is in the position of a sportsman crouching in a butt when beaters are driving the game towards him, and the "bag" must be a heavy one.

Then, next day, you or I or some lumbering cow comes along and that is the end of the web. But what does the spider care? She is bursting with food and the web needed renewing in any case. Later on she will make a new one in the same spot and you, if you are present, will no doubt feel contemptuous pity for her stupidity. Do not waste your pity. The standard of living of that particular spider is probably higher than yours.

Many of the earlier observers found that if the wind stretched a spider's web too much the spider would apparently hang weights, such as pieces of wood or stones, to the bottom strands. If so we have web-making removed from instinct and transferred to intelligence. The Rev. J. C. Wood states that he saw a spider move a piece of wood five feet along the ground until it was directly under its web. The wood was then attached to a thread and hauled up several feet towards the bottom of the web. In the process the thread broke and the wood fell and the spider came down and attached a new and doubtless stronger thread and this time the balance weight was safely drawn up and secured to the web.

Another observer saw the web of an *Aranea sexpunctata* with a bottom strand tied to a pebble which hung seven inches above the ground. In order to see what the spider would do this observer took the rather drastic step of destroying the whole web. Three days later he found the web renewed and (as if the spider had blamed the insufficient weight for things going wrong) the bottom strand secured to two pebbles instead of one. Our thorough-going experimenter again destroyed the whole web. Quite what he expected to happen I do not know—three pebbles this time, perhaps. What *did* happen was that the spider abandoned the site altogether, in which it showed quite as much intelligence as in using pebbles.

Other spiders have been known to hang a block of wood at each bottom corner of their web in windy weather, and when these were removed replace them by others. One could go on and give many further instances of a similar kind but it is not necessary. McCook says, "In accounting for such acts one is compelled to suppose the exercise of reasoning powers of some kind by the spider." A simpler explanation however would appear to be that the spider thought those objects were static in the first place and that they got drawn up by chance.

It is difficult of course for man to know what form the reasoning of an insect, or any animal, takes. By the chance development of a certain lobe of the brain we acquired the power of speech. We talk now of course a lot too much, but, curiously, speech is necessary to thought. We can talk without thinking, and often do, but we cannot think without mental talking. That is why we are so different from other animals, who cannot use speech to help their thought processes.

A love of music does not, in itself, indicate intelligence. One hardly knows what it does indicate, but I read in some old book that "it raises us above the level of the beasts of the field." If that is so, then the spider's alleged love of music ought to come into this chapter.

So many are the tales of the spider's liking for the notes of the violin or the piano that they can hardly *all* be invention. It is a difficult subject for—like smell—we have not yet discovered where the spider's sense of hearing lies. Experimenters have cut off various limbs, the loss of none of which seems to interfere with the spider's response to a tuning-fork. Wherever the sense is situated it is unlikely that the spider appreciates the type of music that appeals to us. Even among ourselves, all possessing a similar type of receiving apparatus, the sounds that please one have the reverse effect on another. When travelling in the remoter parts of interior China I was frequently invited to feasts. Chinese feasts are (or were then) for men only, but "Sing-song" girls would be called in. Each of these ladies would perch behind the guest allotted to her and, twanging on a peculiar instrument, begin to sing. The noise was a mixture of pigs being killed and cats serenading at night; chiefly, I think, the latter.

To repay hospitality I used occasionally to give dinners on my boat, and once, having brought a gramophone along, I thought it would be a treat for my guests to hear some *real* music. I selected a glorious record of Melba singing "Ave Maria." At the very first notes, surprised heads jerked up and my guests looked at each other. I was pleased and flattered— but not for long. As the lovely strains went on giggling broke out, and by the time the record was a quarter way through the guests were lying back shrieking and helpless with laughter.

Similarly in Hongkong when the first of what were then called "Talkies" appeared at the one and only cinema. It was a good film. I forget its title, but it was a reconstruction of the sinking of the *Titanic*. All went well and the Chinese audience seemed impressed until the most serious moment when the band of the ill-fated vessel played the hymn, "Nearer my God to Thee," when at once a roar of laughter went up.

But there is no need to go to China. Often, alas, there is no need to leave one's own home to find out how differently

we are attuned to the sound waves we call music and where
jazz and crooning beget murderous impulses in certain
members of the family. So it seems strange that the spider,
without, in all probability, any ears such as we know them,
should like any form of our music. All the same, unless a
large number of people are lying, it does.

To select one story from a very great number, we have
that of Beethoven. Beethoven when a boy used to play his
violin alone in his room and always, when he did so, a large
spider would let itself down from the ceiling and sit on his
instrument. One day his mother entered, and seeing her
natural enemy sitting there absorbed, took advantage of this
favourable opportunity and killed it. Whereupon Beethoven,
in a rage, smashed up his violin.

One ought to put on record, however, that in later years
the great composer said that he remembered nothing about it.

CHAPTER 13

FEAR OF SPIDERS

SOMEBODY once sent in to the B.B.C. "Brains Trust" the question, "How can I overcome a horror of spiders?" That omniscient brigade were mostly of the opinion that the questioner must accustom himself to spiders, restrain himself from running away from them, keep near them, and even handle them. Then, they said, the horror would go. Only one gave the right answer—that no one can overcome a horror of spiders.

By "horror" I do not mean "dislike." Nearly all women and quite a number of men "dislike" spiders. There is a certain amount of excuse for the women but very little for the men unless the industry of a little creature working so much harder than they do offends them. By "horror" is meant an uncontrollable phobia, and the lot of those possessed by it is not a happy one. At school and in the army I have seen real torture inflicted on them. Spiders are presented to them on every possible occasion, in their hats, cigarette cases, beds, and under their plates, and their horrified reactions noted with glee. Such tricks are not funny.

The phobia may depart at any time in one's life, but whether it does or not one can do nothing about it. It springs from such early sources that it can almost be said to be born with one.

The human infant is helpless and immobile for a year or longer. In primitive days it was always with its mother during this period, secured to her back by straps or carried by her. Nowadays it is left alone for lengthy periods in a cot, pram, or other container. At such times spiders may visit it. Large specimens may even alight on its face and the infant, unlike Miss Muffet, cannot run away. It can scream, and does, and the mother doubtless comes, but finding nothing wrong returns to her work. Out of a large number one or two infants are bound to be unfortunate. They have a very busy mother, or an inattentive one, or are visited by a particularly persistent spider. Their screams are ignored. On the minds of such may be stamped a dread of spiders from which they do not recover.

And not only spiders: there are moth phobias, crane-fly phobias, and others. Writing about wasps I once cited a girl of 18 who screamed and went into hysterics because one wasp got into the room. My thoughts were on the *sting* of the wasp and the unnecessary dread many people have of being stung —as if the wasp's one ambition were to attack them. So I suggested that in this case the girl's conduct was mostly exhibitionism. This brought me an indignant letter from a lady: " . . . I am indifferent to bees and even hornets but in the presence of the common wasp (and I can sense even without seeing or hearing it whether there is one in the room) I am affected with a cold, creeping horror. It's a quite inexplicable thing that I have been fighting without success ever since my childhood. It is certainly not the fear of being stung. I've *been* stung, and the result is no more than a trifling discomfort. It's something much deeper than that, something about the insect itself, the shape possibly."

Here is a typical example of an insect phobia acquired in childhood, and given this time by a wasp. And what more likely than that a wasp should terrify an infant, buzzing round or even alighting on its (perhaps) sticky face? So I apologise for saying that the girl was motivated by exhibitionism.

Fear is a powerful emotion and one of which we understand little. It certainly gives off an emanation, probably a smell, that infuriates the lower animals. Most of the canine tribe will attack any of their members that, through distress of some sort, show signs of it. Indeed, they will often pursue them and kill them, just as if they were different creatures possessing a different scent.

The smell of fear can rarely be detected by the human nose, and when it *is* noticed it is still more rarely tracked down to its source. In Portuguese East Africa I had a native hunter named Jack who always accompanied me when I went out shooting. Since we were chiefly after elephant, rhino, buffalo, or lion, we naturally had one or two rather tight corners, and at such times I always noticed a peculiar smell that came from Jack. It was not sweat—both of us were sweating all the time in that hot and low-lying country—nor was it the normal "native" smell: it was something distinct and different that only came from him in these times of stress. An incident with a buffalo in a dark cane tunnel finally confirmed it. After the event the tunnel simply reeked of Jack's "fear smell," and probably of mine as well.

Now if *our* insensitive and almost atrophied noses can at times smell fear, how potent the fear smell must be to dogs and others. Judging by Jack, it is only very strong fear, positive fright, that gives any emanation *we* can perceive, but a dog or similar creature may well be able to scent a slight uneasiness, a not-*quite*-sure feeling in others. And these animals, remember, are expert analysts of smells; they have them all classified. Many are the stories—quite true stories—of children who have gone straight up to really savage dogs and pulled them about and received no hurt. That infuriating fear smell was absent.

It is only before fellow human-beings that man can "act." A show of bravery gets him nowhere with other animals if any fear at all lies underneath. A lion-tamer knows this: a lion smells fear more quickly even than a dog. Probably a professional rat-catcher does not know it, but if he *had* any fear of rats he would not be able to handle his captives without getting his fingers bitten to the bone. And woe

betide the bee-keeper who takes off occupied supers or who
flings swarms about with the fear smell coming from him.

All this has nothing to do with phobias. I have however
said enough on that subject. I will merely conclude by saying
that if you *have* a genuine fear of spiders do not be ashamed of
it for you are in gallant company. The intrepid Bowers of
the Antarctic was terrified to death of spiders. So were many
other brave men. On the other hand, do not advertise it.
Too many people have crude senses of humour.

But what about the opposite type—people who *like* spiders?
Apart from naturalists few do. Men as a rule ignore them
and women wash them down sinks and do other unpleasant
things to them and only refrain from killing them personally
because spiders make rather a mess when squashed. But *some*
women like them—though not in a way that does any good to
the spider. There was, according to Réaumur, a certain young
French lady who caught and ate every spider she saw. She
found them so delicious she could never resist them. Another
such epicure was the once famous Maria Schurrman who also
gobbled up every spider she could lay her hands on. She
said they tasted of nuts and justified her passion for them
by saying she was born under the sign of Scorpio. "And we
in England," says a writer of the 16th century, " have a Great
Lady yet living who will not leave off eating them." And
not only women: the astronomer Lalande was just as fond
of eating spiders. Bristowe says he can testify that certain
spiders suitably cooked are delicious. Unfortunately although
he gives recipes for certain large foreign specimens he does not
mention his method of cooking the common British spiders
and you will look in vain through Mrs. Beeton for any
directions.
Bristowe, by the way, tells a story of a woman who was

apparently allergic to spiders whom he met on a bus in London. She and her male companion had attracted his attention because of their excessively prim appearance. Suddenly her expression changed to one of frozen horror as a small spider began letting itself down on a thread from the bouquet of flowers she was carrying. Whether it was in a spirit of devilment or in order to help her overcome her dread of spiders Bristowe was unable to decide afterwards—he leaned across, said "excuse me, Madam," gently lifted the spider by its thread, threw back his head, and dropped it into his open mouth. The expressions of amazement and horror of the woman and her companion as he lifted his hat and alighted at his destination are vividly photographed in his memory.

I have seen members of the Matabele tribe roasting and eating dishes of spiders. I pitied them at the time, thinking it indicated starvation, but I have changed my mind since. Indeed the time may come when spiders, like oysters, are one of our most expensive and fashionable dishes. Really, if you eat flesh at all it is absurd to sneer at *any* dish. The whole thing is a matter of custom and has nothing to do with the nature or habits of the animal eaten. One has only to travel in China to see, with horror, what stuff animals like domestic pigs and chickens will eat. Rabbits can be the filthiest of feeders, and so can lobsters and shrimps. Those same Matabele I found eating spiders would have been disgusted had they known that I had ever eaten fish. I knew many men in Africa who, finding a bees' nest, would always eat the maggots before the honey. Hunger had made them do it in the first instance but having once tried maggots they, like the young French lady with spiders, could never resist them afterwards. And I have read that in the old days in China the most princely dish for an honoured guest was one consisting of newly-born *live* mice floating in honey.

One could go on, but the matter perhaps has been pursued long enough. Spiders themselves, compared with men, are *most* particular. True, they eat almost any insect, but rarely touch anything that is dead. And as for eating *decomposed* bodies such as our partridges, pheasants, grouse, etc.—the spider would rather die.

Deliberately to go through life with a spider on one's body, as a large number of young women are doing to-day, would seem to indicate a great affection for that animal. For a famous London tattooist told Bristowe that he is frequently engaged by young women to tattoo a spider on their backs. These ladies, however, are not motivated by love but by a belief that spiders bring luck. This belief is widespread throughout the world and an account of the superstitions in the various countries would occupy a small book.

In medicine too, until quite recent times, the spider was greatly valued. Various diseases were said to be cured by a spider in a box or walnut shell hung round the neck; taken gently bruised" inside a raisin, etc., etc. Spider web is still used, I believe, by some as a dressing for cuts, and I know a lady who goes out nearly every morning collecting dewy webs from the lawn to rub on her face. Whether or not the web is responsible I can vouch for it that the delicacy of her complexion leaves nothing to be desired.

By the way, if you are in China and meet a particularly seductive maiden, be on your guard, for she may be out to ensnare you and treat you cruelly. She may, in short, be a spider that has changed herself into a girl for a short period. This is interesting in that it is the exact opposite of the legend of Arachne.

Coming back to facts, the highest marks for a love of spiders goes, I think, to one of two men, the first a clergyman and the second a policeman. Consider how our womenfolk regard a house spider, and then listen to the Rev. T. Mouffet * talking of the same creature in the sixteenth century.

"The skin of it is so soft, smooth, polished, and neat that

* Quite possibly, says Bristowe, the father of the famous Miss Muffet of the nursery ryhme.

she precedes the softest skin of Mayds, and the daintiest and most beautiful Strumpets. She hath fingers that the most gallant Virgins desire to have theirs like them, long, slender, round, of exact feeling, that there is no man, nor any creature, that can compare with her."

Well, this clergyman lived a long time ago but the police-man is still with us—at least, I hope so. It was in 1936 that he was on point duty at Lambeth Bridge where, in spite of his preoccupation with the traffic of that busy thoroughfare, he did not fail to notice a very large spider about to commit suicide by crossing the road. He immediately held up the traffic while the spider crossed with slow and dignified gait —to the great joy of all the onlookers.

Goldsmith was a spider lover. He wrote once about a spider in his room:

"I perceived about four years ago a large spider in one corner of my room making its web; and, though the maid frequently levelled her fatal broom against the labours of the little animal, I had the good fortune then to prevent its de-struction; and, I may say, it more than paid me by the enter-tainment it afforded.

"In three days the web was with incredible diligence com-pleted: nor could I avoid thinking that the insect exulted in its new abode. . . . The first enemy it had to encounter was another and a much larger spider, which, having no web of its own, and having probably exhausted all its stock in former labours of this kind, came to invade the property of its neigh-bour. Soon then a terrible encounter ensued in which the invader seemed to have the victory, and the laborious spider was obliged to take refuge in its hole. Upon this the victor began to demolish the new web without mercy. This brought on another battle; and, contrary to my expectations, the laborious spider became conqueror and fairly killed its antagonist."

Goldsmith got much pleasure by putting various creatures into the web and noting how his pet dealt with them. It was horrified by a wasp he once introduced, and instantly broke the wasp's bonds and released it.

Perhaps the idea that spiders make only three webs came from Goldsmith, for he started destroying this spider's web to see how many webs a spider could "furnish." He found that this one furnished only three and could then make no more. But he did not know how many it had furnished before or how many the maid had destroyed with her fatal broom.

CHAPTER 14

VERDICT ON SPIDERS

ABOUT three thousand million years ago (scientists are not particular to a thousand million years or so one way or the other) the sun, sailing serenely along, collided or nearly collided with another body. Particles shot from the point of impact (or near impact) and were forced to take up a separate existence, going round and round but never being allowed to rejoin the flaming heaven from which they had been expelled. Exiled thus, the cold of outer space, tempered only by radiation from the parent body, began to lay hold of these unhappy bits and pieces. They lost their glow and gaseity; a shrivelling, cracking crust formed over them.

At airfields when a number of aircraft wish to land they are told to circle and await instructions, and each is given a definite distance at which to make its orbit. The planets now circle after that manner, but the order to land is a long time coming; a fact for which we, personally, must be grateful. Nevertheless they have the urge to do so, and one day, though not in our time, they will presumably receive the message, "You may land"—unless they have previously gone off into space altogether.

Meanwhile we can consider only the particle on which we are passengers, for there is no communication between the circling outcasts.

Earth became so miserably cold that at last the water vapour liquefied and settled in boiling pools in the hollows of the hardening crust. This, to earth, who had never known water before except as an invisible gas, must have come as a great surprise. The boiling water cooled and when it was about the temperature of a warm bath a sort of germ got into it. Where this germ came from we do not know, and the man who finds out will at last possess the key of knowledge.

The germ flourished in the warm water, split up, and developed into many forms, so that in due course the seas teemed with life. Things went well and the various creatures lived more or less happily in the sea and what we would call life everlasting stretched to life still more everlasting. In other words hundreds and hundreds of millions of years went by.

Scientists often say that life on such and such a planet is impossible by reason of such and such conditions. Had any scientist been present on earth at the time of which we write he would have asserted categorically that life on earth's dry land was impossible. No life, he would have said, could possibly live away from water, and subjection to air would kill it almost immediately.

But already certain overcrowded little water weeds were finding that they *could* exist on land from such time as the tide went out until it returned.

And so, over a period of time that our minds cannot even begin to comprehend, life invaded the dry land; the flora paving the way for the wriggling fauna. How paltry compared with this are any invasions Man has ever planned!

There were casualties, but the invaders held on and multiplied and changed their form and habits, and amongst the earliest of these new forms was the spider. The earth too was changing and laying down those strata that enable us to trace the pedigrees of so many forms of life. The spider appeared about 300 million years ago, before the Carboniferous period, and long before those parvenus, the Brontosaurus, the Tyrannosaurus, and the other great reptiles made their appearance. Indeed the latter only commenced their long and mighty reign when the Carboniferous period was drawing to a close. Everyone knows that the great reptiles, some of them almost as big as destroyers, were killed off, possibly by an ice age, but not everyone realises how long they held undisputed dominion of the earth and all that therein was: they reigned supreme for a hundred million years, whereas the present type of mankind has been in existence for only one million, if that.

Through all these changing scenes the venerable spider went quietly about its business, perfecting those traps and designs which we so admire—or not, as the case may be. It saw the birth of many of the insects and the creation of flowering plants. It may even have noticed, towards the end of the age of the reptiles, a small rat-like creature skulking amongst the undergrowth. If it did it probably took little notice of it, for this, the first of the mammals, was very scarce and insignificant then. It led a hard life, too, but that hard life was the secret of its later success.

The ice age (or some other difficult condition) killed off the great reptiles. They had done themselves well for a long time, so they had no cause to grumble. The little mammal survived.

In our own age we value security and comfort. Indeed, the latest idea is that it should be provided for us without any effort on our part. This is not a wise policy. The rocks are full of fossils of creatures long extinct who liked to have everything in the way of food and warmth given to them. The little mammal did not look at things that way. It had learned to be hardy, so it survived and in due time begat cats and horses, apes and men.

Man first appeared about ten million years ago. If one goes to the Natural History Museum there is a room to the right as one enters that makes one a little thoughtful. Here are rows and rows of reconstructed human heads, noble-looking heads many of them, with large brain capacity. These are all types of men that flourished for a time and then became extinct, leaving no progeny. The only surviving type is our own, and that, as I have said, has only been in existence in its present form for about a million years.

Why, it may be asked, go into elementary and irrelevant

details about evolution? It is my round-about way of replying to those who still ask, "What *use* are spiders?" implying with sublime conceit that all forms of life must necessarily have been created for their benefit, even a creature of such ancient lineage as the spider.

It must be admitted, however, that this question is not asked as often as it used to be. Recent events have taken a lot of the starch out of us. But up to fifty or a hundred years ago there was no doubt in men's minds but that all things had been created in order to serve *them*. It was a comfortable feeling and it used to be a sort of game trying to discover the disguised benevolence of difficult subjects, and the disguise with many of them was well-nigh perfect. But it could generally be managed. Lice, fleas, and bed-bugs, of course, were created to teach us to be clean; flies to destroy noxious matter which might offend the human nose or jeopardise human health; flowers and birds were made to please us with their colour, scent and song. And so on. And when really stumped one could always cheat and say that certain creatures were created to teach us patience in misfortune.

All the same there was quite a lot of excuse for this attitude in the old days. Evolution then was but a vague theory and hardly anyone believed in it. Man was on top and he genuinely believed that all the flora and the rest of the fauna had been created with a view to his comfort. Experts, too, had agreed in putting down the age of the world at a few thousand years. It was only radium, ticking away from the dawn of time, throwing little pellets, that showed us the truth.

What use are spiders? Having made it clear that there is no reason why they *should* be of use to anyone except themselves, we can now approach the matter from another angle and put the question in a different way, "Does it so happen that spiders are of any use to *us?*

Well, they do us no harm, either personally or indirectly through our food supplies, and that is saying a lot for an insect —to use the name in its wider sense. But we can go further than that. We can reply that it *does* so happen that spiders are of use to us. Indeed the startling possibility exists that we could not live without them.

The bulk of the insect population, which outnumbers that of the vertebrates by millions to one, is composed chiefly of forces that seem to have a vindictive hatred towards mankind and all his works and associates. They have declared a war, and a by no means cold war, against him. Faced with such odds man has no chance. In spite of his sprays and horticultural and veterinary preparations he would be killed off by starvation did he not possess amongst the ranks of Tuscany certain allies, or fifth columnists, who wage an unceasing war against their own kind. Material assistance is given by such fellow vertebrates as birds, bats, frogs, toads, lizards and others, but their efforts are as nothing compared with those of the insect fifth columns. And of these, which are our most potent allies? Almost undoubtedly, spiders.

Spiders' webs are everywhere and the total number of flies, gnats, and other insects caught must be enormous. But we will ignore the web-weavers and concentrate on the less conspicuous spiders that run about on the ground. Few realise how many of these there are, and it needed a census to find out. They carpet the earth. Let us go to the experts, who have investigated these things in a systematic way. Bristowe tells us that a census of rough grass in a Sussex field showed a spider population in excess of two and a quarter millions to the acre, or about nine millions to a normal sized field. And everyone of those nine millions is killing, or trying to kill, insects, day and night. (It seems incredible that any small insect can remain for five minutes in such a dreadful place.) On this basis Bristowe estimates the ground spider population of England and Wales to be two and one-fifth billions. Assuming that each spider kills a hundred insects a year (which is very far short of what it does kill), we arrive at the staggering figure of 200,000,000,000,000 insects destroyed every year in England and Wales by spiders.

Such a figure, of course, is quite beyond our mental powers to imagine, but some indication may be gained if we switch on to weight instead of numbers. An insect weighs very little; indeed to our senses it weighs nothing at all, yet the *weight* of this insect host that spiders destroy every year exceeds the weight of the total human population, including of course the inhabitants of London, Manchester, Liverpool, Birmingham and the rest. And these insects would breed and multiply though not all, of course, would be harmful to man. Moreover our island is not particularly favoured by spiders. Other parts of the world probably possess more than we do.

Therefore it is not surprising that the American, McCook, states that in many of the inhabited parts of the world man could not live but for spiders. Indeed, it is possible that were spiders exterminated man would follow them, and be wiped from the face of the earth except in ice-bound places.

It is said that people often become rather like the animals they study. So it may be that I am like *Tegenaria domestica* and never know when to stop. Anyway I am going back to the time we invaded dry land and am going to talk about water.

The occupation of barren rocks by creatures from the sea was very creditable, but we must not think that we have yet conquered dry land or adapted ourselves to live on it. In a way we are between the devil and the deep blue sea. On really dry land we perish; back in the arms of our mother ocean we perish too, and even more quickly. We may appear to be dry outside, but we are just a bag of water inside, and most of our senses cannot function unless they are kept bathed in moisture. The hypothetical scientist we mentioned before would have said, amongst other things that creatures from the sea would shrivel up in air. We have avoided this by a protective covering and by keeping our apertures as small as possible. But it is only a temporary measure. We can live away from the sea because our mother has followed us, her truants, and wet-feeds us still and baths us. She baths us so gently that we do not know we are being bathed, but it means that, in a way, we still live in water. One has only to bring a bottle of milk out of the refrigerator to find out how full of water is the apparently dry atmosphere.

This outside bath is almost as important as the inside one; at least, if the air *is* dry we must be very careful indeed not to let the inside water supply get too low. This is well illustrated by an incident recorded by the African hunter, Frederick Courteney Selous in his *Hunter's Wanderings in Africa.*

It was 1879, and he was on a shooting expedition with two friends, Miller and French, in country south of the Zambesi. In these parts, just before the rains, it is always hot, and the atmosphere excessively dry. One afternoon the party came upon a herd of elephants. They blazed away and many of the herd were killed and many, including cow elephants, got away wounded. (The ethics of such slaughter do not concern us here.) French had wounded a cow elephant and proposed to follow it. Selous tried to dissuade him, but French persisted, and taking two natives, one of them carrying water, went off on the spoor.

The account of what happened comes from the natives, both well-tried servants. Shortly, the party lost the spoor and decided to return to camp. They did not strike the camp and, darkness coming on, camped for the night. They had ample water but, not feeling much perturbed, drank the lot of it by daybreak.

So they were well watered when they started off in the morning.

By midday they still had not found the camp, and in the afternoon French lay down, dying of thirst. He scrawled a message on the butt of his rifle to that effect, and died a few minutes after making the message—killed by lack of water in a matter of a few hours.

In the same year (evidently an unusually dry one) three

natives hunting with Mr. Sell in the same district died of thirst within 24 hours of leaving the last water.

Though we have not conquered the dry land certain forms of animal life have made considerable strides towards doing so. The assault is going on and in some hundreds of million years we may perhaps be able to toddle along on land without our wet nurse for ever looking after us.

The spider has certainly not yet learned to do without the nurse, though it is not as dependent on her as we are. It can however get a lot of its fluid from the blood of its victims, a thing we cannot do. This man, French, for instance, not long before his death, had shot a giraffe. Why, I do not know. An animal, I suppose, appeared, and true to the tenets of those days he just shot it as being the normal thing to do. He then left it. Had French been a spider he could have stayed by the corpse of that giraffe and lived in security until those tracking him found him. As it was he died of thirst a few hours afterwards.

But apparently we humans cannot quench our thirst in blood. Perhaps, like sea water, it is salty and only makes things worse. I do not know, but I think that in cases of extreme urgency it might be tried. I knew one man who went through the agony of being lost in the veld in the dry season and who admitted to me that he had drunk his own urine. Of course this made him vomit and lose still more valuable moisture. And yet he had had a rifle and a knife with him, and had met game. Surely blood would have been better. But he never even thought of that.

Mortality from thirst amongst house spiders must be severe, but those living outside fare better than we do as regards water. In places where a man would die of thirst an insect or a spider gets what amounts to a whole jugful from a single drop of dew or a small patch of damp moss. Indeed, anything much larger than this is dangerous. If it drinks at a pool it does so at its own risk—as bathing notices say. The surface film of water, imperceptible to us, acts first like flypaper and after that like quick-sand to an insect. If you keep bees, a pond is the most dangerous thing you can have near your apiary, and the dryer the locality, the more dangerous the pond.

This surface film some spiders, but not others, can run over. But few are able to penetrate it for drinking purposes in safety. In a cage spiders should be given water by means of saturated cotton wool. I once gave a very small though very prized spider a couple of drops of water at the bottom of its jar. It was thirsty, for it went straight to the nearest drop, and I left it drinking greedily. It got caught, however, by the film, for next morning I found it drowned in one small drop of water.

Many, and amongst these are those who ought to know better, think that a spider can live indefinitely on flies and other prey, without water. They can live for varying periods on the fluids of such creatures, but in the end they die of thirst.

This chapter was intended to be a sort of trial or examination of spiders. What have we learnt? We are told that we owe our existence to spiders. If so, it is a very sobering thought. Spiders at least are neutral: at most they are something almost incredible from our point of view. Throughout the ages and in every country there has always been an underlying suspicion in men's minds that spiders are of value—an unknown, mysterious value. Countless old sayings prove this. Let me cite one, the Kentish proverb, "If you wish to live and thrive —let a spider run alive." Taking it all in all however, I am afraid no verdict can be given ; the evidence is too vague.

NOTES ON LITERATURE

COMPARATIVELY few books on spiders have been written and there has been a considerable advance in knowledge since the times of most of them. But the bulk of this new knowledge is scattered in journals where only a specialist can keep track of it.

Nevertheless, those who wish to learn more about the habits of spiders ought not to ignore the pioneers and (if they can get them) should read *The Life of the Spider*, by J. H. Fabre (translated by Alexander Teixeira de Mattos); *Observations on Sexual Selection in Spiders of the Family Attidae*, by G. W. and E. G. Peckham (two papers published by the Natural History Society of Wisconsin in 1889 and 1890); *Harvesting Ants and Trap Door Spiders*, by J. T. Moggridge, 1873; and *American Spiders and their Spinning Work*, by H. C. McCook, 3 vols., 1889. More recent books include *The Biography of Spiders*, by T. H. Savory, 1928; *The Spider Book*, by J. H. Comstock (U.S.A.), 1940; *Spider Wonders of Australia*, by K. C. McKeown, 1936; and *Les Arachnides—Encyclopédie Entomologique A, xvi*, by L. Berland, 1932. The principle work dealing mainly with the habits of British spiders is *The Comity of Spiders*, by W. S. Bristowe (2 Vols. 1939, 1941). In the "popular" class his King Penguin called *Spiders*, 1947, is short but full of interest.

The identification of spiders is difficult and a microscope is needed for all except the more conspicuous species. J. Blackwall's *A History of the Spiders of Great Britain and Ireland* (1864) is beautifully illustrated in colour, but scarce, expensive, and, of course, out of date. O. P. Cambridge's *Spiders of Dorset* suffers from the same disadvantage and lacks good illustrations. A work in two volumes by G. H. Locket and A. F. Millidge describing and illustrating all British species is in preparation by the Ray Society. The first volume is expected in 1950.

INDEX

251